The Night
Witchcraft as transformation

Yvonne Aburrow

for Les and Lin Randall

By the same author

The Night Journey: Witchcraft as Transformation, Doreen Valiente Foundation in association with the Centre for Pagan Studies, 2020.

All acts of love and pleasure: inclusive Wicca, Avalonia Books, 2014.

Pagan Consent Culture: Building Communities of Empathy and Autonomy, co-edited with Christine Hoff-Kraemer, Asphodel Press, 2016.

The Endless Knot, Birdberry Books, 2012.

Many Names, Birdberry Books, 2012.

A Little Book of Serpents, Birdberry Books, 2012.

The author at Wayland's Smithy.
Photo by Bob Houghton.

The Night Journey: Witchcraft as Transformation

First edition published by Birdberry Books, 2018.

Second edition revised and updated, 2020, published by The Doreen Valiente Foundation in association with the Centre for Pagan Studies.

www.centre-for-pagan-studies.com

www.doreenvaliente.org

Praise for *The Night Journey*

The Night Journey utilizes the historical legend of the witch's flight to the sabbat to expand Aburrow's notion of a modern witchcraft which is "queer, transgressive, and resistant to authoritarian versions of reality." In the spiritual world of *The Night Journey*, witchcraft isn't seen as some sort of rarefied practice isolated from the messy mundane world, but as a beautiful, viable, and practical way of living in the world as a person of power and integrity. Taken together with *Dark Mirror*, these two texts comprise something quite special: a revolutionary vision of traditional Wicca which looks to the Craft's future while simultaneously honoring its traditions.

> **- Misha Magdalene, author of *Outside the Charmed Circle: Exploring Gender & Sexuality in Magical Practice***

There's a real shortage of good books on advanced witchcraft. *The Night Journey - Witchcraft as Transformation* is therefore a much-needed new publication aimed at Wiccans and witches who have reached second degree or who are running their own covens. ... The work at second degree involves looking at the darker sides of our own psyches, confronting our fears and challenging our perhaps long-held beliefs. The goal of this is transformation, and this book is a guide to ways of enabling that to happen.

> **- Lucya Starza, www.badwitch.co.uk**

The Night Journey takes us on a wild ride through Witchcraft of the past, present and future. While so many other books focus on the 'how' of Witchcraft, Aburrow gives us a much-needed dive into the 'why', and champions the diversity that is so necessary for the continuation of the Craft.

> **- Thista Minai, founder of Spectrum Gate Mysteries, author of *Casting a Queer Circle: Non-binary Witchcraft* and *Suffering for Spirit: Empowerment Through Ordeal***

This book is a cornerstone for every modern Pagan's library, or for anyone at all interested in a valid inner reality and how to develop and cope with and enjoy it. ...This isn't a book for the mystically minded, more a kicking, scratching fight on the road to a modern Wiccan spirituality. Paganism is Green, and this is Pagan politics, ecologically and spiritually, the microcosm and the macrocosm. We were right all along, and now is the time to chant our many chants to be heard around the world. However you identify, this book provides well-stated explorations of all aspects of Pagan life. Read it and become an active part of the debate.

> **- Geraldine Beskin,**
> **The Atlantis Bookshop, London, UK.**

Yvonne Aburrow has done it again! In *The Night Journey: Witchcraft as Transformation* Aburrow takes their readers on a journey into the inner working of Wicca, ritual, and magic. They are always careful to consider the ways in which folks of different backgrounds understand, internalize, or experience the Craft, Aburrow is wonderfully honest when it comes to their relationship to the gods while also being refreshingly informative about group and coven dynamics. With a keen eye for issues surrounding mental illness, Aburrow shows their readers, with careful precision, how to spot groups that are supportive, inclusive, and spiritually motivating. This book will be of special interest to coven leaders or to those who wish to understand the role a healthy coven may play in the lives of a new or seasoned witch.

> **- Tim Landry,**
> **anthropologist and occultist.**

An insightful and accessible guide to the theory and practice of contemporary Pagan witchcraft. The author writes from their extensive personal experience and presents their views in a thoughtful and enthusiastic style that are suitable for experienced practitioners and those taking their first exploratory steps. Each chapter concludes with some excellent discussion topics, suggestions for self-reflection, and practical exercises. Like all good books, it presents some challenging views, which offer much food for thought.

> **- Julia Phillips, Postgraduate Researcher,**
> **University of Bristol, author of *Witches of Oz* and**
> ***Madeline Montalban, Magus of St Giles.***

The night journey: witchcraft as transformation

A deep dive into the roots and meanings of contemporary Wiccan and Pagan practices, and how they can be updated for the 21st century. Essential reading for covens and groves.

Sabina Magliocco,
Professor of Anthropology and Chair, Program in the Study of Religion, University of British Columbia, and author of *Witching Culture: Folklore and Neopaganism in America.*

The night journey

Slipping out of the body, sliding up the chimney
Out over the moonlit land, along the ghost-paths
The witch flies to the meeting place on the lonely heath.
The ancestors glimmer softly in the moonlight,
And the fair folk ride out across the woods and fens.
Hecate gathers the wild hunt about her,
And the hounds of Annwn raise their voices to the Moon.
Come to the feast, the Horned One is here,
The witches are gathered at the crossroads.
The cauldron of possibility comes to the boil,
Anything is possible in this twilight realm.
Shadows and dreams made manifest,
Spilling over into the waking world.

Yvonne Aburrow, 2017

The Night Journey
Witchcraft as transformation

Yvonne Aburrow

Contents

Foreword by Steve Dee

Most of the books that I have read on Witchcraft in the last five years have tended to be either focused on history (e.g. Ronald Hutton's *The Witch*) or the spookier reimagining of its Traditional, Non-Wiccan manifestations. In contrast, *The Night Journey* offers something different in its radical re-visioning of initiatory Wicca as a path of personal and political liberation.

I first encountered Yvonne's writing in their excellent *All Acts of Love and Pleasure: inclusive Wicca*, which I experienced as a vivid attempt at bringing inclusive and Queer perspectives to forms of Paganism that may have become stuck in our ableist and heteronormative views of human expression. This new work feels like an expansion of inclusive Wicca; a conscious fleshing-out that provides a deeper, more theological appreciation of what Witchcraft has to offer as a contemporary religious path.

Yvonne has been an initiate of Gardnerian Wicca for almost 30 years and this work represents a distillation of their thinking regarding how Wicca can speak to the challenges of the 21st century. The structure of the book covers a range of themes regarding the validity of Wicca as a religious path and the way in which its initiatory structure helps manage issues such as ego-inflation and spiritual burn out.

The first section of the book "Between the Worlds" moves beyond a simple "how to book" and provides a rich theological reflection on how Wicca provides a living process of shared ritual work via which a relationship with divinity can be evolved. They provide a nuanced engagement with how Pagan magical paths can address our deepest psychological need for contrast and polarity, whether these are between darkness and light or silence and sound. Yvonne has a background in academic religious studies, and this feels very present in their deep description of how their own spirituality and beliefs have evolved within the framework that Wicca has provided.

For Yvonne, Witchcraft is an innately Queer path. The Witch is one who inhabits "a liminal zone between the worlds." This path offers us a shimmering multiplicity of sexual and gender expressions and the Witch by their very definition bends, shapes and adapts. Their theology is unapologetically one of immanence and this is a one of the unique features that they believe Wicca (and Paganism more widely) has to offer in the spiritual marketplace.

In many ways Yvonne's writing has many parallels with that of Starhawk in very consciously seeing the Witch as an adversarial figure that "endangers the status quo." Yvonne explores the more Left-Hand Path adversarial dimensions of the Witch path, not as a preoccupation with Gothic aesthetics, but as the outlaw-tricksters who are "the eternal outsiders, the eternal critics." The Night as the realm of dreams and the Sabbatic journey represents a need to work with ecstasy, wildness and even our own madness as a means of empowering our activism.

The second section "Bringing it all back home" provides us with an engaging set of reflections on Yvonne's experience of running a coven and these insights regarding ritual forms and working with power in leadership hold relevance across many spiritual paths. How do we seek to work towards more flattened hierarchies while retaining our awareness of the power that we hold via experience and time within a tradition?

Yvonne explores the differing ways that people learn and how we support people in plugging into an Egregore while also allowing them to retain the rich individuality that will ultimately add to a tradition and allow it to evolve. For Yvonne, the ability to co-create and change is at the heart of their magic and their self-description as "a relational polytheist" evokes for me the image of a shared cauldron into which people bring their own unique contributions towards a common goal.

Toward the book's conclusion, Yvonne returns to the theme of liberation in the longest essay "Challenging Oppression" in which they ask us to consider the implications of our Paganism:

"I became a Witch, a Pagan, a Polytheist because I believe all life is interconnected, interwoven, interpermeable."

If such connection is central to our religious identity, then it has to have implications for our ethics and how we pursue liberty at both a personal and collective level. Yvonne's work is unapologetically anti-oppressive and anti-racist. Well-meaning inaction is no longer viable. In order to move forward we have to face the implications of racism and colonialism and it is inevitable that such unlearning will be deeply uncomfortable. The chapter also provides some really helpful reflections of the complexities of cultural appropriation and how we might integrate wider traditions in a slow, respectful syncretism.

The Night Journey never promises to be an easy one! As you would expect it can be both disturbing and challenging. At times I felt almost overwhelmed by the concentrated punch of Yvonne's insights and I consciously chose to slow down to allow a healthier process of digestion! Thankfully, Yvonne provides a series of helpful reflective questions and exercises at the end of each chapter to allow us to consider the implications of these issues in our lives. The brew in this cauldron is a potent one and I could imagine myself spending a year and a day working with these chapters so as to allow the type of reflection, soul searching and deep change that Yvonne's work is promoting.

Steve Dee.

Steve Dee is the author of the books A Gnostic's Progress: Magic and the Path of Awakening *and* The Heretic's Journey: Spiritual Freethinking for Difficult Times. *He is also the co-author of* Chaos Craft *with Julian Vayne. His writing has also appeared in* Queer Magic, *edited by Lee Harrington and Tai Fenix Kulystin, and* Gods and Monsters *edited by Michael Kelly. He is a spiritual freethinker with a deep interest in contemplative practices and is an initiate within the east/west Tantra tradition AMOOKOS. He blogs with his friends over at https://theblogofbaphomet.com*

Introduction

The night journey was one of the key themes of medieval witchcraft legends. Witches were believed to travel out of their bodies to attend a nocturnal feast in some wild place and consort with faeries, devils, daemons, and deities of the night and the underworld. It involved leaving everyday reality and entering a liminal zone between the worlds. Here the witch could learn new knowledge, consort with otherworldly beings, and perform rituals and magic to transform reality. This liminal world was queer, transgressive, and resistant to authoritarian versions of reality. In the world of the *treguenda* (the witches' feast) and the Game of Benevento, everyone was equal.

The aim of this book

I wrote this book because I wanted to explore the structure and purpose of ritual, the stages of the spiritual journey, the practice of witchcraft as resistance to imposed norms and structures of oppression, and how folkloric witchcraft connects to the land. I believe that witchcraft is inherently queer and has always resisted authoritarian structures and oppressors. If these vital elements are removed from witchcraft, it becomes safe, sanitised, and dull. Witchcraft should be countercultural and transgressive. That is why we should be wary of self-appointed leaders and elders, and why we need to work to dismantle internalised biases and oppressive tendencies, as well as resisting systemic oppressions.

Who is the book for?

Anyone who is interested in how witchcraft relates to queerness, resistance to oppressors, the land, the ancestors, and legends and folklore will enjoy this book. It will also be useful for people who have begun to experience the descent into the depths of the psyche that is part of the spiritual journey, and people who are preparing to lead a coven and teach the Craft to other people.

About this book

The first section of the book, *Between the worlds*, is aimed at witches who have grasped the basics of ritual practice and want to deepen their engagement with their Craft. The first chapter looks at modes and types of ritual, and some theories of how rituals work to bring about transformation and mystical experiences. The next chapter looks at the uses of sound and silence in ritual. The following chapter deals with the witch's journey through life, and the stages and pitfalls of the inner work, including spiritual bypassing, ego inflation, and spiritual burnout. Next, we look at Queer Witchcraft, and how this is actually an inherent aspect of the archetype of the witch. Then we look at how witchcraft relates to the land, witchcraft as resistance to oppression; and how we can work with ancestors. The next chapter relates the old idea of the witch's pact with spiritual powers to the more recent ideas of relational polytheism. Then we look at the relationship between madness, shamanism, and witchcraft. Finally, we explore the concept of the night journey, another very old image from the history of witchcraft.

In the second section, *Bringing it all back home*, the focus is on how we can use insights gained from the practice of witchcraft in everyday life. The first chapter looks at group dynamics and how they impact on the life of a coven; next we explore being a coven leader, and the process of teaching and learning in a coven, including learning styles and differentiation. Then we explore the concepts of egregore, lineage, upline, and downline; followed by the uses and abuses of power and authority. The next chapter explores the process of challenging oppression (racism, homophobia, transphobia, biphobia, sexism, and misogyny), both within your own life and within the community. Then we look at how to evaluate your Craft and its impact on your life. Next, I reflect on the meaning and purpose of 'spirituality', religion, and magic. Finally, I reflect on the archetype of the witch and what it means.

I finished writing this book in November 2016, just before the American election; things are looking worse now than they did then. I have attempted to revise the text where it references current events, but there may still be inconsistencies.

About me

I have been practising Paganism since 1985 and was initiated into Gardnerian Wicca in 1991. I got my second-degree initiation in 1996, and my third degree in 2014. I started my first coven in 2003, and have trained a dozen people in Wicca, each with their own unique perspectives. This book is the product of my experiences of ritual and training witches.

I started thinking about how to make Wiccan ritual more inclusive of LGBT+ people in 1995, as I am bisexual and have been genderqueer since before there was a word for it. I am still not sure if I am nonbinary or genderqueer or genderfluid (it depends on the day), but nonbinary is a good catch-all term.

I started thinking about how to make the Craft more inclusive of neurodivergent people in around 2003, when I was working with people with dyslexia. The product of both strands of thinking was my previous book on Wicca, *All Acts of Love and Pleasure: inclusive Wicca.*

It was quite a while before I realised that there were things about the Wiccan and wider Pagan communities that were excluding of People of Colour – not least the way that deities tend to be represented as white-skinned.

From 2006 to 2008 I studied contemporary religions and spiritualities at Bath Spa University, and carried out research on queer spirituality, syncretism and dual-faith practice, and Pagan attitudes to science. The course also explored feminist spirituality, Paganism and the New Age, and the encounter between East and West.

I have been seeking for a long time to explore the more transgressive aspects of the Craft, such as the night journey, the pact with spirits, and the archetype of the "Devil", and I have always been interested in basing rituals on folklore and legends. These more transgressive aspects of witchcraft are joyfully embraced by traditions which draw on traditional folklore and legends.

I believe that witchcraft traditions have something important to say about human nature and our place in the world, and that these ideas can be used to undermine structures of oppression such as systemic racism, homophobia, transphobia, and misogyny – because that has been the role of the witch for centuries.

Part 1: Between the worlds

This section is aimed at witches who have grasped the basics of ritual practice and want to deepen their engagement with their Craft. It explores modes and types of ritual, and some theories of how rituals work to bring about transformation and mystical experiences; the uses of sound and silence in ritual; the witch's journey through life; the stages and pitfalls of the inner work, including spiritual bypassing, ego inflation, and spiritual burnout. It discusses Queer Witchcraft, and how this is actually an inherent aspect of the archetype of the witch; how witchcraft relates to the land; witchcraft as resistance to oppression; and how we can work with ancestors; the witch's pact with spiritual powers and how it relates to the more recent ideas of relational polytheism. Next it explores the relationship between madness, shamanism, and witchcraft; and then the concept of the night journey, another very old image from the history of witchcraft.

1. Religion, spirituality, and the inner work

There are several memes doing the rounds on the internet which dismiss religion as a conformist and dull activity and claim that spirituality is much more enlightened. These memes ignore the concept that religion involves wrestling with tradition, seeking to make a connection with the divine, deities, or Nature, and that there are many different forms of religion – esoteric, exoteric, liberal, conservative, literalist, metaphorical, ecstatic, liturgical, and so on.

David Webster has offered an extended and brilliant critique of the "spiritual but not religious" brigade in his book *Dispirited: How Contemporary Spirituality Makes Us Stupid, Selfish and Unhappy.* He points out some of the same issues that I have outlined in this chapter.

If someone claims to be religious, spiritual, not religious, or not spiritual, ask them what they mean by the term they are using. These terms have been bandied around in so many different contexts and discourses that in order to use them to communicate (often across vast philosophical divides), we may need to unpack what each participant in a conversation means by the term, if we are not to end up with a failure to communicate.

At its best, "spirituality" (whatever that term means [1]) is a spur to greater compassion, engagement with social justice, and trying to make the world a better place. This used to be called mysticism, which meant something and sought to

---

[1] L Bregman, Spirituality: *A Glowing and Useful Term in Search of a Meaning,* http://ome.sagepub.com/content/53/1/5.full.pdf

wrestle and engage with the wider tradition in which it was situated. Many times, organised religion sought to crush the mystics, with their call to genuine compassion, and their speaking truth to power, and their direct engagement with the divine other (or others).

At its worst, "spirituality" is a mess of cultural appropriation, exploitation of the vulnerable, silencing of dissent, sweeping justified anger under the carpet, and offering a pabulum of spurious advice, airy-fairy sayings, and consumer offerings of easily-digested "wisdom" and manufactured artefacts to make you feel "spiritual" and get in touch with your feelings. Many 'spiritual directors', 'life coaches', and other self-styled spiritual leaders – most of whom are not even qualified therapists – prey on the vulnerable to make them feel that they cannot have self-worth without succumbing to a rigorous programme of self-help, self-examination, and generally beating themselves up for not being spiritual enough. They keep their 'followers' as perpetual neophytes, never empowering them to lead groups themselves.

Every time I have an encounter with someone who has an interest in spirituality, and also possesses power over others, I find that they want to silence my anger at injustice because it is "not spiritual" to be angry. I find myself bruised and diminished by their criticism of my way of being in the world. Any engagement with the intellectual or theological or historical context of an issue is also silenced by these people because that is "not spiritual" either. These people are so convincing with their "peaceful" mien and unfurrowed brows, untroubled by actual social injustice or the suffering of others. These are the type of people who silence those who complain of racism, sexism, and homophobia, claiming that they are "obsessed" with race, gender, and sexuality.

Some of them do engage with the suffering of others, but in my view, they only exacerbate it by placing the blame squarely on the shoulders of the sufferer, convincing them that they must "work on themselves" and buy whatever the latest self-help book, video, course, life-coaching, etc happens to be. Some of them even say that the first step to being more spiritual or loving or whatever is to accept oneself. The natural response of many people to this is to feel guilty for not loving themselves. However, the lack of self-love and self-esteem that many people suffer from is caused by alienation from other people, from nature, and from life. It will not be solved by increased introspection, but by going out and doing what you love. If you are an introvert, that might be different from what extroverts love to do, and that is just fine. The first step to accepting yourself is to stop worrying about yourself so much.

The blame for social ills is constantly shifted from the collective to the individual in many contexts. Instead of preventing bullying in the workplace, employers hire stress and time-management consultants to 'fix' individuals who have not 'adapted' to the workplace. The same applies to dieting, where the fact that it is difficult to avoid eating fattening food, and difficult to get enough exercise to burn it off, is laid squarely at the door of the overweight individual, and hardly anyone bothers to look for social or societal factors that might contribute to obesity.

Whenever you see a self-help book, or a person who sets themselves up as an authority on spiritual matters, ask

yourself what qualifies them to be such an authority. I am
not saying their life must be totally organised (whose life is
not subject to misfortune and the vagaries of
circumstance?) – but rather, how do they respond to
disaster? Do they curl up in a welter of self-pity, or do they
get out and do something, perhaps getting involved with
trying to right the social injustice that caused their
misfortune (if applicable)? As the wonderful saying has it,
"if you meet the Buddha on the road, kill him". Anyone
claiming to be a Buddha is not a Buddha. The Tao that can
be named is not the true Tao. Indeed, Siddhārtha Gautama,
the Buddha himself, allegedly remarked that if the things
he said did not make sense to his hearers, they should
ignore him. [2]

Subjecting advice to scrutiny and reflection about whether
it applies to your own life is of course a principle that you
should apply to anything that I write as well. Nothing is
exempt from this principle. My perspective is mostly
limited to my own experience, as is that of every other
writer.

Do without doing, and everything gets done

If all the money and energy that was expended on trying to
become more spiritual was expended on trying to make the
world a better place for everyone, think how much better
the world would be. I am not saying that people should not
indulge themselves in a bit of pampering like a massage
and a bath with some nice candles and a bit of tinkly music,
but do it unashamedly because it makes you feel good, not

[2] http://www.goodreads.com/quotes/1815-do-not-believe-in-anything-simply-because-you-have-heard

because you think you ought to, or because you think it will make you a more spiritual person.

Personally, I derive more benefit from going for a nice walk in the woods, doing a ritual, going on a demonstration about a social justice issue, or having a nice evening with friends, than I ever have from any attempt to "be more spiritual". I am not a naturally introspective person in any case. You can derive a great amount of self-worth and connecting with others by going to take part in conservation work, or feeding the homeless, or helping animals, or doing something creative – you don't need to sit around worrying about whether you are spiritual enough. I also derived a great deal of benefit from being a trade union caseworker, because I learnt to speak truth to power, but I became a caseworker because it was the thing in front of me that needed doing, and I knew it was the right thing to do, not because I particularly hoped to gain anything from it.

There is a brilliant and hilarious video by J P Sears, *How to be ultra-spiritual*, [3] which sends up the "spiritualler-than-thou" types (as I call them): the people who speak ultra-softly and go about dispensing unsolicited "wisdom". It is a merciless send-up of the "ultra-spiritual", and a critique that needed to be out there.

And then I saw an article by a "life-coach" giving women contradictory advice about how to be irresistible to men, where one of the pieces of advice was a blatant piece of slut-shaming. Fortunately, several people had posted hilarious comments on the piece.

---

[3] https://www.youtube.com/watch?v=1kDso5ElFRg

I vividly remember my first encounter with a "life-coach" and I remember thinking it was a load of pretentious tosh and quite possibly a sugar-coated version of "how to be a capitalist bastard and succeed in the rat-race".

I feel much the same about most so-called "self-help" books, which again locate the source of suffering in the individual and fail to offer any remedy that we might all undertake as a society. There are a few excellent exceptions, such as *Taking care* by David Smail, and *Women who run with the Wolves* by Clarissa Pinkola Estes (brilliantly satirised by *Women who run with the Poodles*, however).

Therefore, I have been trying to eliminate any talk of "spirituality" from my speech and writing, and instead talk about the inner work, embodiment, and connecting with the body. This too might become problematic if we assume that there is only one right way to be embodied, but at least it is more earthy, and takes actual physical and emotional needs into account and makes a connection between them. Writers on embodiment that I have seen do seem to engage with the world around them.

Spirituality as a commodity

Nevertheless, it strikes me that the elephant in the room, and what really ails us, is the commodification and marketisation of everything – also known as capitalism. Value is no longer seen as intrinsic to an experience or a thing, but only as a marketable commodity. "Spirituality" has become yet another marketable commodity – a thing that should be our birth-right, that should be as natural as breathing, has been packaged and marketed back to us as something that can only be mediated by experts.

People often say that "the best things in life are free" and it is true. Having a consensual hug or a massage with someone you love, or a stimulating conversation with a friend, or a lovely walk in the woods, or some other experience of shared beauty, is much more effective than hours of "spirituality"-related activities.

One of the things that has made me a more empathetic person, and possibly a nicer person to be around, is reading novels, because novels teach you about the nuances of feeling and allow you to empathise with someone else's pain in a safe space (the privacy of your own mind) before going out and practising compassion in the real world. The trick is to make the connection between the character in the novel and real people, of course.

Connect the inner to the outer

Many people have emphasised the idea that you need to love something greater than yourself, and/or other than yourself, to find happiness. Of course, many people who aspire to be spiritual do love God, or Nature, or something beyond themselves; but then they spend a lot of time worrying about how to be more spiritual and fall back into introspection and self-doubt.

Viktor Frankl explains that the only way to find meaning and peace is to look beyond the self.[4] This implies that relentless self-examination is counterproductive. The Muslims say that "Allah is closer to me than my jugular vein. The great mystery of life is always available, always present, always pouring itself into reality at every moment, waiting to be experienced and enjoyed.

---

[4] https://www.goodreads.com/work/quotes/3389674

For me, the central mystery of my religion is love. The word religion comes from the Latin word, *religio*, which I interpret poetically as meaning 'to reconnect'. (Its literal meaning is probably more to do with being bound to sacred laws and customs.) Love is about connection, connecting fully and deeply with another human being. There are many types of love involving different types and depths of connection (*eros, filia, storge,* and *agape* are some that have been named).

Our culture has also sought to commodify love, and reduce it only to romantic love, but it is much broader and deeper than that. In Hebrew, one of the words for love is *Ahava,* meaning 'I will give'. The Tanakh (Hebrew Bible) contains an extended meditation on the meaning of Ahava in the story told in the *Book of Ruth*. Another is *Chesed*, meaning steadfast love, loving-kindness. This term is often translated into Greek as *eleos*.

The goddess Eleos is the personification of compassion in Greek mythology. Her Roman counterpart was Clementia. Ancient paganism had thought about love, compassion, and forgiveness, and these were among the virtues they cultivated.

All the best writing seeks to broaden our humanity by encouraging us to connect, to have compassion, to love (both ourselves and others). If we cannot be compassionate to ourselves, how can we have compassion for others?

And if we have compassion for others, then we will desire social justice (and not just a few cosmetic fixes to the system, but genuine deep and transformative change. In the Jewish tradition, the practice of restoring social justice is known as *tikkun olam*. [5]

This concept of repairing the world, and cleansing the doors of perception to be able to apprehend the infinite - to see angels in the trees, as Blake did: it seems to me that this is the purpose of religion and the inner work.

What is religion? Some have derived the word religion from the Latin word *religare*, to reconnect; others have derived it from *relego*, to re-read. I like both these meanings, as the first implies compassion and connection, and the second implies the living of the examined life, the interpretation of experience, and the pursuit of knowledge. Religions have been compared to languages, in that they are embedded in specific cultures; even when a religion claims to be universally applicable, it is still modified by each new culture that adopts it. A religion is a set of shared practices, values and narratives that make the world meaningful for its adherents. Most of the world's religions are not based on shared beliefs in the same way as Christianity, but rather on a shared worldview: a set of values and practices embedded in a symbolic and mythological understanding of the world.

Even in the traditions that have codified beliefs that their adherents are supposed to subscribe to, individual interpretations of their creeds can and do vary wildly. In Christianity, individual believers do not all believe the same things, even if they pay lip service to the idea that they should do. Even though Islam has a set of beliefs,

---

[5] Jennifer Noparstak, *Tikkun Olam*,
http://learningtogive.org/papers/paper169.html

there's still room for interpretation of the *Qu'ran*. The word *fatwa* means an interpretation or an opinion. So, if you are unsure about what to do about a thing, you go and ask a mullah or a qadi for an interpretation of the Qu'ran. It is not assumed by most Muslims that there is only one possible interpretation of the *Qu'ran*.

Judaism is mainly focused around observing the *mitzvot* (commandments). That is why a Jewish coming of age ceremony is called a Bat Mitzvah or Bar Mitzvah (daughter or son of the vow). Many Liberal Jews are atheists. Also, Jews (Orthodox and Liberal and Reform) say that there are many different interpretations of the *Torah* - they really enjoy debating them in the *schul* or *yeshiva* attached to the synagogue.

There is religion as it is officially supposed to be according to the doctrine of the tradition in question; and then there is the reassuringly messy, fuzzy, and human way that people actually do it. The problem is that no-one apart from liberal religionists will admit that the fuzzy messy human way of doing it is the best way.

I see religion as rituals practised in community, whose goal is to create a sense of mystical connection with the universe and all beings within it. In feeling this sense of connection, we experience compassion for the sufferings of other beings, and empathy with their joys. We can enhance this sense of connection by finding a community with whom we can practice compassion and mindfulness; if we do not engage in ritual in a community setting, it can become self-centred and shallow, disconnected from everyday reality. We need the experience of living and sharing with others to enable us to grow and become our authentic selves. This can be done by the creation of a community of shared values, which models in microcosm the desired qualities of human community. Of course, there will be conflicts and tensions, but it is in how these are resolved that the real values of the community will be tested and refined. It is only by this kind of radical openness and humility that the beloved community can become strong and genuinely inclusive.

I believe that the religious life is a shared journey towards greater communion with the cosmos, where Spirit descends into matter rather than escaping from it – but this communion does not involve the effacement of individuality; rather it is the celebration of diversity and the quest for authenticity, because the "divine" (the vision of ultimate worth) is the potentiality of all life to share in mystical communion. But we must expand our compassion to all beings, not just to those whose values we share, and we do this by engaging in social action – caring for the poor and the oppressed, protecting the environment, standing up for human rights, and promoting freedom, peace and justice.

Indeed, we cannot really expect others to be convinced that we are 'mystical' unless we put compassion into practice by helping others. The two aspects of religion go together: without a sense of connection there is no basis for compassion, and without the expression of compassion in the form of caring, the life of a mystic can be barren and unproductive.

The inner work is intimately related to the outer work - the inner work is the ever-welling presence of life-giving waters, and the outer work is the carrying of the water to the parched and thirsty land.

Love is a fierce and joyful thing

Love does not mean complete negation of the self. I am a human being with needs and desires, and I deserve love and compassion as much as the next person. Transcending the ego is not the same thing as erasing or negating the ego. All that happens is that one becomes aware of a reality beyond the ego and seeks to connect with that greater reality.

Love is not a mealy-mouthed, weak thing that allows others to walk all over one. Love is a fierce and joyful thing that seeks the greatest well-being for all – bearing in mind that another person's well-being may look quite different from yours. As many sages have said, "love thy neighbour as thyself" – in other words, love your neighbour as much as you love yourself.

Buddhism talks about 'foolish compassion' – the type of compassion that fails to involve the mind as well as the heart, to try and assess what would really help the suffering other. [6] Love is not afraid to speak truth to power, or to tell the schlemiel that he is a fool.

Love is out on the front line telling the world that Black lives matter, standing up for the rights of LGBTQIA+ people, Indigenous Peoples, immigrants, asylum seekers, and the marginalised. Love may be gentle and kind, but it

---

[6] Ed and Deb Shapiro, *Wise Compassion*, http://www.huffingtonpost.com/ed-and-deb-shapiro/wise-compassion_b_841019.html

is also fierce and joyous, and angry and sad, and embracing diversity.

Discussion

What do 'spirituality', 'religion', and 'the inner work' mean to you?

To what extent have contemporary Pagan traditions succumbed to the commodification of religion and spirituality?

What are the aims or purposes of your religious / spiritual practice?
Have they changed over the years?

What is the central mystery of your Craft?

Exercises

Draw a mind-map of the term spirituality and your associations with it

Meditate on the experience that you have identified as the central mystery of your Craft

Meditate on the aims of your religious / spiritual practice

2. Queer Witchcraft

The Queer Ones are rising. We are rising out of the woods, out of the ocean, out of the cracks between the concrete. Genderqueer, transgender, glorious peacock-shimmering, rising out of the darkness, the healing and sacred darkness, into the many-hued light of day. Queer deities, genderqueer deities, transgender goddesses and gods. Inari the fox deity; Vertumnus the changeable and ever-changing; tricksters and healers, poets and seers and shamans.

Gender is not a binary, not even a spectrum, it is a vast glittering field of possibility, many genders, many hues, many different expressions of being and love.

We are rising, out of the silence, out of the hidden places, daring to be, to shine forth our glorious queer radiance, because we are the holy ones, the liminal ones, the dreamers and the creators of possibility.

Our freedom is frightening to some who want there to be a binary, a set of limitations. We call them out of their fear and into the radiant and glittering field of stars, into the joy of expressing all that you are – joy, magic, dreams, anger at injustice, diversity in unity, unity in diversity. We call them to embrace their humanity and ours, not to cling in fear and loathing to a diminished, fearful, restrictive, and destructive vision of womanhood, that excludes the childless as much as the transgender and the non-binary.

The glorious diversity of the human body, the glorious diversity of life journeys and intersecting identities, is to be enjoyed and celebrated. Different people have different journeys. The penis is not a symbol of the patriarchy. The gun is the symbol and the weapon of patriarchy and kyriarchy. The penis is a symbol of life, celebrated and venerated as such by many ancient cultures, along with the yoni, the vulva, the vagina. Both are fountains of life and creativity. The kyriarchy wants to distort and desecrate these sacred places, by turning the penis into a weapon and the vagina into its sheath, a place to be violated. But we reject and resist the violence of the kyriarchy, and affirm the sacred beauty of transgender, genderfluid, and genderqueer in all their gentle and fierce beauty and glory. We embrace the witchery of genderblending [7].

Gender essentialism and separatism is the mirror image of patriarchy. We reject the patriarchy and the kyriarchy. We reject all binaries. There are men who reject rape culture and women who excuse rape. Let us promote consent culture and gather our beautiful diverse tribe. Let us include people in, welcoming and celebrating and affirming diversity, not sowing hate and fear and division. Let us create spaces that are safe for every person of every gender. Pagan traditions (both ancient and contemporary) affirm the queer as sacred, as liminal, as being touched by the gods. All magic is magic. All love is love. All people are people.

We are all images of divinity. As a polytheist, I affirm trans and queer deities among the vast range of deities. The Sun is both fierce and hot, gentle and warming. The Ocean is both gentle, rocking the cradle of dreams, and destructive,

---

[7] Laura Tempest Zakroff, *The Witchery of Genderblending*, 6 June 2016, http://www.patheos.com/blogs/tempest/2016/06/the-witchery-of-genderblending.html

storming and raging and destroying. Neither of these moods has any essential gender. The Moon is the lover of the hidden ones, calling to us of wildness and wilderness, dreams and intuition. These experiences are available to all genders – we all carry the tides of the Moon in our blood and in our bodies, regardless of whether we menstruate. Let us celebrate the tides of our blood with all who venerate the body, regardless of their anatomy or ours.

Let us magnify and glorify the images of divinity within ourselves and each other. Show forth love and beauty and creativity; celebrate the radiance of the many-hued multiplicity of gender expression, sexuality, and the human body.

Darkness, nature, and queerness

Edward Carpenter was an enthusiastic advocate of Nature as a place of freedom, and following him, his friend E M Forster made the hero of his novel *Maurice* feel "at one with the forests and the night" as soon as he had made the decision to adopt an actively gay lifestyle. Harry Hay, founder of the Radical Faeries, who was a Carpenter enthusiast, also stressed the importance of communing with Nature.

The celebration of darkness, which we have been told by mainstream culture is the realm of evil, allows us to transcend boundaries.[8] It also allows us to escape the hierarchical view of the cosmos which is associated with

---

[8] Hawley-Gorsline, R. (2003) 'James Baldwin and Audre Lorde as Theological Resources for the Celebration of Darkness.' *Theology and Sexuality* 10(1) pp 58-72

the exclusive honouring of the light. [9]

Wicca is partly about the interaction of light and darkness, played out in the Wheel of the Year (the cycle of Wiccan festivals). Instead of being opposed, light and darkness interact in a dance or sexual union. This is the basis of the idea of polarity. One way to make the idea of polarity more inclusive is to regard the primary polarity as being the interaction of self and other, lover and beloved (rather than as male and female). Lynna Landstreet sees the first touch of lightning on the primordial waters as being the "true Great Rite, of which all other enactments, sexual or not, are merely symbolic".

It could be argued that Wicca is inherently queer, but most practitioners are unaware of this. The word *wicca* (Anglo-Saxon for a male witch) apparently derives from an Indo-European root meaning 'to bend' or 'to shape' - and the actions of bending and creativity are both frequently associated with same-sex love. The emphasis on the need to become psychologically androgynous (frequently couched in terms of developing men's feminine side and women's masculine side) and the use of the *Dryghtyn Prayer* add to the feeling of queerness at the heart of the tradition. In addition to this, the figure of the witch, derived in part from the spae-wives and *seiðr*-workers of Northern Europe[10], is often associated with sexual and gender

[9] Hawley-Gorsline, R. (2003) 'James Baldwin and Audre Lorde as Theological Resources for the Celebration of Darkness.' *Theology and Sexuality* 10(1) pp 58-72

[10] Blain, J. (2002) *Nine Worlds of Seid-Magic: Ecstasy and Neo-Shamanism in North European Paganism*. London and New York: Routledge.

transgression. These ideas may not be very current in Wicca generally, but they are apparent in other witchcraft traditions, and are part of the historical discourse about witchcraft.

LGBTQIA+ people have reclaimed the word 'queer' as a badge of resistance to heteronormativity and as a tool for liberation. Irshad Manji[11] defines queer as 'being unpredictable', rather than 'rigid and absolute, and frankly dull'. Similarly, Wiccans and other contemporary Pagan witches have reclaimed the word 'witch' to mean a shaper, a changer of consciousness, and a radical. There is a strong strand of ecological, political, and sexual radicalism in witchcraft.

Queer spiritual roles

In his book, *Coming Out Spiritually*, Christian de la Huerta identifies ten queer spiritual roles or archetypes which we have traditionally expressed. However, it must be noted that these roles are not the only roles that queer people can occupy, and they are not necessarily exclusive to queer people. It is not helpful to tell people that they must express their queerness in a particular way, either in ritual or out of it. Nor is it helpful to insist that specific groups of people ought to honour specific deities just because of their gender, sexual orientation, or ethnic group.

Catalytic transformers. Queer people are highly aware of what needs changing in our societies, and so we participate in movements for change and transformation.

---

[11] Summerskill, B. ed. (2006) *The Way we are now: Gay and Lesbian Lives in the 21st Century.* London and New York: Continuum.

Outsiders: Mirrors of Society. We live on the edge, and force society to look at things it does not want to deal with.

Consciousness scouts: Going First and Taking Risks. Queer people are often pioneers in spirituality, religion, the arts, discovering new art forms, dreaming new dreams, coming up with new ways to interact with the unseen.

Sacred clowns and eternal youth. There is a playful, camp, puckish, tricksterish quality to queer culture. We are the ones who believe in magic and add a sprinkle of fairy dust to every situation.

Keepers of Beauty. We are often the movers and shakers in music, art, poetry, theatre, design, and fashion. These are all aspects of life which give pleasure and relaxation.

Caregivers. We are often counsellors, nurses, doctors, massage therapists, flight attendants, personal trainers, food servers, teachers, and parents. Our marginalised status perhaps gives us more empathy for the vulnerable.

Mediators: The In-Between People. Many cultures view queer people as "the in-between people" because we seem to perform multiple genders. This has meant that we have been mediators between the sexes, and between the seen and the unseen worlds.

Shamans and Priests: Sacred Functionaries. In many cultures throughout history, queer people have been honoured as spiritual leaders and advisers.

The Divine Androgyne. Many occult authors, from Edward Carpenter to Carl Jung, have suggested that the archetype of the Divine Androgyne (inherited from the Western Mystery Tradition), a being who includes both

41

genders, perhaps even transcending gender. Occultists at the end of the nineteenth century regarded psychological androgyny as the aim of the Adept, partly because of a belief that humans were androgynous before the Fall, and partly because of a belief in the androgyny of the divine. As Wicca draws in part on the Western Mystery Tradition, it has inherited these ideas, which are expressed in the Dryghtyn Prayer, which is addressed to an entity that is "male and female, the original source of all things".

Gatekeepers. Among the Dagar people of Africa, gays are believed to have a higher vibration which allows us to access higher spiritual realms. They believe that our purpose on earth is to keep the gates open to the Otherworld.

Some of these roles are perhaps stereotypes rather than archetypes, but it is great to see an exploration of these roles, and how being queer can illuminate the inner work. The manifestation of these roles may be because queer people are marginalised and transgress the heterocentric norms of our society - so maybe they would disappear if being queer came to be viewed as normal.

Queer rituals

Our passage through life is marked by a series of rituals - birth, coming of age, initiation, marriage, divorce, retirement, death. But as a society, we lack rituals for coming out as queer. There should be a ritual for transitioning, and a ritual for coming out of the closet and being welcomed into the community - both the queer community and the wider community - as your new identity. Perhaps there should be coming out rituals for heterosexuals too, as we gradually cease to take heterosexuality as a norm or a given. A coming-out ritual is offered in *Appendix II* - feel free to adopt and adapt it as you see fit. Chapter 42, *Rites of Passage*, offers some thoughts on how to create meaningful rituals to mark the phases of life.

One of my favourite queer rituals is one I call the queer tunnel of rebirth. People tend to associate the mysteries of birth with people who have wombs; but we can all symbolically give birth to each other. The way that the ritual works is that all the participants form a tunnel of pairs of people by holding their hands up to form an arch. The participants can be of any gender and sexual orientation - preferably including lesbian, gay, bisexual, transgender, genderqueer, nonbinary, polyamorous, kinky, asexual, intersex, cisgender, and heterosexual, to include all acts of love and pleasure. The last pair at the back of the tunnel then walk through the tunnel and are "reborn" from the other end. This is then repeated by every pair of people, until everyone has been "reborn". This is a lovely ritual to do if you want to strengthen the sense of community in a group.

I have always taken the view that the Great Rite is any pair of lovers either making love (with freely given and enthusiastic consent) or performing a symbolic representation of making love (an athame placed in a chalice, or a chalice poured into another chalice. I believe that the central mystery of Wicca is love, and that all acts of love and pleasure are rituals of the Goddess of Wicca.

Discussion

What does the word 'queer' mean to you?

How is queerness associated with witchcraft?

Does being queer give you a unique perspective on witchcraft and magic?

Which deities do you associate with being queer?

Exercises

Try the queer tunnel of rebirth with your coven

Write your own coming-out ritual

Write your own transition / gender recognition ritual

3. The witch's journey

The witch's journey from initiation, through the depths of the psyche and up to the heights of apotheosis, from trials and tribulations to joy and communion with deities and divinity, is fraught with perils and pitfalls. The sudden reversals of fortune are reminiscent of the game of Snakes and Ladders, which originated in India as the game of Moksha Patam and was intended to illustrate the pitfalls and triumphs of the spiritual journey. [12]

The goal of the journey is different in left-hand path and right-hand path traditions. This implies that the techniques and approaches necessary to facilitate reaching the goal will be different, too.

Right-hand path traditions stress self-negation, and in some cases self-emptying (*kenosis*), to assist with the process of divinisation or *theosis* - being filled with the divine or remade in the image of the divine. In some right-hand path traditions, the aim is union with the divine. (Obviously, this is a massive oversimplification of a complex topic, but this broad-brush picture will suffice for our purposes here.) The Gnostics' aim was to free spirit from matter entirely (whereas mainstream Christianity - rightly in my view - rejected this goal).

Left-hand path traditions stress self-actualisation, becoming more authentic, more powerful, and eventually

---

[12] "Snakes & Ladders History", *The Museum of Gaming Newsletter*, No 2, February 2015.
http://www.museumofgaming.org.uk/documents/Newsletter2.pdf

becoming a deity in one's own right (*apotheosis*). I would also suggest that this means that their aim is for more spirit to descend into matter, for a *hieros gamos* (sacred marriage) of spirit and matter. This may be why they are often represented with an inverted pentagram, which symbolises the descent of spirit into matter. This is why the virtues stressed by Doreen Valiente of the Wica (honour and humility, strength and beauty, power and compassion, mirth and reverence) and by Victor Anderson of the Feri (Sex, Pride, Self, Power, Passion on the Iron Pentacle; Love, Law, Knowledge, Liberty, Wisdom on the Pearl Pentacle) are virtues that facilitate self-actualisation, and not self-negation.[13] Both of these traditions emphasise the self as divine. [14]

Similar ideas are found in the Wiccan tradition, and doubtless in other witchcraft traditions too. We are gods, we just need to realise our divine natures. So, the pitfalls on our path will not be pride, sex, power, passion, or self (as they would be on a path of self-negation). Our pitfalls will be unrealistic or misplaced pride; sex and power used unethically; blind passion not tempered by the other virtues; a failure to balance our needs with those of others, a failure to know the boundaries of self. Or, to express this in terms of the eight Wiccan virtues, an excessive sense of honour not balanced by humility; excessive humility that fails to honour the self; too much of one virtue and not

---

[13] See chapter 9 of *Dark Mirror: The Inner Work of Witchcraft*, for a discussion of the Iron Pentacle and the Pearl Pentacle.
[14] Jason Mankey (2015), *American Paganisms: the Feri Tradition* [interview with Anaar Niino], http://www.patheos.com/blogs/panmankey/2015/08/america n-paganisms-the-feri-tradition/

enough of its balancing virtue.

Why witchcraft is a craft

A craft is a system of knowledge that unites practical and theoretical knowledge. In the West, we have tended to divide knowledge between art and craft, scientific knowledge and technical knowhow, and regarded the practical side of things as somehow lesser. But as Michael Shanks and Randall McGuire [15] have pointed out, "a craft [is] a socially engaged practice which is not alienating, which edifies and provides diverse experience." It is not alienating because it unites the work of head and hand, the theoretical and the practical. The Arts and Crafts Movement (circa 1900) wanted to restore the unity of thinking and doing; they wanted craft to become art put into practice in society, not separated from life. They wanted to create a unity of intellect and emotion. Witchcraft rituals are better when they are performed as a physical activity: there is dance, movement, gesture, all of which mirror the movement of energy in the circle; a movement which creates change in the practitioners, and (we hope) in the world. To create magic, we must have a concept, to which we then give form. We direct the energy into a specific shape or outcome. [16] *Visualize the outcome you want.*

The crafting of good ritual cannot be reduced to a set of abstract rules or procedures – it requires skill and creativity. In any craft, there are three considerations: purpose; viability; and expression.

---

[15] Michael Shanks & Randall H McGuire (1996), "The Craft of Archaeology", *American Antiquity*, 61 (1), pp 75-88.
[16] *Ibid.*

The needs of the community, aesthetics, ethics, and a dialogue within the craft community all contribute to a definition of purpose.

Creativity is a response to the situation, the raw materials to hand, the integration of art and craft, tradition, and the sharing of knowledge and skills. All of these contribute to the viability of the work.

Expression is determined by personal style, technique, tradition, effectiveness, oneness with nature, resonance in the moment, and aesthetic, emotive and ethical considerations.

The point of a craft is not to have a formalised method; there is no substitute for skill – hence the emphasis on apprenticeship and the journey. In craft traditions, wisdom is valued more than knowledge (wisdom involves a combination of knowledge, insight, judgment, and a wise course of action). A craft is a form of storytelling: it makes cultural meanings and provides a structuring narrative and set of symbols to help the practitioner relate to the world in a meaningful way.

In a craft, there is no single "correct" route to the outcome; each person develops their own technique – so witchcraft is unified as a body of practice, but not reduced to a single technique. Theory is not regarded as more useful than practice – the separation of theory from practice is a capitalist phenomenon (compare Marxist theories of the division of labour). The concept of a craft is subversive; it resists capitalist structures of work. It is not just knowledge for its own sake, nor technique isolated from knowledge; rather, it considers the spiritual and material needs of the community it serves.

The importance of a craft approach to knowledge is that it is an embodied knowledge, involving an awareness of the properties of materials, and how to interact with them. It is also worth noting that the guild system that evolved to regulate the crafts had three stages: the apprentice, the journeyman, and the master. These three stages are in many ways like the degree system in Wicca.

The degree system in Wicca

The degree system in Wicca appears to me to be an attempt to mirror the stages of the inner work. I have seen similar stages of development described in the writings of people in other religions who are on some kind of spiritual journey - a period of expansion, followed by an encounter with constriction, followed by some sort of inner union. The Druidic system of initiations (Bard, Ovate, Druid) is similarly structured, but with different symbolism. Interestingly, though, the Ovate grade is very similar to the Wiccan second degree.

Many people are confused or misinformed about the Wiccan degree system (including some Wiccans). The degree system is not a hierarchical structure, nor is it about keeping secrets for the sake of secrecy. It is more like an apprenticeship system.

One would hope that students would respect their teacher and show up on time, help out with setting up and packing away the temple, do their homework, and put in the effort required to progress in the Craft - but respect does not equal subservience.

The point of the encounter with the mysteries that the degree system represents is an unfolding of a journey rather like the progression of ideas in the Tarot deck.

I have spent 17 years offering progressive and inclusive Wiccan training, and everyone I have trained is encouraged and empowered to become a fully fledged witch as soon as possible.

The metaphor that many covens and lineages use for the degree system is that of the guild system of apprentice / journeyman / master. The apprentice learns a craft (such as stonemasonry) by watching and imitating the master craftsperson. After completing their apprenticeship, apprentices become journeymen, who travel around different workshops learning from different master crafts-persons. Masters are regarded as having mastered their craft.

In the past, masters had authority over apprentices by virtue of their craft knowledge. The authority stemmed from their knowledge, not from the hierarchy. The more modern view of this is that the authority is to elevate apprentices and journeymen to the next level, based on their progress in the craft. Extra knowledge and skill also empower the practitioner to train others and determine who is suitable to be trained.

In magical systems, some of the stuff we do can be psychologically damaging if handled incorrectly. That is why there is a build-up to more advanced skills. You start with relatively easy stuff and work your way towards the more challenging stuff.

Learning Wicca is not like a university degree. The most

important skills and experiences are difficult to test. You can see and hear whether someone has called a quarter elegantly with words and gestures, but the important thing is that they made a connection to the spirit of the element. That is an internal process, which feels different to different people.

An even better metaphor for the degree system would be exploring a garden when you move into a new home.

For the first year, you just enjoy the sights and smells and sounds of the new garden. You wait to see what will grow as the seasons unfold, and where the birds will nest. You tend the flowerbeds and the grassy area (which could be a meadow instead of a lawn). You do not bring in very many new plants (in case you displace existing ones). You work with the garden as it is.

The next year, once you know where everything is, you experiment more: moving plants around, introducing new plants, maybe creating a new path. Maybe things get difficult when you start digging more.

In subsequent years, when you have really got the hang of your new garden, what will grow there, and what will not, you start to achieve a new level of comfort and confidence with your garden. A new synthesis has been achieved. A sacred marriage, one might say.

The first year of a new garden is like the first degree. You are just enjoying the flowers and the new experience.

The second year is like second degree; things get a bit more challenging, but you are also more familiar with the new environment. You are also able to share gardening tips with the other people who work on your garden.

The subsequent years are like third degree, when you are confident with your garden and maybe ready to show other people some gardening tricks, and perhaps extend your gardening wisdom to other areas of life.

The first degree

The first degree is traditionally described as an encounter with the Goddess. In other words, an encounter with the principle of expansion, life, and growth. At the beginning of the inner work, the psyche and consciousness seem expanded, more alive, more aware and awake. Everything is shiny and exciting and renewed. The initiate embarks on a journey of discovery (of the self, of magical techniques, and of feeling connected to All That Is). The first degree is (or should be) like a honeymoon period when everything is hunky-dory.

The first-degree Wiccan is a priestess, priest, or priestex unto themselves, but not yet a priest, priestess, or priestex to anyone else. In many covens, they can cast a circle, call the quarters, invoke and be invoked on. Some covens prefer people to wait until second degree before invoking or being invoked on. It is usually preferable for first degrees to ask the advice of their high priestess, high priest, or high priestex before guesting with another coven (and many covens prefer their first degrees to ask permission). The coven leaders will have experience of other covens which will be invaluable. The first degree is like an apprentice, learning the Craft.

The second degree

It becomes apparent that someone is ready for second degree when the principle of constriction becomes apparent in their life. The second degree is traditionally regarded as an encounter with the Horned God. The initiate becomes aware of death in a new way. They descend into the underworld of their own psyche. Again, this seems to be a universal stage in the inner work. They learn that everything is finite, that change and death are inevitable. They experience a 'little death' - the loss of innocence, the death of a loved one, sometimes even a loss of the feeling of connection to Nature and the deities.

The second-degree Wiccan is now a priest, priestess, or priestex to others in the coven, as well as to themselves. They are expected to be able to lead a ritual, to train others, and to offer support to people within the coven. They are encouraged to visit other covens and find out how they work. A second-degree Wiccan may initiate others.

The second- and third-degree initiation does not necessarily mean that someone is 'higher' than a first degree. The first degree is sufficient to make you a witch; the other degrees are recognitions of inner transformation and deepening of commitment.

The third degree

At third, the initiate has experienced some sort of inner marriage: the unity of dark and light, the integration of the unconscious, the coming together of their inner and outer work. The ritual of initiation is a recognition of the first stirrings of that inner unity; it does not mean that their psyche is now at peace and there is no more work to do. There is a new sense of unity of purpose, however: that what you do in the physical world has meaning in the spiritual realms, and vice versa; that you are one with your Craft. It does not mean giving up on action in the physical world: as a great Buddhist sage once said, "Before enlightenment, chop wood, carry water; after enlightenment, chop wood, carry water." It does not necessarily mean that you are now enlightened, either.

In some Wiccan lineages, it is not necessary to have attained third degree to lead a coven; in others, it is. Certainly, a person who has attained third degree should be a competent ritualist, and with any luck, a competent human being. For me, the definition of a true priestess, priestex, or priest is a person who can do the work of that role (ritual, healing, comforting others, dealing with a crisis) even when they are not feeling up to it. They are a person who can transform the atmosphere in a room with the right words or ritual actions, even when the room is full of fractious, nervous, or irritable people.

Different traditions of Wicca have different views on how soon it is appropriate to elevate someone to the next degree, and on what the criteria for elevation are, and on the aspects of ritual it is appropriate for different degrees to do.

However, if someone asks you to do something that you are uncomfortable with for them to give you the next level, check out their behaviour against checklists for abusive behaviour. If there is a pattern that looks abusive, run away.

The role of the coven leaders should be to keep coveners feeling safe and empowered, not unsafe and cowed into submission.

I believe it is very important to create a safe space with healthy boundaries in covens.

The journey of life

Life is a journey through many different situations and stages of growth. We mark these stages with rites of passage, designed to help us and other people adjust to the new situation. These rituals are important for both the individual and the community; it helps the individual to adjust to their new role and helps the community to recognise them as having that new role. It is both a celebration, and a way of balancing the state of things, and reconnecting the person to their community after a period of transition.

When a baby is born, it is welcomed into the community, given a name, and people establish relationships to the new person such as parent, aunt, uncle, godparent. When the child comes of age, it enters a new phase, and some religious traditions (notably Judaism) have coming-of-age rituals to acknowledge and celebrate their new role in life. Coming out is another significant moment when the young adult declares their sexual orientation. In families where the parents do not automatically assume that their child is cisgender and heterosexual, coming out is not restricted to LGBTQIA+ people. Marriage is another significant shift in role; now the person is part of a couple, but still an individual. Later, they may get divorced; this is another change which ought to be marked by some sort of ritual.

The process of becoming a parent is also a significant shift and brings new responsibilities as well as joy. Then a female body begins to change with the menopause, and this can also be marked with a croning ritual. Entry into old age can also be marked by male and non-binary people with a suitable ritual.

The journey of life can also be represented by a pentacle: birth, initiation, consummation, repose, and death. These five stages were identified by both W B Yeats[17] and Robert Graves[18] as five faces of the Goddess. Between birth and initiation, a person rests under the care of their parents. The journey from initiation to consummation goes by way of a death (the death of the old way of life), and the journey from consummation to repose often includes a birth (the creation of a literal or symbolic child - a book, or a work coming to fruition). As the person journeys from the repose of old age to the gates of death, another initiation, into the mysteries of letting go, is required. The journey from death to rebirth is presided over by both the consummation of encountering what is beyond death, and by the fact that a consummation is required for there to be a birth.

Perils and pitfalls of the inner work

What follows are some of the pitfalls I have observed on the journey (in myself and others), with some thoughts on how to deal with them. They can occur at any stage of the inner work - even highly experienced people are not

---

[17] *The Living Stream*: Yeats Annual No. 18, edited by Warwick Gould. pp 114-115.
https://books.google.co.uk/books?id=hPTKdUNVXhcC
[18] Robert Graves, *The White Goddess*, p 398.
https://books.google.co.uk/books?id=XHwaVK17cf0C

immune to them. Some are extremely subtle; others will hit you in the face like a wet towel. Either way, it is best to be prepared.

Spiritual bypassing

Spiritual bypassing is a term coined by John Welwood and means the avoidance of painful feelings by focussing on spirituality instead. It can be very subtle and takes many forms and is the shadow side of spiritual practice.[19]

The symptoms of spiritual bypassing include a refusal to look at 'difficult' emotions like anger, because they are 'not spiritual'. It can also include overemphasis on one's negative traits, and an excessive focus on oneness at the expense of individuality. It may also manifest as a view that the physical, fleshly aspects of life (food and sex being the most obvious examples) are somehow 'not spiritual'. People who are engaging in spiritual bypassing are just too nice, too compassionate, too tolerant, and often dismiss those who express anger and sadness as intolerant or lacking in compassion. Spiritual bypassing is often accompanied by the view that 'all is one', and this results in weak boundaries and a lack of self-protection characterised by being too ready to forgive and forget.

The cure for spiritual bypassing is doing the real inner work. Expressing and working through difficult emotions, using safe means of catharsis. More authentic forms of religion and spirituality have techniques for doing this.

---

[19] Robert Augustus Masters (2013), *Spiritual Bypassing: Avoidance in Holy Drag.* http://robertmasters.com/writings/spiritual-bypassing/

Real, embodied spirituality (or the inner work) can be hard work. The good news is that being hard on yourself does not need to be part of that process; being compassionate with yourself, but at the same time being real and working with the wounds in your psyche, is the way forward.

Pretty much anyone who sets out on the spiritual journey will encounter this pitfall in one or several of its forms; but forewarned is forearmed. Identifying the likely causes and symptoms of spiritual bypassing is a big step towards avoiding it. Working with your shadow side, rather than repressing it, will be a helpful thing; and expressing anger, sadness, melancholy, regret, even bitterness, will help to prevent the festering of wounds, and instead start the process of cleaning them. By all means be forgiving if it helps to prevent simmering resentment, but make sure that you set boundaries and clear expectations for better behaviour next time; don't keep allowing the person to commit the same transgression over and over again, forgiving them each time. If they cannot mend their ways, then you need to set up some boundaries for your own protection, like avoiding seeing them, or not seeing them in situations where the violation is likely to occur.

Ego inflation

Quite a common phenomenon resulting from a magical initiation is the idea that the new initiate now knows everything there is to know about the occult, and is far superior to all Muggles, cowans, mundanes, and other 'lesser' beings, including other Pagans, armchair occultists, and other dilettantes. This symptom is often accompanied by a penchant for black turtleneck jumpers, an excess of gothic accessories, and lots of occult jewellery.

The best cure for this symptom is time, patience, and gentle ribaldry. If you wish to hasten the end of this tiresome phase, you could buy the person suffering from it the excellent book *Bluff your way in the Occult*, by Alexander Rae [20], which ably skewers some of the more pretentious guff put about by sufferers from this malady.

This pitfall recurs at other seasons of the journey in more subtle forms. Those moments when one is convinced that one is right about some abstruse occult point and will not back down or compromise. Those moments when one is convinced that one is suffering more than everyone else (though sometimes this may be true). The sensation that one is the lone voice of reason in a sea of flaky people. Again, a quick reality check is required.

Wobbling

Wobbles can take many forms - doubt, despair, disillusionment - and can be caused by spiritual burnout. It may result in some sort of conversion process, or eventually to a deeper engagement with witchcraft.

Some Pagan and polytheist traditions will tell you that you should have a patron deity, and a close relationship with that deity. The internet is full of people with deep and fulfilling relationships with their personal deity. One of the

---

[20] Sadly now out of print, but still available secondhand. ISBN 10: 1853040576; ISBN 13: 9781853040573

causes of my personal wobble [21] was my lack of such a relationship.

Another thing that I personally found difficult was the possible effect of oaths in altering the structure of the psyche, creating a block.

I also began to wonder if the problems of the world could ever be solved by human means, since everything is so entangled – capitalism leads to war and oppression and environmental degradation, and if you fix one problem, you're likely to cause another one.

It is also difficult if you have previously been involved with fundamentalist Christianity, or another fundamentalist group. There may be a lurking fear that their beliefs are true. In my own case, I had had a huge reservoir of anger in my psyche that was directed against Christianity, which would well up and spill over about almost anything. After the anger was removed, there was a locked box underneath it marked "do not open" which contained my fear that the Christian explanation for how the universe works was true. Even though I knew in my rational mind that it was not, the idea that it might be true still lurked in some pre-rational area of my mind. The fear caused me actual physical pain in my chest.

John Beckett suggests that the best cure for the lurking fear that fundamentalist Christianity may be right is to continue with Pagan practice, encountering the Pagan deities in powerful and transformative rituals, and contacting Pagan

---

[21] Yvonne Aburrow (2015), *Wobbling but not falling off,*
http://dowsingfordivinity.wordpress.com/2015/08/wobbling-but-not-falling-off/

deities daily. He says that debunking the Christian mythos and deconstructing it will help, but it must be accompanied by an emotional and spiritual process, otherwise the lurking fear will remain, because the subconscious works with emotion, not reason. [22]

During my wobble, I think I temporarily lost the balance of my mind, because I re-enacted the development of religious thought in Europe over the last 2000 years in the space of six months. I went from polytheism to Christianity, to universalism, back to atheism, and then eventually back to polytheism. It was a theological roller-coaster ride and I do not recommend taking it so fast.

I am so grateful to the members of the Pagan community who held me steady during this time. One of those people was Cat Chapin-Bishop. The members of my coven at that time were also tremendously supportive, despite it being difficult for them that their new high priestess [23] had a different theological perspective every time we met up. The other thing that was very important was Pagans saying that if I was on the right spiritual path for me, that was fine with them. That remains one of the great strengths of Paganism – that we do not believe it is cosmically necessary to be a Pagan, and that the same spiritual path may not be right for everyone.

---

[22] John Beckett (2015), *Escaping Fundamentalism*, http://www.patheos.com/blogs/johnbeckett/2015/09/escaping -fundamentalism.html
[23] Although I am nonbinary and genderqueer, I like the term priestess because it feels entirely Pagan to me. We do not allocate roles by gender in our coven; a person of any gender may perform any role.

Another very common issue is people who come over all rationalist and cannot see how atheism can be compatible with Paganism and witchcraft. As I was perfectly happily atheist for the first twenty years or so of my Wiccan journey, and so are many other witches, I am here to tell you that it can and does work. John Halstead and Mark Green have written a lot on being a Pagan atheist, or atheist Pagan, whichever you prefer. The one thing where it might be difficult to do witchcraft would be if you didn't believe in or experience energies, but I have even come across people who have managed to enjoy Wicca even though they do not have any experience of magical energies. The best cure for this type of wobble (or difficulty getting started) is finding other atheist Pagans and witches and discussing with them how they see Paganism and witchcraft. Many atheist Pagans see the deities as archetypes or energies; some do not work with deities at all; still others do not believe in or work with energies, only with archetypes.

Another possible cause of disillusionment is infighting and unethical behaviour in the Pagan community. A good cure for this is to go and observe a different religious community for a while, and observe the same infighting, arguing over how many angels can dance on the head of a pin, and unethical behaviour occurring there too. Doubtless each religious community has its own shadow issues, but many of these are the same, and it is very instructive to observe.

There may be other wobbles that I have not identified, but with all of them, I suspect, the cure is to work on the emotional causes as well as the intellectual aspects. This may involve a period of journaling, creative writing, music-making, art, or whatever you happen to find eases stress and helps you to access the contents of your subconscious.

Sometimes, to truly experience a feeling, you must go away from it and approach it from a different angle. You must try to do without your connection to beloved community to know that they are really your tribe, your people. Having tested my faith in Paganism, the deities, and the power of Nature, I found that it bent but did not break, it tore but did not disintegrate.

There are numerous spiritual stories where the hero goes past the thing they seek, mistaking it for something else, and then must double back to find it again by accident. This is especially true of the story of Moses and Al-Khidr [24]. In this story, Moses and Khidr are on a quest for the water of life, and they have given up on their quest and turned back. They stop for the night and decide to have supper by the sea. Their servant, Nun, catches a fish, and fetches some water to cook it in. However, when Nun puts the fish into the water, it jumps out, having been brought back to life. They found the water of life in an unexpected way, after they had given up and turned back. That is often the nature of 'spiritual' treasure. It is not immediately obvious that it is treasure, and sometimes we find it by luck or instinct, rather than by searching.

---

[24] *The Parable of Moses and Khidr in the Holy Qur'an: an Ismaili Interpretation.* http://simerg.com/parables/the-parable-of-moses-and-khidr-in-the-holy-qur%E2%80%99an-an-ismaili-interpretation/

Many people find that they arrive at a universalist perspective on spirituality, only to find that it is really difficult to sustain the idea that "all is one" (perhaps because your mountain is not the same as my mountain, perhaps because spirituality works better when it has a specific context), and then move once again into their own spiritual perspective and homeland, with a new appreciation of its worth.

So, whilst having a wobble on your spiritual journey can be very painful and difficult: if you are having one, follow your bliss, whatever that turns out to be. Pay attention to what your body is telling you. Where do you feel most comfortable, most nourished? Who are the people who really support your journey, and who are the people who just want to control you?

Dry seasons

Every now and again, probably caused by living too much in one's head and not paying enough attention to one's body, the creative juices dry up, the magic seems barren and rote, lifeless and dull, and everything seems a bit pointless. This can often be the early warning sign of spiritual burnout, so it is best dealt with immediately.

The best cure for this is to reconnect with the body and with Nature. Get off the internet and go for a walk in the woods or by the sea (if you can). If you can't get outside or walk very far, find another way to pamper yourself - a nice bath with candles and incense, a massage, even listening to some beautiful music, snuggling up with your cat or dog, watching a film about Nature, reading a children's book, especially if it involves magic and dragons and all that sort of thing. The key thing here is to revive your sense of wonder at the beauty and magic of the world.

Spiritual burnout

Spiritual burn-out is a real risk for spiritual leaders, counsellors, caregivers, healers, and psychics. I have found in the past that if I was getting nurtured by others, setting clear boundaries, practicing self-care, and receiving energy from the universe, it didn't happen, whereas if you fail to do these things, you will get burn-out, and the symptoms can be quite nasty.

The symptoms of spiritual burnout or psychic burnout can include exhaustion, depression, dread before or after working, feelings of unbearable responsibility, feeling overwhelmed, crying for no reason, crying often, being overtired, insomnia, difficulty getting out of bed, restlessness, procrastination, avoidance, constant illness, problems with the heart, difficulty breathing, anxiety and panic attacks, extreme weight loss or weight gain, hair loss, irritability, and a desire to avoid people.

In an excellent article on spiritual burnout, Grace, a psychic, describes the symptoms, how to avoid them, and how to deal with them if you already have spiritual burnout. Her advice can be summed up in six key points:

Take a break and rest - she says, "take a sabbatical from everyone and everything, and really nurture yourself physically, emotionally, mentally and spiritually".

Make sure your needs are met - physically, emotionally, mentally, and spiritually. Breathe properly.

Draw your energy from the universe - do not use up all your personal energy; make sure to be replenished from the source.

Charge for your services - either in money or in kind - Grace says "there always has to be an exchange of energy, which is what money is - it is the energy of worth and value given in exchange for the service received."

Maintain strong boundaries - visualise yourself surrounded by white light; set aside a special room for your clients; set fixed working hours. If there is an emergency, calm the client down first. Have a website which answers all the obvious questions about what you do.

Only work when you can give 100% - do not deplete yourself by working when you are ill, distracted, etc.

If you think you are suffering spiritual burn-out, get help - do not leave it until you are completely exhausted.

Self-care

 Above all, take care of yourself. Get the right amount of sleep, food, water, massage, pampering, hugs, sex, and intellectual and emotional nourishment. (The right amount of these things may vary from person to person, depending on individual needs and preferences.) Take the time to smell the flowers along the way, say kind words to others, smile, snuggle with your lovers, friends, and companion animals. Take a hot bath with essential oils; go for a walk in the woods, or by the sea, or a river. Read the kind of books that make you happy; watch the kind of films that make you laugh, because they are quirky and individualistic. Magical and transformative rituals are also refreshing and healing. I am not saying you should pretend that the world is all sunshine and rainbows, as it clearly isn't, and that would be a form of spiritual bypassing, but make sure you get your fair share of sunshine and rainbows.

If you are an activist, self-care is especially important. Be aware of how much arguing and campaigning for social justice you can cope with before you must recharge your batteries by doing some self-care. The same applies if you are a coven leader; holding a safe space for others can be surprisingly tiring, especially when conflicts occur in the group. Set good boundaries. Self-care is very important to prevent dry spells, wobbles, and spiritual burnout.

If you can afford psychotherapy, go for it. It can be very helpful to explore your personal issues in a safe and non-judgmental space. It has been suggested that psychotherapy is a way of constructing a new narrative of your life, retelling your story, and sending it off in a new direction, no longer hampered by the wounds of the past. If you cannot afford therapy, do not try to 'roll your own'. A magical group is not therapy, though it may have therapeutic benefits. Instead, go for a long walk with a trusted friend and take it in turns to talk about your issues.

If you are angry, feel your anger, and then channel it into a constructive solution (if one is available). Unrecognised or repressed anger can be a cause of depression, so don't shove it down the back of the sofa and ignore it: do something to express it, even if it's a bit of a stomp about and a shout. Sometimes I burst into tears when I am angry; sometimes I hit a pillow.

However, it is best not to dwell on or feed the anger. If the situation that is making you angry continues to exist, can you escape from the situation, or do something to improve the conditions or behaviours that are making you angry? If not, then rather than continuously stoking and feeding the anger, expressing it in ways that diffuse your feelings can be helpful. Anger is not actually a negative emotion - it is your psyche's way of telling you that you are in a negative and potentially dangerous situation that needs fixing. The situation may also be pressing on an old psychological wound, and that may be the real cause of the anger - especially if the anger seems excessive in relation to the thing that is making you angry.

Robert Masters writes that suppressing anger is one of the symptoms of spiritual bypassing [25] (I call these people the 'spiritualler-than-thou').

Some people derive satisfaction from helping others, but do not give and give and give without receiving anything in return. Healthy boundaries are important to prevent you from feeling drained and exploited.

Do not ignore the warning signs of spiritual burnout and other pitfalls; do something to take care of yourself before the symptoms worsen.

Once again, the watchword is balance. Take care of yourself at the same time as you take care of other people, and of Nature.

---

[25] Robert Augustus Masters (2013), *Spiritual Bypassing: Avoidance in Holy Drag*. http://robertmasters.com/writings/spiritual-bypassing/ (an outstanding article, highly recommended)

Discussion

How have you experienced the different stages of the inner work?

What are the causes of spiritual burnout, wobbles, dry seasons, ego inflation, and spiritual bypassing?

What are the symptoms?

How can they be mitigated or prevented?

Exercises

Do something creative - make poetry, art, or music

Start a journal in which to record your feelings (if you find it helpful - I am not naturally introspective, so I am not sure this would help me)

Looking at the six defences against spiritual burnout, identify the areas where you are not helping yourself, and fix them

Go for a walk in Nature

Pamper yourself - have a bath, massage, manicure, pedicure, haircut, whatever makes you feel good

Read a children's book

Engage in genuinely transformative ritual

4. Sound and silence

The use of sound in ritual

As all actions in ritual are metaphors for actions on the inner realms, so any action in a ritual can be accompanied by a sound. And when I say sound, it does not necessarily have to be music. In many respects simpler sounds are more powerful, such as the simple ringing of a bell to clear the air and denote the pause between important parts of the ritual.

The method of making the sound influences the ritual space e.g. a sistrum used for sweeping. The quality of the sound will affect the quality of the energy; possibly the frequency of the sound equates to the frequency of the energy.

For evoking, you can make a sound that is like the thing being evoked, such as a crackling noise for fire, a trickling noise for water (using a rainstick for example), a stamping sound for earth, and a whooshing sound for air.

For banishing, you could make a sound that disrupts the space, such as rattles, bells; a falling pitch (where the sound gets lower); or you could use sound as a boundary marker. To make sure that everyone in the circle is grounded, you can use stomping, or a low-frequency sound.

For raising power, associated sounds could be inhaling, chanting, using a rising pitch (where the sound gets higher). For sending power, suitable sounds are exhaling, and abrupt sounds. Healing is associated with soothing, caressing sounds.

Sound made within the body has a powerfully direct effect on the body and spirit-body. Also, the sound itself is a vibration not only in the medium of the air, but also in the medium of your body. It directly and indirectly affects mind, body, and spirit. Sound touches everything, whereas light does not necessarily reach in or through.

Recorded music can also be very powerful (particularly if it is a piece you know well and that 'gets you going') and can be used actively as a method of raising energy. Recorded music can also be used passively as a guide to stimulate visualisation. Soundscapes are as fluid as the landscapes of the inner realms.

Sound is very powerful in spell-work. A simple sound made after words at the end of the spell can give the energy the extra push that it needs (for example, exhaling to send energy). The breath is very powerful. It can be used to store and then send energy, which can be accompanied by a sound if needed.

Sound can also be used as a boundary marker (for example, a bell to indicate a change of mood, pace, or part of a ritual); it is used in this way in many cultures.

Sound was used in at least two folklore rituals of the past. In the annual wassailing of the apple trees, people would sing to the trees, and beat pots and pans to wake them up. They would fire shots through the branches to scare off the evil spirits.

In the Skimmington Ride, also known as Charivari or Rough Music, people would beat pots and pans outside the house of a wife-beater or an adulterer to let them know that they were no longer welcome in the community. This would also be done outside the house of unmarried mothers or a couple who were not married, to encourage them to get married (when you consider that a woman was particularly socially insecure whilst unmarried, the latter was not such a bad thing). There is a Hogarth engraving of a Skimmington Ride. The offending individual would be placed backwards on a donkey or a riding pole (sometimes in person, sometimes in effigy). The Skimmington was often organised by the women in a community.

The basic rule of thumb for using sound in ritual is to make the noise that corresponds to what it sounds like in your head. If it sounds like whooshing, make a whooshing noise. Do not be afraid to sound like a child playing, because it is the same state of mind that we are aiming for.

According to folklore, witches used many chants and songs to accompany their dances. Some of these can be found in the excellent book *Earth Air Fire Water* [26] by Robin Skelton and Margaret Blackwood. The use of repetitive chant can be a powerful way to bring about a shift in consciousness, as the use of rhythm and rhyme can switch us over to the twilight side of consciousness. Another method is to make eerie sounds, which are associated with the spirit world. One traditional chant was the use of the vowels as a long-drawn-out sound: AAA EEE III OOO UUU. This would presumably have used the 'pure' vowel sounds, as they are in Italian for example, pronounced Ah, Eh, Ee, O, U in English.

---

[26] Robin Skelton and Margaret Blackwood (1990), *Earth Air Fire Water: Pre-Christian and Pagan Elements in British Songs, Rhymes and Ballads*. Arkana Publishing.

Varying the pitch, volume, and tone

A ritual is like a piece of music. It has different movements (*allegro, andante,* and so on) - fast and slow, rhythmic and melodic. The performance of a chant or spell is very effective if you start by whispering, and then build up gradually to louder chanting. Sometimes it works better if you end with a whisper too. If you have a large group of people, it sometimes means that everyone ends up chanting loudly and not paying attention to the energies in the circle.

When planning a ritual, I try to start with a visualisation or meditation to get everyone into a magical frame of mind, and then alternate between activities of different intensities. A highly focused activity is followed by something lighter and frothier; physical and embodied activities give form and expression to words and imagery; sounds and stillness can divide the ritual into sections if necessary.

The dynamic of a ritual is usually (to continue with the musical metaphor) from *piano* (soft), to *mezzoforte* (medium), rising in a crescendo to *forte* (loud), back to *mezzoforte,* and back to *piano* again - not just in terms of sound, but also in terms of the amount of magical energy that is raised at any point in the ritual.

Silence in ritual

Silence can also be a very powerful thing in ritual. There are different qualities of silence: a companionable silence, an angry silence, an expectant silence, a peaceful silence. There is the silence of meditation, the silence of absence, the silence of awe in the presence of something greater.

When I teach people how to call the quarters, I ask them to silently contact the energy of the direction before they start saying any words. They need to reach out and feel the energy, and this is best done silently and with focussed intention. The words are merely the outward confirmation that something has happened.

It can be good to do an entire ritual silently, to emphasise that the inner work can and does happen, with or without words. It is an excellent exercise in paying attention to what is happening inwardly. Many parts of ritual can be done silently - grounding and centering, calling the quarters, raising energy. I sometimes create a series of pictures as *aide-memoires* of what we plan to do in the ritual. A certain amount of sign-language is also necessary. Mime can also be a good way to do silent ritual. I once facilitated a Lammas ritual where I divided a group of thirty up into five groups of six, then asked them to come up with a mime describing an aspect of the John Barleycorn story. One group mimed the death of the Corn King; another group mimed the wheat being cut down by reapers; and so on. It was very moving. You could also do this for Autumn Equinox, perhaps with the story of Hades and Persephone.

Another very effective use of silence in ritual is the Quaker silence, also known as gathered silence. The members of the meeting come together to create a silence. They sit quietly and wait until the silence runs together like a pool; that is when it becomes a gathered silence. Once that has happened, they feel a sense of Presence: Spirit has come to join them. For Christian Quakers, that Presence is Christ; for non-Christian Quakers, it is Spirit, or the Limitless Light, or some other way of describing an energy which is more than the sum of those present. Once the silence becomes a gathered silence, it is then possible for utterances to emerge from it. These utterances are not from the ego of the speaker, but rather, they are messages from spirit. Of course, the Quakers say that "the water often tastes of the pipes" (that the personality of the speaker is often imprinted on the utterance). The utterances do not necessarily have to follow on from each other, but sometimes they fit together, or complement each other in unexpected ways. I have tried this technique with groups of Wiccans, and we have had some very interesting experiences of gods and spirits, and sometimes just a sense of coming together in the silence.

It is very important to test whether your utterance is from ego or is really from spirit. The way that I do this is, when I first feel the urge to speak, I lean forward. If the utterance is from ego, I find that I physically cannot say it, so I lean back again. If I feel the urge again, I lean forward again, to test it in the same way. If it is from spirit, then I find I can say it. It usually takes two or three of these tests to make sure. Others may experience the process of testing differently. It may be that you will experience an overwhelming urge to say whatever it is, or that it somehow bypasses your brain and comes straight out of your mouth. In some ways, it is rather like the experience of being invoked in a Wiccan ritual. You know in that situation whether it is the deity talking, or your ego. Sometimes your voice changes, or the style of your speech is different.

The Western tradition of spirituality, magic, and religion is very wordy, so the use of silence, gesture, mime, and indeed sounds without words, makes a refreshing change. It gets us into the twilight half of consciousness and makes us more aware of the movement of subtle energy that we might otherwise miss. The quality of sound and silence can change the vibration in a space and affect the mood in a room.

Discussion

Which sounds do you associate with different magical events and qualities (invoking, banishing, healing, opening and closing the circle)?

How do you experience the effects of silence?

What gestures are associated with different sections of a witchcraft ritual?

Exercises

Create a silent ritual with silent casting and sweeping, silent consecrations, silent quarter calls, silent meditation, spell-work, visualisation, cakes and wine, and use of gesture, mime, and movement to convey meaning. (You don't have to have a silent feast afterwards, though it might be interesting!)

Create a gathered silence out of which prophetic utterances may emerge.

Gather all the percussion instruments you own (if you don't own any, find some kitchen utensils to play with) and make sounds with them. What do you associate each sound with? How could you use this sound in ritual?

5. Witchcraft and the land

My witchcraft is intimately connected with the land. The hills, valleys, trees, stones, burial mounds, and rivers. The geology beneath our feet. These are our sources of energy: these are what sustains life. The air, the waters, the heat of the sun, the gravitational pull of the Moon, governing the tides. The bees that pollinate the flowers. If the bees die out, we all die for lack of food.

No wonder the witchcraft of Alkistis Dimech and Peter Grey is apocalyptic: we live in apocalyptic times. The earth is being poisoned by capitalism: the myth that unbridled economic growth is possible on a single planet with finite resources. The very idea that the Earth is a 'resource' to be plundered; that other animals, even other people, do not have as much of a right as we do to habitat and food and air and clean water.

That is why we urgently need to change the foundational myths of our culture. We need to understand the land, the Earth, and Nature as sacred. We need to stop worshipping money and start worshipping life. What does worship mean? It means 'honouring that which is of highest worth', from worth-ship, as the *Abraxan Essay on Worship* [27] tells us.

Worship, then, is the practice of reconnecting our alienated selves back to all that is: the trees, the animals, the birds, the land, the waters. We are alienated from meaning by our fragmented and discordant social and economic structures;

---

[27] "Vern the Void" et al (1976), *The Abraxan Essay on Worship* (originally hosted on uua.org).
http://pagantheologies.pbworks.com/w/page/112082326/Worship

many of us are engaged in meaningless work, that is not craft, but repetitive production of separate and standardised parts.

How do we reconnect to Nature, the land, the Earth? These are three separate concepts, so it is best to look at them separately. Nature is perhaps the least helpful of these as a concept, as we tend to regard it as separate from ourselves, everything that is not man-made; but we need to consider our dwellings and activities as part of the ecosystem, because they have a massive effect on ecosystems. We ourselves are part of Nature, although we often fail to behave as if that were the case. The *Oxford English Dictionary* has as its first definition of Nature, 'The phenomena of the physical world collectively, including plants, animals, the landscape, and other features and products of the earth, as opposed to humans or human creations', followed by 'The physical force regarded as causing and regulating the phenomena of the world'. The first of these definitions neatly sums up the problem: that we see ourselves as outside Nature, as not subject to the laws of Nature, and as being able to 'subdue' or 'tame' Nature. Try telling that to hurricanes, or to rising meltwater and floods.

Seeing the Earth as a whole living being is important, but perhaps also unhelpful in some ways, because then we might miss the complexity of the many ecosystems and organisms that form part of the Earth. We need to think about geology, soil ecology, water, wind, plants, animals, and birds as part of the great complexity of living systems, and we need to recognise them as beings with inherent rights to life.

Talking about the land as a living entity is perhaps more immediately affecting, as it is at a scale that we can comprehend on a human level. Now we are talking about a specific biosphere, our local landscape, its geology, ecology, hills, rivers, lakes, estuaries, woods, marshes, and fields. Now we are talking about the land as it has been lived on and shaped for millennia by humans, some living on and with the land in a sacred manner; others exploiting it. [28]

Perhaps we need to be able to conceptualise our relationship with the web of life in all these ways. One particularly useful way of doing this is to think about bioregions, which represent the overall pattern of natural characteristics, and how they form a continuous geographical terrain or system. Examples include Cascadia, the bioregion of the Pacific Northwest of North America; and Laurentia, the bioregion of the Laurentian Shield.

We urgently need to reconceptualise Nature, and the Earth, as a living system of which we are a part. If we make the ecosystems of this beautiful planet unliveable for ourselves and other species, life will undoubtedly continue in some form: but we may well not be part of it.

There are, however, some encouraging signs. New Zealand recently declared that lands and rivers can count as people

---

[28] *Cascadian Bioregionalism,* Cascadia,
http://www.cascadianow.org/about-cascadia/cascadia-bioregionalism/

in legal terms [29], with the possibility that the idea may
spread to Canada.

The same view of water and land as sacred can be found in
Indigenous worldviews everywhere. The Standing Rock
Lakota tribe [30] resisted the building of a pipeline across
their sacred lands, which would pollute and decrease their
water supply. Their slogan is 'water is life'. Similarly, the
Wet'suwet'en resisted the building of a pipeline on their
sacred and unceded land in Canada, the Yintah. Many
land disputes around the world centre on supplies of clean
water, include the conflict between Israeli settlers and
Palestinians.

The view expressed in Starhawk's novel *The Fifth Sacred
Thing*, that water, earth, air, fire, and spirit cannot be
owned or treated as a commodity, needs to become the
central tenet of a new way of looking at the world. For far
too long, the land, which ought never to be regarded as
property, has been parcelled up and sold as a commodity.
This practice is completely alien to the Indigenous
worldview, and to the worldview that would have held
sway in prehistoric times in our own lands. Only with the
coming of "civilisation" - literally, the creation of cities -
did it become necessary to control land in order to ensure
that those not directly engaged in the gathering or growing
of food would get fed. Hunter-gatherer societies, and even

---

[29] Bryant Rousseau (2016), *In New Zealand, Lands and Rivers Can
Be People (Legally Speaking)*. New York Times.
http://www.nytimes.com/2016/07/14/world/what-in-the-
world/in-new-zealand-lands-and-rivers-can-be-people-legally-
speaking.html?_r=0
[30] http://standingrock.org/

early agrarian societies, had complex arrangements of land usage, but did not own the land. The gradual process of enclosures turned the land into private property, instead of ensuring it was justly apportioned to everyone in the community.

The problem, of course, with a 'back to the land' approach to Paganism, is that the countryside is usually socially conservative, and therefore unsafe for People of Colour and LGBTQIA+ people. Cities are where innovation and change tend to happen; they are where artists and creative people gather and flourish, where craft-workers come together and form trades unions and guilds.

This means that we need to stop conceptualising cities and countryside as inherently different. Cities need to become sustainable places of beauty, using wind and solar power generated locally, with urban farms and permaculture. We need to stop the industrialisation of agriculture, where animals are kept in huge sheds with hardly any space to move, or natural light. Land can have multiple uses, and farmed animals would be part of a permaculture ecosystem, not a separate commodity.

Therefore, Pagan and Indigenous worldviews urgently need to become part of mainstream thinking. Paganism and witchcraft need to avoid being co-opted or assimilated into the 'business as usual' of capitalist exploitation of the Earth, and start forming alternative ways of interacting with Nature, the land, the Earth, our local bioregions. Starhawk's excellent and decades-long activism in promoting permaculture and sustainability is a significant step towards realising a Pagan vision of the land as sacred.

The seasonal rituals of the Wiccan Wheel of the Year are a good start towards reconnecting with Nature as sacred: with Earth, Air, Fire, and water as sacred, and with the cycles of the seasons. However, we must look deeper, and examine our worldview root and branch, if we want to really be in tune with the land, and with our local bioregion. Are you living sustainably? Hardly any of us are - and it is very difficult in a consumerist, capitalist culture. All you can do is live as sustainably as you can, and try to make your ecological footprint as small as possible, whilst raising awareness, campaigning for ecological sustainability, and doing everything you can to bring about the shift in consciousness that is needed if we are to stop screwing up life on this beautiful planet.

Whenever I confront my personal ethical choices around sustainability and ecology, I realise that everything depends on everything else. One choice may be more sustainable than another, but it may have other deleterious effects. You fix one part of the ecosystem, another gets broken. You try to fix poverty by donating clothes to charity shops (thrift stores) and then discover you have undermined small-scale Indigenous clothing manufacture. You buy fair trade goods and then discover that they have been shipped over vast distances.

This interconnectedness of everything shows that we need a massive global paradigm shift, not merely a cosmetic fix to our already broken system. Capitalism - the practice of creaming off profits to give to shareholders and investors who do not contribute directly to the enterprise - created the opportunity to exploit people and resources and got us into the mess we are in now. I recently watched a documentary on the origins of the industrial revolution, and it was very clear that it could not have got started without capitalism to fund it, and consumerism to drive demand for the commodities that were produced. Manufacturing snowballed in response to the stimuli of investment and consumer demand.

We are in a huge mess right now, and we need action. Climate change is already happening, sea levels are rising, species are dying off. It might be worse if there had not been an environmental movement, and if Pagans had not existed. This is also the premise of the excellent book *Hope in the dark: The Untold History of People Power*, by Rebecca Solnit.

Two things give me hope: deep ecology and trophic cascade.

Deep Ecology is the radical idea that all life has the right to exist, that no one species is more important than another.

Environmental justice and social justice go together. You cannot solve world poverty unless we are all in right relationship with the Earth. [31] You cannot solve the climate emergency without giving land back to Indigenous Peoples.

So, we all need to change our perspective to one of deep ecology, rather than seeing environmentalism as some kind of 'add-on' to our existing lifestyles.

---

[31] Organic is Beautiful: *Vandana Shiva on Deep Ecology.* http://organicisbeautiful.wordpress.com/2011/09/24/vandana-shiva-on-deep-ecology/

How will this change of perspective come about? Like any paradigm shift, it started with individuals who were ahead of their time and has gradually been building momentum. Sadly, so has climate change, but this means more people will wake up and smell the coffee. We can take action to speed up the process of change. We can re-enchant the world that capitalism and the industrial revolution disenchanted.

There are also interventions that can be made to restore ecosystems.

One of the most interesting discoveries of recent years has been trophic cascade. This is the discovery that if you restore a major predator to an ecosystem, other species recover.

For example, restoring wolves to Yellowstone Park resulted in a decrease in elk, but an increase in the tree species that elk would otherwise have eaten, and consequently an increase in beaver and bison, as well as carrion birds which benefit from the remains of the wolves' kills.[32]

Restoring beavers to river systems in Scotland has resulted in the creation of more pools, and hence more habitats for fish and plants.

The problems that climate change has brought, is bringing, and will bring will be severe and disastrous. Maybe we can ride out the storm; maybe it is too late; but if we despair and do not act, it will be too late.

[32] http://www.sciencedirect.com/science/article/pii/S0006320711004046

first thing we need to do to get into right relationship
h Nature is to get into right relationship with our
ᴗᴗ dies. How you conceive of being in right relationship
with your body may vary according to the shape of your
body, any conditions you have, and what being kind to
your body looks like for you. As Mary Oliver wisely wrote,
"Let the soft animal of your body love what it loves." If you
have Ehlers-Danlos Syndrome, arthritis, cerebral palsy,
rheumatism, sleep apnoea, Parkinson's Disease,
hemiplegia, autism, and any number of other
neurodivergent and physically divergent conditions (which
are called disabilities because society fails to create an
environment which would enable people to live
comfortably), then being in right relationship with your
body may look very different from how it looks for a non-
divergent person, and will often include various drugs and
physical assistance to enable mobility and a relatively pain-
free existence. Being in right relationship with your body
may include coming to terms with the fact that you are fat.
I am fat, and whilst I am not particularly ecstatic about it, I
love my body, and I do not think that fat-shaming is a
healthy or helpful way to relate to your body. The point of
being in right relationship with your body is to listen to its
needs: the aches and pains, the need for food, water, water,
rest, sleep, cuddles, exercise, stretching, consensual and
fulfilling sex (or not, if you are asexual), intimate and
consensual touch, the right kind of touch, and the feeling of
warm sunshine, or cool water, or a refreshing breeze, on
your stretched-out body.

Once you are in some sort of communication with your
body's needs, the next step is interpersonal relationships.

Maintaining healthy boundaries and consensual relationships with other people (friends, coveners, family, and colleagues) is important for everyone's well-being. Forgiveness is good for the soul, they say, but forgetting what has happened, and failing to set clear boundaries and expectations for future interactions, is not healthy.

The next step is to look at your relationship with the environment. Do you really need a car? (If you live in a remote location with a lack of regular public transport, or are disabled, then yes, you need a car.) How much living space do you really need? Is your house well-insulated and using a sustainable source of electricity? Is the food you eat imported over vast distances? Check your environmental footprint (you may need to use more than one online calculator for this, as the results can vary depending on whether the emphasis is on carbon emissions, or another environmental factor).

Personal responsibility towards the environment is great, but it will not make any difference if there is not a general change on a governmental level. The Paris accord on keeping global temperature increases below 1.5 degrees Celsius was a hopeful step, but there was no concrete plan on how to implement it, or how to protect vulnerable low-lying countries from flooding, or equatorial countries from drought. We need to keep the political pressure up on these issues, as well as trying to do something about the current lurch to the extreme right.

It looks as if global capitalism is about to go into a massive global meltdown, and the consequences are going to be ugly. I hope that something can emerge from other end of the coming upheaval, but things are looking bleak right now. That is why we need action on all levels: personal, interpersonal, political, environmental, and magical.

When I first got involved in Paganism back in the late 1980s and early 1990s, it was clear that upheaval was coming. The top-down authoritarian worldview of fundamentalists and right-wingers would become entrenched in a small diehard minority who would feel ever more besieged and beleaguered, before it became apparent that their approach to life is ultimately futile and barren. And that is exactly what has happened, except the scary thing is that they are gaining power again. Britain has just voted to leave the European Union - a project which, whilst flawed in many ways, has prevented war in Europe for decades, and promises a vision of something above and beyond petty nationalism. The 'alt right' (the far right in new trappings) is becoming increasingly powerful in the USA and in Europe. The government of the UK is seeking to lay the blame for decades of government-imposed austerity at the door of 'foreigners'.

But another world is possible. Humanity has emerged from worse times than those in which we currently find ourselves. In 1999, Canada created the territory of Nunavut, which is the largest Indigenous land claim settlement, after a process of discussion and negotiation which started in the 1970s. However, there is still a vast amount to be done to create equality and justice for the First Nations. They are still hugely disadvantaged by systemic racism, underfunding, bad housing, bias in the justice system, and the destructive legacy of the residential schools.

As mentioned earlier, New Zealand has embraced the idea of land and water as legal entities or persons. In the USA, the Obama administration agreed to consult Native American tribes before starting major construction projects (as they should have done before starting to build the Dakota Access Pipeline, or DAPL). Some governments have started to accept the reality of climate change and do something about it, however slowly and dilatorily. Sadly, with the resurgence of right-wing rhetoric, fake news, climate change denial, and the dismantling of environmental protections and workers' rights, all this progress is threatened.

As Rebecca Solnit points out in her excellent book, *Hope in the Dark: The Never-Surrender Guide to Changing the World*, if activists had not constantly campaigned for social and environmental justice over the last hundred years or so, we would not have made any of the gains in these areas that we have, and things would be much worse than they are.

However, those of us who insist that capitalism is breathing its last must offer alternative visions of how the economy and society might be organised. The co-operative movement provides one such alternative.

Over many decades, the *Two Cows* joke has evolved through several different iterations. The first recorded instances appeared in 1936. Before the internet (yes, there was a time before the internet), people circulated jokes like *Two Cows* on photocopied sheets. Then they got passed around in email and bulletin boards and mailing lists; then they found their way onto BuzzFeed and Facebook. The joke always starts with "you have two cows" and imagines what would happen to them under different political and economic systems, including capitalism, communism, state communism, anarchism, and so on. Some versions are incredibly detailed. But they very rarely include two very promising economic practices, the creation of cooperatives, and microfinance.

Interestingly, the latest version of "Two cows", Modern Capitalism Explained,[33] only presents different flavours of capitalism. It is as if the other socio-economic systems had simply ceased to exist. One of the problems with capitalism is that investors inject capital into businesses, and then demand a profit. There are several issues with this:

They have not done any of the work to produce the profit.

They can withdraw their investment at any time.

They can sell their shares to the highest bidder, thus creating instability in financial markets.

They usually have no personal connection or involvement with the company they have invested in.

The need to make a profit inflates the cost of goods and services.

The creaming-off of profits creates massive economic inequality.

The short-termism of demanding a quick return on investment leads to the degradation of the environment, the destruction of habitats, and the overuse of resources.

Capitalism is *not* small traders who make and sell their own goods, or who buy the products of others and sell

---

[33] http://www.freerepublic.com/focus/chat/3329106/posts

them on. Such merchants existed before capitalism, and they will continue to exist after capitalism has collapsed under its own weight. So, what are the alternatives to capitalism?

One way to remove the problem of investors out to make a quick buck is to use the co-operative model. In this model, the business is co-owned by its employees, though non-employees can often become members. This business model is very popular in Europe, and several well-known businesses in the UK (the Co-operative group, John Lewis, and Nationwide) use this model.

The co-operative system means that ownership is spread amongst many people who all own a small share in the business and who receive dividends, rather than amongst a small group of powerful shareholders.

Another useful idea is the practice of micro-finance. This has been very successful in helping to empower women and other small traders in the developing world. It means that people can borrow very small amounts of money that large banks would not be interested in lending and pay them back incrementally without being charged exorbitant levels of interest. I currently have a small amount of money with Kiva, a microfinance non-profit, which I have lent out to people in Armenia, Dominican Republic, El Salvador, Guatemala, Haiti, Honduras, Kenya, Liberia, Mexico, Nigeria, Pakistan, Peru, and Vietnam.

Various movements around alternative ways to think about land ownership and housing are springing up, such as House of the Commons. Alternative economists are looking seriously at how to tax land ownership to ensure fair distribution of land, which is after all a finite resource.

Those who stand to benefit from capitalism want us to believe that there are no alternatives to capitalism – that because state communism collapsed, and there are very few successful anarchist societies, there is no alternative to capitalism.

This is part of the baneful magic of capitalism; it weaves a fog of confusion and obfuscation around the very tools and concepts that might liberate us from its spell. That is why we need to liberate ourselves from the illusion of its permanence as soon as possible and educate ourselves about the alternatives.

It is hard to be part of the solution when we are so entangled in the problem, and just trying to make a living and survive the daily grind. But even if the only part you can play is to raise awareness of climate change, systemic racism, and to do magic to bring about a more just and sustainable society, that is a big help.

The thing you need to remember is that Pagan, polytheist, magical, occult, animist, and Indigenous worldviews are not merely the mainstream worldview with a few leaves and some nice stories bolted on. They are a completely different view of the world: not identical to each other, to be sure, but with significant overlap and an understanding of the land, bioregions, Nature, and the Earth as sacred beings in their own right, with their own particular stories, ways of being, and ways of interacting. If humanity wants to survive as a species and not wipe itself out, it had better start listening to Indigenous Peoples, who know how to live in harmony with the land, and the other species and beings with whom we share this planet.

Remember when you were a kid, and you wrote your address as "my house, my street, my district, my city, my country, the world, the universe" (or some variation on that theme)? We need to recover that view of existence as a series of nested and overlapping spheres, an appreciation of the multiple scales of existence from the microcosmic to the macrocosmic, and to remember that it is all interconnected: "as above, so below" as the Hermetic philosophers put it.

Discussion

What are the alternatives to capitalism?

How can we help to create a more sustainable and just society?

How is witchcraft connected to the land, ecosystems, bioregions, Nature, the Earth, and the Universe?

Exercises

Take some time each day to really listen to your body, and to relax each bit of it (sometimes it is easier to tense a part of the body and then relax it). Send your awareness, and imagine sending your breath, into each part of the body in turn.

Take up gardening if you are able to, and learn about permaculture.

Find out about the ecology, geology, flora, fauna, and waters of your local bioregion.

Adopt some of the practices in chapter 20 of *All Acts of Love and Pleasure: inclusive Wicca.*

Adopt some of the embodied spirituality practices outlined in *Dark Mirror: the inner work of witchcraft* (the previous volume in this series).

6. Witchcraft as resistance

The witch is the ultimate figure of resistance to power. When the powerless have no more material means to hand of resisting the powerful, then they resort to witchcraft. The witch in history is frequently marginalised and associated with wild sexuality, queerness, "perversion", resistance to authority, undermining the patriarchy, and generally causing trouble to rulers and oppressors. That's why the English authorities labelled Joan of Arc a witch: she was a gender-divergent and woman-loving woman. Clear signs of witchcraft, according to all the folklore. If we let go of this symbolism, we lose something quintessential of the power in the archetype of the witch.

Another very significant figure in the history of witchcraft as resistance to the authority of the Church is the Devil.

The Devil and witchcraft

Some folkloric Craft practitioners have always honoured both Lucifer and Jesus, regarding them as brothers (from the reference in the *Book of Job* about Samael being among the Sons of God). Cain is also an important figure in their mysteries and is viewed as the son of Samael and Lilith [34]. And Tubal-Cain is viewed as the earthly vessel of Azazel [35]. They place a lot of importance on the smith-gods such as

---

[34] Michael Ford (2009), *Luciferian Witchcraft: Book of the Serpent.* Lulu.com https://books.google.co.uk/books?id=H44yAgAAQBAJ (page 43)

[35] American Folkloric Witchcraft (2012), *Tubal Cain: an introduction.* http://afwcraft.blogspot.co.uk/2012/04/tubal-cain-introduction.html

Prometheus, Tubal-Cain, Hephaestos, Wayland, and Vulcan.

I can understand why some Wiccans completely denied that they even believed in the Devil, as I vividly remember the fear instilled in us by the Satanic Panic of the late 1980s. It is much easier to say "we don't believe in your mythology at all" than it is to say something more complicated, such as "we don't accept your dualistic cosmology, but we do believe there is a place for acknowledging the darker aspects of the psyche, and deities associated with them, and rather than demonising them, it would be better to integrate those forces into consciousness and work with their energies". Some Wiccan and Pagan writers actually did attempt to convey this more complicated message.

Various concepts and images of these entities are lurking about in the basement of the Western psyche - but we are not powerless to change them. Some people will prefer to ignore them altogether; others feel the need to change these images by working with them. That is their prerogative.

However, there is no need to throw Satanists under the bus when stating that Wiccans do not worship the Devil. There are at least three different flavours of Satanism, the philosophical and anarchist variety allegedly espoused by Mikhail Bakunin, the inversion-of-Christianity variety, and the people who are worshipping the Egyptian god Set. Therefore, claiming that Satanism is "just an inversion of Christianity" is an inadequate explanation of what it is.

I have not met that many Satanists, and many of the ones I have met have taken considerable pleasure in being self-consciously "dark" and very left-hand-path. Some of the ones I have met were very right-wing. There are nasty people in every group, but that does not mean that all of them are like that. I also know a couple of Setians and some left-wing Satanists.

It is worth pointing out that an acknowledgement of the possible existence of Lucifer, or Samael, or any other such entity, does *not* mean that we are suddenly Satanists. Some Wiccans have been acknowledging Lilith for years - so why is Samael so taboo?

I think that Wicca and Satanism are two separate and distinct traditions, but we are not being fair and reasonable if we demonise Satanism in the same way that some Christians have done to us.

There is also a positive side to acknowledging that the Horned God has a whiff of the Devil about him. The Christian image of the Devil was partly created from the image of Pan, god of sexuality, wilderness, wildness, and resistance to hierarchy and civilisation. When traditional witches referred to the Devil, these were the ideas they were trying to connect with. The oppression of the Church and its attempt to crush the joy out of life by imposing fasts and penances, and punishing people for 'deviant' sexuality, seems an excellent reason for a medieval person to investigate the possibilities of devil-worship.

Who cleft the Devil's foot?

From a hard(ish) polytheist point of view, I would argue that Lucifer, Satan, Samael, Asmodeus, Beelzebub, and various other entities are different beings. They may have got lumped together as one by the monotheists, but then I think we would all agree that monotheists have a tin ear when it comes to mythology. One of the Pagan deities whose image fed into the Christian concept of the Devil was Pan, and it is thought that that is how the Devil acquired his cloven hooves (unless it was from the image of Azazel as the scapegoat).

Some people have argued that neither Jesus nor Satan have a place in contemporary Paganisms, because we do not accept the dualistic and antagonistic worldview of Christianity. However, I do not have to accept that monotheism's assessment of the stature or nature of a being is true in order to accept that the being (or at least, its archetype) exists. I think Jesus probably exists as a god-form, but I certainly do not accept monotheism's view of who he is. So why not his brother Lucifer? We do not accept fundamentalist Christianity's assessment that all our deities are the devil in disguise - so why should we accept their view of Lucifer?

The various deities that were some form of adversary (and a necessary source of creative conflict) in the pre-Christian pagan religions all got lumped together to form the Christian version of the devil as the main adversary of Yahweh. Furthermore, the Jewish concept of Samael or Satan was quite different and existed alongside other figures such as Lilith as necessary aspects of the cosmic order.

I think the Christian view was probably influenced either by the two gods of Zoroastrianism (Ahura Mazda and Angra Mainyu), or by the good and evil entities of Manichaeism. Manichaeism was essentially a Gnostic view of the world that held that matter was created by an evil demiurge, and that the source of all good was the creator, to whom light and spirit seek to return by escaping from matter. Zoroastrians, on the other hand, say that the world was created by Ahura Mazda, the good god. However, both systems have an ultimate force of good pitted against an ultimate force of evil. Contrast this with Judaism, where Samael was essentially under the control of Yahweh - in this view, Samael existed to punish transgressors. If you look at the history of Jewish mythologisation of Satan, Samael, Azazel, Asmodeus, and other characters, it is clear that they are much more nuanced than the Christian versions. I really wish people would not conflate Judaism and Christianity, or back-project Christian attitudes onto Judaism, which is a completely different religion that Christianity is a massive distortion of. (And as far as I know, it is a heresy in Christianity to regard the Devil as being of equal power with God.)

As I do not accept monotheism's view that there is only one god and one adversary, I have room in my concept of deities for some that like to promote conflict for whatever reason they think it necessary (even if they don't happen to be among the deities with whom I have a personal relationship, because I do not like conflict). If I acknowledge the existence of Lilith and Loki and Set and Yahweh and Asherah, then I am prepared to accept that Lucifer, Samael, Baphomet, and Asmodeus also exist.

My polytheism consists of acknowledging the existence of many deities and honouring and/or worshipping those that have called to me. So far, only one of these entities has come knocking at my door, but if one of the others shows up, I think I would make my own assessment of their character. After all, Christianity was very rude about all our other deities - why should I take their word for it about any entity?

As to whether the Wiccan Horned God contains a bit of the Devil in his DNA... I think he probably does. If the Devil is equated in the Christian worldview with prancing about naked by moonlight, joyous love-making, and wild shenanigans - then the God of the Witches *does* represent these things.

What is interesting is that Pan, who may have informed some of the Christian idea of the Devil (because he represents wildness and wilderness and unbridled sexuality) is one of the few beings involved that was not an adversary figure in ancient mythology. (Though the Devil's horns and hooves may have come from Azazel the scapegoat rather than from Pan.)

In Charles Godfrey Leland's *Aradia: the gospel of the witches*, Aradia is presented as the consort of Lucifer, and it appears that Gerald Gardner and Doreen Valiente replaced Lucifer with Cernunnos when they were forming Wicca - in part because they believed Margaret Murray's theory that the being worshipped by witches was an ancient pagan Horned God (but also because they were well aware of the media furore that would result if they admitted to devil-worship). However, it appears from some research by

Sabina Magliocco [36] that the legend of Aradia pre-dates the association of witchcraft with devil-worship.

Horned deities in India were possibly associated with shamanism and animism, both of which have been viewed as transgressive by established religions.

It is also worth noting that the word demon (*daimon* in Greek) originally meant a spirit of place, or the genius of a gifted person, and had no negative connotation in ancient paganism.

My personal theology celebrates the marriage of spirit and matter, and not their separation. I celebrate wildness, and chaos, and the celebration of physical pleasure. I do not think that blind obedience is a virtue. I think a deity that represents anarchy, and rebellion against absolute authority, is worth looking into.

yes. For when understanding is impossible, too complicated.

Adversaries in ancient paganisms

Some ancient paganisms had the concept of a struggle between two groups of deities (in Greek mythology, the clash of the Olympian gods with their rivals, the Titans; and in Norse mythology, the clash of the Aesir and Vanir with the giants) but these were not so much conceived of as a struggle of good and evil, as a struggle between natural forces such as fire and ice, some of which were more inimical to humans than others. But things were complicated in the Greek myths because Prometheus stole fire from the gods to give to humanity (an impious act, but

---

[36] Sabina Magliocco (2005), *Who Was Aradia? The History and Development of a Legend.*
http://www.stregheria.com/MaglioccoAradia.htm

one for which we can be grateful). And in the Norse myths, the gods were born from the primal giant, Ymir, and then slew him to make the heavens and the Earth.

Some ancient religions of the Near East had powerful beings who were slain by the creator god (for example in Sumerian mythology, Tiamat the serpent goddess was slain by Marduk, who formed the Earth from her body - probably the original of many dragon-slayer stories). We can trace some of the motifs that went into the making of the archetype of the Devil back to some of these figures.

Be careful

I have got to admit that the name 'Satan' makes me really uncomfortable. I am much more comfortable with 'Old Nick', 'Lucifer', or even 'the Devil'. But then I am curious to delve into the depths and find out *why* it makes me uncomfortable.

However, given the enormous weight of negativity attached to the archetype of the Devil, anyone invoking these entities needs to be really careful to invoke the aspects of the complex that they want (the freedom, anarchy, hedonism, and sex-positive aspects) and avoid the negative associations with it (selfishness, greed, destructive impulses, etc). I find it very interesting that most people work with lesser-known names and beings such as Samael and Lucifer (arguably the bright side of this archetype) and avoid the more negative aspects. So much negativity has been loaded onto the archetype that it may be difficult to recover the bright aspects of it. If you do invoke or evoke such a being, are you a powerful enough magician to handle it?

Civilisation and its discontents

It is easy to see how gods of the wildwood (symbols of the wilderness and therefore opposed to civilisation, with which Christianity strongly identifies itself) may have fed into the Christian archetype of the Devil. Recently, I read *Lolly Willowes, or the Loving Huntsman* by Sylvia Townsend Warner, and in that book (written in 1926), the god of the witches is unequivocally represented (with considerable glee) as Satan. He is quite kindly, and the freedom of the countryside where he holds sway is contrasted with the stifling atmosphere of middle-class respectability from which the heroine escapes.

Many myths and legends (from ancient times until very recently) are about the struggle to establish civilisation and order, set against the urge to return to a state of nature and chaos. The myth of the dragon-slayer is one such story. One of the oldest of these myths is the slaying of the dragon Tiamat by the hero-god Marduk. Tiamat is the embodiment of the primordial waters, the great ocean. She represents the salt waters, and her consort Apsu is the sweet waters. When Marduk slays her, he builds the mountains from her bones, and the waters of the earth from her blood. This represents the establishment of order. In many Christianised dragon legends, the dragon represents the Devil. In Pagan mythology, the dragon represents earth energy. In Chinese mythology, dragons are spirits that guard sources of water. It has not been universally agreed that the imposition of law and order and civilisation is necessarily all good.

If someone were to draw a mindmap or a family tree describing all these entities and their mythological relationship with each other, it would get quite complicated. The massive number of references to the Devil in popular culture add an extra layer of complexity.

So - when you say that you do not worship the Devil, you might need to be a bit more specific. Do you mean Old Nick, Satan, Asmodeus, Azazel, Beelzebub, Baphomet, Samael, Lilith, Tiamat, Lucifer, Mephistopheles, Angra Mainyu, Iblis, Loki, Set, Apep, Prometheus, or some other adversarial figure? The Devil really is in the details.

The outlaw

Another hugely important figure in witchcraft is that of the outlaw - specifically Robin Hood, Maid Marian, and their Merry Men. There are some very interesting themes in the legends of Robin Hood. He is an archer, and an outlaw, a hero of the people who represents freedom and defiance of authority.

He may have been based on more than one historical individual. According to legend, he and his band of merry men lived in the 12th or 13th century. The legend became popular in the mid-14th century. Margaret Murray suggested that there was a connection with the witch-cult, as the Somerset witches (in 1664) called their god Robin, and Dame Alice Kyteler (in 1324) worshipped a spirit called Robin Artisson. There may also have been a connection with Robin Goodfellow. Plays about Robin Hood were performed as part of the May Day ceremonies. The ballads of Robin Hood place great emphasis on the idea that Robin Hood was devoted to the Virgin Mary, and treated women with great courtesy on her account. He disliked corrupt clergymen and priests in the extreme, though, and often ambushed them. So here we have a figure who is opposed to authority, yet devoted to a goddess, and who lives in the forest, defying normal social conventions and structures - robbing from the rich to give to the poor.

The historical person who was supposed to have been Maid Marian was a lady called Matilda Fitzwalter. She had refused to marry King John, so he confiscated her father's land. When she went into the forest with Robin Hood, she is supposed to have adopted the title "Maid Marian" to indicate that she was leading a pure and spotless maiden life, until such time as he could give up his outlawry and marry her. After Robin's death, she is said to have retired to Little Dunmow Priory, where she was poisoned by King John. Because of the manner of her life and death, she was viewed as an English heroine resisting the tyranny of the Normans, so it seemed only natural to link her with Robin Hood. She was also an important character in the May Games, and in some places, the May Queen was called Maid Marian, which might even precede the tradition of her as Robin's wife.

The Merrie Men were attached to the legend of Robin Hood gradually. The earliest mentioned was Little John, in 1341. Friar Tuck, probably a Franciscan friar, presumably symbolised resistance to the rapacious greed of the Church. Will Scarlet joined the outlaws after Robin Hood rescued the woman he wanted to marry from a forced marriage to someone else.

The medieval forest was a refuge from law and order: for odd cults, hermits, refugees from war, fugitive serfs, murderers, soldiers of fortune, outlaws, exiles, brigands, and wolf's-heads. Robin Hood and his Merrie Men epitomise the wild and free life of the forest outlaw, an alternative subculture living by different rules. They are subversive because they rob from the rich and give to the poor. This reversal of the order of things was a popular element in folk festivals, from the Saturnalia of ancient Rome, to the Lord of Misrule in medieval Yule festivities. Fugitives from the oppressive Normans could flee to the wildwood, and from there, conduct a sporadic guerrilla war against the authorities, with the help of the peasantry, who were also groaning under the yoke of tyranny.

The festival of May Eve was traditionally associated with Robin Hood, Maid Marian, the May Games, and Morris dancing. They represent an inversion of hierarchies, the renewal of life, sexuality, the growth of greenery, and dancing - all joyful things associated with subversion and anarchy.

One thing to be wary of here, though, is that such festivals were ways of letting off steam, having a holiday from the hierarchical order of things, which was viewed as normal and natural. The inversion of this 'natural' order worked to reinforce the hierarchy by associating a less hierarchical way of being with chaos and disorder. If we really want to get away from a hierarchical view of the world, we need to do more than invert the hierarchy: we need to imagine new ways of being.

The Fool

Another important tool in resisting the encroachments of authority is the figure of the fool or trickster, which is often linked with the Devil. Humour is the best weapon against authoritarianism.

Fools are more compassionate than tricksters; tricksters exploit human frailty, fools send it up, to release the healing power of laughter. The fool carries a bladder, perhaps as a symbol of pomposity, whose puffed-up balloon the wit of the fool will pop.

The seeker of wisdom should always be prepared to take the piss out of themselves and their delusions of grandeur. This is the reason why kings would license a fool or jester: so that when they were about to do something stupid, there was one person who was not afraid to tell them it was stupid. I have a small posse of people whom I have encouraged to kick me up the arse if I ever start getting too big for my boots. I hope their arse-kicking services will never be needed, but I feel it is wise to be prepared.

The Fool in the Tarot is depicted as setting out on the spiritual journey, without a care in the world. He carries all his belongings in a bundle, with a little dog prancing at his feet. Sometimes the dog has bitten a chunk out of his trousers, exposing his buttocks to the world. The dog represents the wiser instincts, warning us that we look ridiculous in our pretensions. In the Rider-Waite Tarot, painted by Pamela Colman-Smith, the Fool is dancing towards the edge of a cliff. The cliff represents the edge of the abyss, the gulf between innocence and experience, perhaps.

The wisest and most compassionate character in Shakespeare's *Twelfth Night* is Feste, the fool - quite possibly my favourite Shakespeare character of all. He skewers the pomposity of Malvolio, the drama of Orsino, and the self-pity of Olivia, but when the other characters (Maria and Sir Toby) turn the jest into cruelty, he takes pity on Malvolio. He also sings beautiful and poignant songs.

The fool was and is an ambivalent figure. Are they truly mad, or are they saner than the rest of us, having seen through the charade of maintaining the *status quo*, where all the most humane values are scorned in favour of turning a quick profit?

The Fool in Jan Matejko's painting, *Stańczyk*, is the only person at a 1514 royal ball who is troubled by the news that the Russians have captured Smolensk. His is a deeper wisdom than the superficial people around him.

Stańczyk by Jan Matejko [Public Domain]

I am also reminded of the Welsh story of the three causeless blows [37], also known as *The Lady of the Lake*. A faery woman married a human and said that she would leave him when he had struck her three times without cause. The first time was when she left her gloves behind; the second time was when she cried at a christening; the third time was when she laughed at a funeral. Each time it was because she knew something that the others present did not. Her wisdom ran contrary to that of the world, and so she was deemed a fool.

Witches, fools, and harlots were often seen as being in league with the Devil and the Fair Folk. The song *Tom o' Bedlam* [38] makes this connection:

> I went down to Satan's kitchen,
> for to beg me food one morning
>
> There I got souls piping hot,
> all on the spit a turning.
>
> There I picked up a cauldron,
> Where boiled ten thousand harlots
>
> Though full of flame I drank the same,
> to the health of all such varlets.
>
> My staff has murdered giants,
> my bag a long knife carries
>
> For to cut mince pies from children's thighs,
> with which to feed the fairies.

---

[37] http://www.sacred-texts.com/neu/celt/wfb/wfb03.htm
[38] http://thebards.net/music/lyrics/Bedlam_Boys.shtml

To be "in league with the Devil" is to celebrate wildness and sexuality, queerness and quirks, unbridled lust, revolting against authority.

Humour skewers the powerful and the pompous, pricking their bubble of self-importance. That is why authoritarians do not like humour and seek to control it, to turn it as a weapon against the powerless. But the joyous wildness always breaks through the cracks, like ivy and creepers bringing down stone and concrete.

The authorities want us to remain divided, frightened, and alone. They want to establish hierarchies, keep the poor downtrodden and enslaved by debt, crush the possibility of love and joy. They want women to be seen merely as walking wombs, and men as drones that fight and fuck. But we are more than that: half angel, half animal. The animal in us demands to be loved, to feel the wind on our faces, to snuggle with our beloved, and to laugh and dance and make love. The angel in us is a messenger, a communicator, a poet, a transformer, who yearns for the connection of minds.

The Fool calls us to our full humanity, both animal and angel, lover and beloved, dreamer and maker.

That is why being open to the queer, the wild, the exuberant, is inherently dangerous. It endangers the *status quo*, the drab everyday reality, and threatens to replace it will full colour and radiance and overflowing exuberance.

Witchcraft is resistance

Witchcraft is, essentially, resistance. Resisting oppression, resisting hierarchy, transforming consciousness, living on the edge of civilisation, offering an alternative way of being. That is why folklore has it that the witch lives in the last house in the village, on the edge of the forest. In some folktales, the witch's house is in a glade in the forest - in these stories, the witches and the wild people are embodiments of the forest and of wilderness.

Hedge witch.

We resist the notion that magic does not exist, that the world cannot be changed, that the oppressors cannot be overthrown. We will skewer their pomposity and arrogance with all the weapons at our disposal: with satire, with humour, with magic. In the ancient world, a good satire could raise boils on the person it was aimed at.

We resist heteronormativity, cisnormativity, hierarchy, patriarchy, and kyriarchy. We resist colonialism and racism. (Well, some of us do.)

We resist the idea that the Earth, or any being upon it, is a resource to be exploited. We resist the depredations of capitalism upon the common treasury. We resist the notion that everything has a price.

We are the eternal outsiders, the eternal critics. That is why Lilith, the scorned one, is a goddess of witches, and Hecate, lady of the crossroads and the underworld. That is why we are associated with liminal creatures of the night: frogs and toads, owls and bats, goatsuckers and nightjars, and cats. We are the people of the night, the hidden children of the Goddess. We are the honoured ones and the scorned ones.

Discussion

How is the image of the Horned God like, or different from, the image of the Devil?

To what extent is witchcraft a form of resistance to authority, or an alternative to civilisation?

How does the image of the fool fit in with the inner work?

What weapons are at our disposal in resisting authority?

Exercises

Meditate on the figure of the Devil. What does it represent for you? What feelings does it evoke - repulsion, fascination, something else? How could you integrate the positive aspects of this archetype (freedom, wildness, sexuality) into your psyche?

Meditate on the figure of the Fool. What does it represent for you? How does it link with the Wiccan virtues of mirth and reverence? How can we use the power of humour as part of the inner work?

Meditate on the figures of Robin Hood and Maid Marian. What do they mean to you? What does the wildwood symbolise for you?

Meditate on the archetype of the Witch. What does it represent for you? How does it empower you? Do you feel that it represents resistance to authority? How do you embody that?

7. Working with ancestors

It is good to know where we came from, and to honour those who struggled to give us the freedoms that we have today – freedom to love, live, laugh, and learn. I do not think we owe it to the ancestors to behave in a certain way, or to live in a specific place — but we do owe it to them to remember their struggles and their achievements. Without the feminists, queers, Dissenters, Pagans, and many others who struggled for freedom and rights, we would not have those rights and freedoms today.

Ancestors of blood, spirit, and place

What is an ancestor? First, and most obviously, it is someone from whom you are genetically descended. If you go back far enough, of course, your ancestors multiply exponentially and you could be descended from *anyone*. You can even have your genome mapped now, so you can see where your ancestors came from generations back. Some Druids refer to family ancestors as "ancestors of blood". Focussing exclusively on "ancestors of blood" can be problematic if your ancestors were in the habit of colonising and subjugating other peoples (which is true for just about everyone who is of European descent). For these ancestors, you may need to do work of healing and restoration of the damage they caused. It is also deeply problematic if you go around claiming that only people of a specific genetic background can follow certain religions. A person is part of a culture because they have been immersed in that culture, not because they are genetically related to the people whose culture it is (or was).

An ancestor may also be someone from the past whom you admire or feel an affinity with. Perhaps they were an activist for a cause you support (feminism, LGBTQIA+ rights, the environment) or created beautiful art or literature, or made an amazing discovery in the sciences. Some Druids refer to these ancestors as "ancestors of spirit".

An ancestor may also be someone who lived in the place where you live now (no matter where your family came from originally). Some Druids call these "ancestors of place". If you are a descendant of people who colonised a region, then the concept of "ancestors of place" needs to be treated with considerable sensitivity. And if you are a descendant of people who were persecuted by the inhabitants of the country where you live, then you might not feel like honouring ancestors of place – though some of them might have been defenders instead of persecutors.

The Beloved Dead

In many forms of witchcraft, including Reclaiming, Feri, and Wicca, there is the concept of honouring witches who have died, especially at Samhain. In Reclaiming and Feri, they are called the Beloved Dead. These may also include non-Craft family members who have died.

Companion animals

Companion animals who have passed on can also be remembered at Samhain. I remember the cats our family had as a child, Shandy and Spicy, my cat Harry, who died in 2011, and my cat Ziggy, who died in 2019.

Previous incarnations

If you have a clear idea of who you were in previous incarnations, you could also honour your previous lives as ancestors.

Beliefs about life after death

Most Pagans believe in reincarnation, with a period of rest in the spirit world between incarnations. In Wicca, the region where the dead go is referred to as the Summerlands. Some of the dead are believed to stay in the spirit world to watch over other Wiccans, or their families.

Samhain and ancestors

At Samhain (31 October), many Pagan traditions believe that the veil between the worlds is thin, and that the Beloved Dead can visit this world. Rituals are held for people to connect with the Beloved Dead. This can include putting up pictures of them or creating a shrine for them; reading the names of all those who have died since the last Samhain (this is done by Reclaiming witches); meditating and communing with them; and setting a place for them at the feast.

Some people find that the veil is thin all year round, not only at Samhain; for them, Samhain provides an opportunity to focus on the beloved dead and having a ritual to remember and honour them.

Every Samhain, I take the opportunity to commune with my friends, fellow witches, and family who have died, and to tell others about their lives. It is a beautiful ritual, and important to remember those who have passed on. There is a saying in the Reclaiming tradition: "What is remembered, lives."

Rituals for connecting with ancestors

Many people create a shrine for their ancestors of blood, spirit, and place, and their Beloved Dead. These may be photographs of the dead, and items they owned in life. Offerings of food, incense, and wine may be placed at the shrine. Some people do this all year round; others do it for the season of Samhain.

Another way in which you can honour your ancestors is by researching your family tree. The stories that emerge from this research can be fascinating, and there are many surprises to be discovered.

A traditional ritual at Samhain is the 'dumb supper'. Patti Wiginton[39] recommends making "the traditional Soul Cakes, as well as serving dishes with apples, late fall vegetables, and game if available. Set the table with a black cloth, black plates and cutlery, black napkins. Use candles as your only source of light -- black if you can get them."

As the name implies, the Dumb Supper is held in silence, and there is a chair and a place setting for the dead. As each person enters the room, they offer a silent prayer to the dead at the 'spirit chair', which is often shrouded in black. This chair is reserved for the dead.

A small offering of each serving of food is left on the plate for the dead - usually a portion from each diner's plate.

---

[39] Patti Wiginton (2016), *The Dumb Supper: A feast with the Dead.* http://paganwiccan.about.com/od/samhainoctober31/p/Dumb_Supper.htm

Each person may also bring a note (whose contents are private to them) in which is written what they would like to say to a person in their life who has died. At the end of the meal, they burn their note in the candle next to the spirit chair. Finally, everyone joins hands in silent prayer.

Another Samhain ritual is the litany of names of people who have died in the preceding year, which is practiced in the Reclaiming Tradition.

Most Samhain rituals include some form of communion with the Beloved Dead, as it is believed that the veil between the worlds is thin at this time.

The remembrance of the victims of war takes place on 11 November and includes a period of silence and meditation.

An important ritual which takes place on 20 November every year is the Transgender Day of Remembrance, to commemorate the lives of the many transgender people who are murdered every year. The event was started in 1999 and is now commemorated around the world.

The Transgender Rite of Elevation is a ritual created by a small group of Pagans and performed by many transgender and queer Pagans.[40]

Participants in the Transgender Rite of Ancestor Elevation pray and offer water for nine nights from 12 November to 20 November, the Transgender Day of Remembrance. After preparing themselves by washing and censing with incense, participants offer prayers for the transgender

---

[40] Alder Night, *So you want to honor the trans dead?* (Gods and Radicals) https://godsandradicals.org/2015/11/09/so-you-wan-to-honor-the-trans-dead/

ancestors, reading their names aloud, and building an altar, starting with a white cloth on the first night, and placing a book on the cloth, then stacking up one book on each night. The ritual is very powerful and needs to be done with focus and commitment. The ritual was devised through divination and consultation with the spirits of the transgender dead for whom it is performed – a very important point, I feel.

Similarly, after the shooting of 49 LGBTQ+ people, many of whom were of Latinx origin, at the Pulse nightclub in Orlando, Florida, Salvatore Caci, a Pagan from Italy, wanted to create a ritual to commemorate the dead and bring the LGBTQ+ Pagan community together. Sorita d'Este put him in touch with me, and together we created a ritual to commemorate the dead. Various friends translated it into French, German, Polish, Spanish, and Italian.[41]

The commemoration of queer ancestors is incredibly important, because queer people were marginalised, persecuted, and killed, and their lives and achievements are even more scintillating and amazing considering the obstacles they faced. It also makes LGBTQIA+ people aware that we have always been around, and we are not a new phenomenon, as some cisgender and heterosexual people would like to believe.

An ancestor is a person from the past with whom you feel an affinity: not necessarily genetic ancestors, but ancestors of spirit - people with whom you share ideals and values, or who are part of your community (LGBTQIA+ people, other witches, other Black people, Indigenous people, and

---

[41] https://wandsup.wordpress.com/

People of Colour); and ancestors of place - people who lived in the place where you live.

Discussion

Who is an ancestor?

How can I relate to my ancestors if they were colonisers and enslavers of other people?

How can we create ritual for connecting with ancestors?

Exercises

Create an altar for your ancestors of blood, place, and spirit

Research your family tree

Create a ritual to honour the ancestors of your community (BIPOC, LGBTQIA+, witches)

8. The pact in witchcraft and relational polytheism

A pact in witchcraft was originally the creation of a relationship with the Devil. This pact (much like the pact that blues singers were said to make at the crossroads) conferred the power of the Craft on the witch. According to Michael Clarke[42], a witch's power came from making a pact with a spirit or entity, sometimes called Old Harry, Old Scrat, Old Ragusan, or Old Horny. This entity was rarely referred to as the Devil. Such a pact could be made in a variety of ways, sometimes by writing it down, but in a semi-literate society, this was relatively unusual. One of the key rituals for making a pact was the toad ritual.

The toad ritual was an elaborate magical procedure for gaining occult power, and conferred power over fellow creatures on the person who successfully completed the ritual.

Of course, the Devil of the old Craft was quite different from the Christian Satan, or any of their other demons. Witches probably began by worshipping the old country gods - as people in out-of-the-way places had always done. But then the new religion, Christianity, said that the gods and goddesses of the old religion were "devils".

Sabina Magliocco, in a fascinating article on the development of the Aradia mythos, has shown that there was a "diabolical turn" at some time around the twelfth

---

[42] *East Anglian Folk Magic and Witchcraft* by Michael Clarke, http://mandox.blogspot.co.uk/2007/05/east-anglian-folk-magic-and-witchcraft.html

century.[43] Throughout Europe, beliefs in nocturnal spirit journeys, folk healing and fairies started to shift during the 12th century. Strongly influenced by the diabolical interpretation of witchcraft promoted by the Church, folk beliefs started to change, and to include stories of congress with devils, night-time feasts known as the *treguenda*, and consorting with Herodias and Diana.

The same process occurred with the god of the witches, the Horned One. He is the god of sexuality, physical pleasure, death, and resurrection. All of these were anathema to the Church. (See chapter 6, *Witchcraft as resistance*.)

The pact made by a witch with a deity was one of exchange, and as such the witch formed a relationship with that deity.

Deities, familiars, and daemons

There are many different categories of spirit in a polytheist and/or animist worldview. There are deities, demigods, gods of natural phenomena, deified humans, spirits of place (*daemones* or *genii loci*), land-wights, spirits of the home, *lares* and *penates*, familiar spirits, ancestral spirits, elemental spirits, and the Fair Folk. Some of these categories may overlap. Some of them may be friendly to humans; some may be indifferent; others may be hostile. Hostility or indifference does not necessarily mean that the spirit is evil; it just means it has a different agenda. The slugs that eat your lettuces are not evil; they just have an agenda that conflicts with your agenda. The hurricane and

---

[43] Sabina Magliocco, *Who Was Aradia? The History and Development of a Legend,* http://www.stregheria.com/MaglioccoAradia.htm

the volcano do not mean to destroy everything in their path; it is just their nature. could be applied to anything evil.

My working definition of a spirit is a conscious entity or identity. In non-dualistic worldviews, matter is just a denser form of spirit, so there is no separation between spirit and matter. In the West, we tend to see spirit as either inhabiting matter, or we deny spirit and see consciousness as an epiphenomenon of biology. A spirit is the consciousness of a place, person, or complex phenomenon. A deity is a more powerful spirit, perhaps not as dependent on place, but able to manifest anywhere. Both deities and spirits may choose to show themselves to us in human form (or perhaps they latch on to the human-shaped images in our heads), but that is not necessarily their 'true' form. Perhaps they are pure energy or consciousness and do not have a form.

or 'beingness'
denser, more concentrated.

A familiar spirit in traditional folklore was an animal who accompanied a witch. Familiars were often creatures of the night, such as cats, frogs, toads, owls, and mice. There are various explanations for this: that they were some sort of totem animal, spirit animal, or power animal; that witches have an affinity with the natural world, and that's why they were drawn to these creatures; or they were just lonely old women who needed a companion animal. In the *His Dark Materials* trilogy by Philip Pullman, everyone in Lyra's universe has an external soul or *daemon,* which takes the form of different animals while they are a child but settles on one particular form when they finish puberty. People from other alternate universes have their daemons on the inside.

Originally, a familiar spirit was a spirit that was particularly attached to a family, like the *lares* and *penates* of Roman religion, or the house spirits of various folk religions, or the *bean sidhe* (banshee) of old Scottish families. Somehow, these concepts mutated into the familiar spirits of witches.

Spirits of place also come in many different types: spirits of wood and field, hill and valley, lake and river, hearth and stove, barn and bath house. There are many stories of these spirits from folklore and mythology all over the world. There are also the Fair Folk, or elves and faeries, some of whom are helpful to humans, and some of whom are not.

Witches might sometimes enter pacts with such beings, usually to gain occult knowledge. There are numerous stories of gifts of magical artefacts from the Fair Folk which give supernatural assistance. When entering into a pact, it is best to be very clear about the terms, and to make sure that you are able and willing to fulfil your end of the bargain, because that is a courteous response to help from any source.

The desire for a relationship between a deity and a human needs to be mutual. If a deity seeks a relationship with you, and you are not interested in that deity, it is perfectly acceptable to say no. Similarly, if you want a relationship with a deity, and they are not interested in you, they also have a right to say no. Not every polytheistic religion takes this view, and some religions are closed, in the sense that it is not advisable to contact their deities except through their specific religious practices. If this is the case, it is not a good idea to devise an eclectic ritual calling on one of their deities, as it is likely to be seen as disrespectful (either by the religion, the deity, or both).

Relational polytheism and Wicca

I believe the gods are real and have agency. I am not sure if the gods are made of energy or consciousness or both, but I am sure that they are distinct identities. I do not see any conflict between polytheism and Wicca.

In the UK and Europe, Gardnerian and Alexandrian Wicca do not have a standardised theology. I have Wiccan friends who are polytheist, animist, henotheist, archetypalist, duotheist (an increasingly rare view in the UK and European Wiccan community), atheist, non-theist, and unclassifiable. I cannot speak for the USA, but I think the same is true there. American Wicca *may* be largely duotheist (I have insufficient data) but in the UK and Europe, I would say it is *probably* majority polytheist – though as I do not often ask for people's theological views, I am not sure. But you can often tell by what people do in rituals. I am happy to do ritual with people with varying theological viewpoints, as long as they are respectful towards the deities and each other.

The key aspects of Wicca for me are that we practice in a circle – a symbol of the equality of all the participants (like King Arthur's Round Table); that the circle becomes a microcosm to mirror the macrocosm (because we call the quarters); and that Wicca is both a religion and a magical practice. In other words, its purpose is to connect us with the numinous (*religio*, meaning to reconnect), and to transform us and the world for the better (that is the purpose of the magic). Working skyclad is also important to me, as a symbol of freedom and equality.

Witches do not serve the gods; we are largely a left-hand path religion and seek to become divine - to take our place among the gods. In his ode, *Nemea*, the classical poet Pindar [44] wrote:

> There is one race of men, one race of gods;
> both have breath of life from a single mother.
> But sundered power
> holds us divided, so that the one is nothing, while for the other
> the brazen sky is established their sure citadel forever.
> Yet we have some likeness in great intelligence, or strength, to the immortals,
> though we know not what the day will bring, what course after nightfall
> destiny has written that we must run to the end.

So, according to Pindar, humans and gods are related, and we have the "breath of life from a single mother". This passage is part of the basis of my (relational) polytheism. The gods have different powers, being immortal – they are non-local and do not have a physical form. So, they need our temporally focussed and physically located consciousness to be able to affect events in the physical world; and we need their eternal and non-local perspective to be able to access the divine realms.

---

[44]

http://archive.org/stream/odesofpindar035276mbp/odesofpin dar035276mbp_djvu.txt

One of the many things I appreciate about witchcraft is that the theology is fuzzy, and there is a greater focus on experience than on theology. If people and deities have a mutually satisfying encounter in a ritual, then I would regard that as a successful ritual. There is plenty of room for mystery in witchcraft. We do not know what the nature of the gods is, so all our theorising is probably inadequate, and most witches acknowledge that. There is room for apophatic theology in witchcraft: an acknowledgement that we don't know everything about the gods, and that we only see the faces they choose to show us; that sometimes it may be more illuminating to say what the gods are *not* than to attempt to say what they are.

For me, Wicca is the religio-magical framework in which I engage with the gods and Nature. Wiccans are my tribe and I love them – even the ones who annoy me and/or who find me annoying. Witches of other paths are related tribes.

The way I see my relationship with the deities I work with is that they are allies. They are not our masters and we are not their servants; we are not their masters and they are not our servants. We are co-creators with them of reality. Sometimes the realities that humans create are frightening and harmful, as in the current ecological and climate crisis. Sometimes the realities that the gods are said to have created are frightening and harmful, as in the Trojan War (though I am sure it was all too easy for the ancient Greeks and Trojans to claim that "the gods made them do it").

Whilst the gods are important, because they are the consciousnesses of specific places and natural phenomena, they are not more important than the ecosystem, Nature, the Earth, and other species who share the planet with us.

As a relational polytheist, I feel that it is our job to focus on right relationship with other beings, starting with other animals, including humans, and with the ecosystem in which we live, of which the deities are the conscious emanations. This can mean that we need to engage in restorative justice, such as the Black Lives Matter campaign, or by supporting the Idle No More protests of Indigenous Peoples, or campaigning for asylum seekers to be treated fairly by the UK.

Being in right relationship with our fellow embodied beings, and in right relationship with our ecosystem, will do more to bring us into right relationship with our deities than any amount of worship. Yes, we need to make that inner connection with the spirits of place, the spirits of the land, and the deities, as part of our awareness of all the interconnected relationships of the nested interconnections of being in which we live. But deities, land-wights, animals, humans, are all part of that web of relationships. The deities are not more important than other aspects of that interconnectedness, any more than humans are.

I stand *beside* my deities as an ally and a co-worker. They are more powerful and far-seeing in the realms of spirit, consciousness, and the timeless, so I need their help to access that mode of consciousness. They, on the other hand, need my finite, time-bound, and physically embodied mode of consciousness to bring about change in the physical world.

Wiccan liturgy and openness to mystery

If you look at Wiccan liturgy, there are some bits that refer to multiple deities, and some that refer to two deities. However, Wiccan liturgy does not define or prescribe Wiccan theology; for one thing, the materials written by Gardner, Valiente, *et al* are not strictly duotheist; and for another, we have a lot of other material, written by many different Wiccans. If other people use duotheist concepts in their rituals, I tend to "translate in my head". I know that they are expressing their understanding of how divinity works, and that it is sacred to them. There are many different traditional words for casting the circle, calling the quarters, and so on, so there is plenty of choice, and many people have adapted them or written their own to suit their specific perspective. Most Wiccans in the UK, Europe, and Australia write our own rituals, drawing on the body of existing material and on broader Pagan themes and ancient pagan source texts, so we can please ourselves as to the theology thereof.

I am aware that many 101 books on Wicca talk about "the Goddess" and "the God". That is one of several reasons I wrote my previous book, *All acts of love and pleasure: inclusive Wicca* – to try to promote some more nuanced ideas on theology, polarity, fertility, and so on.

The gods with whom I have a relationship are from several different pantheons, so Wicca provides a setting where I can honour them.

The things that I love about Wicca are the combination of magical practice and entering relationship with gods and spirits. I am a relational polytheist (a term coined by Niki

Whiting and Aine Llewellyn) – I enter relationships and alliances with the gods.

I love the idea, suggested by Niki Whiting, that we are in a guest/host relationship with the gods, and the fact that the words for guest and host are derived from the same Indo-European root word. Hospitality is a sacred relationship.

I am devoted to the interconnectedness, to bringing about heaven on earth, to creating right relationships and beloved community. If the gods are allies in that process, then they are my allies and my friends.

Mystical Polytheism

In ritual, we express our deepest yearnings towards what we hold to be of greatest worth. Some rituals can be shared with people who see the world differently; other rituals cannot be shared. Life is like that sometimes. In Wicca, it is possible for a polytheist and an atheist and a duotheist and an animist to circle together, if we share the same values and a similar practice. I would not circle with someone who was a racist or a homophobe or a transphobe – but I am fine with people with different theological perspectives, *as long as they respect my theological perspective.* We might even refine our working hypotheses of how it all works by engaging in dialogue. But one of the guidelines of interfaith dialogue is deep listening and being open to the other person's perspective.

This is the sacred ethic of hospitality: if I invite you into my space, I have certain obligations as the host, and you have obligations as a guest. The ethic of hospitality is one of mutually respectful behaviour.

We can learn from different perspectives

The reason why I welcome different perspectives on deities, and reality in general, is that I think our perspective is limited by our finite and localised nature in space-time. If we have an encounter with a deity, they are often kind enough to appear in a form that we can recognise, such as a vision of a humanoid form (I say humanoid so as not to exclude Ganesh, Pan, and other theriomorphic deities). I do not think for a moment that the gods' only form is a humanoid one. Someone once described deities as "possibly anthropomorphic interfaces of vast cosmic forces" – a description that sums it up well for me.

I think we need to approach the gods with a certain humility, and with an awareness that their nature is a mystery. Whilst deities are not merely archetypes, they do include archetypal qualities (I am not merely an archetype, but I include archetypal qualities – I am a fairly typical geek, for example; I'd quite like to be a femme fatale, but sadly I failed the exam).

People's beliefs and hypotheses do wax and wane; after all, we live in a highly rationalist and materialist culture – it is hard to maintain a faith in conscious cosmic forces in the face of all that. There is room for honest doubt, and apophatic theology, and mystical approaches, and people who think the gods are archetypes.

What is real?

The nature of reality can be viewed from many different perspectives: on the quantum level, everything is quarks and leptons and bosons and strangeness and charm. At the level of chemistry, it is all about the chemical interactions;

on the cellular biology level, cells join and divide and exchange chemical signals. On a psychological level, no-one would deny that love and hate and other emotions are real, and only the most reductionist person would insist that they are merely biochemical signals. Then there are interpersonal relationships, social movements, discourses, historical trends, and other macro-level processes, all the way up to the movement of galaxies and the expansion of the universe. From the perspective of the universe, our little lives are somewhat insignificant; from my personal perspective, my life is very significant to me.

I would say that something is "real" if it has a real effect on existence. In this view, ideas are real because they affect people's lives. However, ideas are not things, and they are not people. That is why the "gods have agency" part of contemporary polytheism is important, because gods are not just ideas or archetypes, but beings with will and agency. Overall, though, that is a matter of faith; although there are plenty of people experiencing the gods as beings with will and agency, they cannot provide irrefutable evidence that this is the case.

Most Pagans view the deities as immanent in the world, rather than existing only on some other plane of reality. If they are both immanent and many, then they must be the consciousnesses of natural phenomena.

I have always thought that the deities of Nature are the emergent consciousness of complex phenomena, such as sacred places, mountains, trees, storms, forests, and so on. If this is the case, then any anthropomorphic appearance they choose to adopt is only one aspect or facet of their vast and complex nature. And we cannot say with any certainty that we know them fully, or that we know exactly what they are. We can only say that we do experience them as distinct beings with agency, and that when we experience the presence of a deity, we know that we are blessed by their presence.

When I feel the presence of a deity, I feel their unique personality and energy. Some are reassuring and comforting; others feel more remote and challenging; but all are beings of majesty and power.

Apophatic and cataphatic theology

Apophatic theology attempts to describe the Divine only by negation. For example, we might say, the gods are not physical, they are not infinite, they are not energy, they are not light (though they may be *like* light or energy in some respects). By this process of negation, the aim is to arrive at a more mystical understanding of the Divine. The ninth century apophatic theologian, John Scotus Eriugena, wrote:

> "We do not know what God is. God Himself does not know what He is because He is not any thing. Literally God is not, because He transcends being."

The apophatic approach was first described by Plotinus, the Neo-Platonist:

> "Our thought cannot grasp the One as long as any other image remains active in the soul...To this end, you must set free your soul from all outward things and turn wholly within yourself, with no more leaning to what lies outside, and lay your mind bare of ideal forms, as before of the objects of sense, and

forget even yourself, and so come within sight of that One."

Similar ways of approaching the Divine also exist in Buddhism, Hinduism, Islam, Judaism, and Taoism. They attempt to free the Divine / deities from our limited human ideas about them. Because we cannot fully know the nature of the gods, it is hubris to assume that we know the will of a deity on all matters, especially those concerning other people. That is why, if you believe you have been given a command by a deity, it is wise to check it with insights received by others, both in the past and in the wider community, to see if it is consistent with that deity's other reported communications.

Cataphatic theology is statements about what the Divine *is,* such as "God is good". Similar approaches to cataphatic theology are also found in Hinduism and Buddhism. Historically, much of Pagan theology was cataphatic, in that it described the attributes and qualities of deities. Cataphatic statements are helpful in some ways, but apophatic and mystical theologians take the view that they need to be tempered with apophatic statements (a classic example would be that God is *like* light but is not *actually* light).

When we speak of the Mysteries in Wicca as something that is ineffable which cannot be described in words, but only experienced directly, that is an apophatic insight.

Discussion

Does the making of a pact have relevance in today's witchcraft?

How do we enter relationships with specific deities or spirits?

Must the desire for a relationship between a deity and a human be mutual and reciprocal?

Can we do ritual with people with different theological perspectives?

How does a mystical or apophatic approach to the nature of the Divine / deities help us?

How does a mystical approach relate to our experience of the Mysteries?

What do we know about the Divine / deities?

Exercises

Meditate on the qualities and attributes of your favourite deity, and then negate them, realising that they are more than their revealed nature.

Invoke a non-specific deity or energy; how does this feel different from invoking a specific one? Does a deity manifest?

9. Madness, shamanism, and witchcraft

The history of madness and attempts to treat it is long, convoluted, and fascinating. Different theories and treatments have come and gone, depending on the mood of the age. I think it is worth remembering that in many cultures, such episodes are not seen as mental illness, but a blessing from the gods. Many magical practitioners have had similar experiences to what western medicine dismisses as mental illness. That is not to say that mental illnesses are not actually illnesses; societies that recognise forms of shamanism also recognise and treat mental distress - but they are often better at distinguishing between the two. Mental distress and illness are frequently a response to the trauma of living in a hierarchical, capitalist, racist, misogynist, homophobic, and transphobic society.

The causes of mental illness are both environmental and internal. Fluctuations in brain chemistry are an internal response to external circumstances, so if you need medication as part of the treatment for your trauma, do not let anyone tell you that you are wrong. Treatment should be a combination of restoring the balance of chemicals in the brain and fixing the external circumstances that triggered the imbalance. Some imbalances are a result of systemic factors that are resistant to being fixed; so a careful examination of the situation is needed. Different people will need a different combination of medication, therapy, and a change in circumstances.

In the Middle Ages, people thought that madness and learning disabilities were of supernatural origin. Holy fools were 'simple' and were blessed and protected by God. The mad were either possessed or saintly, depending on the symptoms and how easily they could be fitted into the prevailing paradigm.

After the Reformation, people sought to control madness, and a medical model developed, and the mad were incarcerated. Various 'therapies' were tried, some quite drastic.

By the twentieth century, various drugs had been developed, and both social and medical models of the causes of mental illness were discussed. The disciplines of psychotherapy (using the 'talking cure' to treat the social causes of mental illness) and psychiatry (for treating mental illness with drugs) developed.

In India, mental distress of various kinds was traditionally treated by giving the person a story or folktale to meditate on. The tale was a form of therapy which would help them to solve the issues which had given rise to the distress.

In the 1960s, the anti-psychiatry movement examined the ways that other cultures (both past and present) have treated mental illness of various kinds. Michel Foucault wrote a history of madness, *Folie et Déraison: Histoire de la folie à l'âge classique,* which was translated into English by R D Laing as *Madness and Civilization: A History of Insanity in the Age of Reason.* Some of the key insights of the anti-psychiatry movement were:

- that madness can be a consequence of the disenchantment of living in a capitalist society

- that regulating the mad is a form of social and political control

- that seeing visions, hearing voices, and magical thinking are the traditional attributes of shamans and witches

- that behaviour which is considered normal in one culture may be classified as 'mad' by another culture (people who differ from cultural norms and expectations are often incarcerated unnecessarily)

- and that different societies classify and treat mental illness in different ways.

Several social historians analysed the content of the visions of witches and saints from the Middle Ages and concluded that these would be regarded as "madness" in the modern context. One member of the anti-psychiatry movement analysed the content of schizophrenics' visions and found recurring images of the cosmic axis (the world mountain and the world tree) and the cosmic hero.

Clairaudience and clairvoyance

Psychic abilities are a much-disputed area of psychological functioning. Many people hear voices and see visions, and have these experiences well-integrated into their lives, and can function normally. Others find hearing voices and seeing visions traumatic and difficult. The difference between these two groups appears to be mainly in whether they can 'turn off' the clairaudience or clairvoyance at will, or not. If you cannot shut down these abilities and focus on something else, it can be overwhelming.

Many psychiatrists claim that any sort of magical thinking is dysfunctional. Millions of occult practitioners leading balanced and happy lives would differ strongly from that view.

If you have these abilities, it is important to be able to ground and shield, and distinguish between what you think is happening, and what is happening. Are you sure that another person is impinging on your psyche, for example, or is it just paranoia on your part?

Psychic abilities are really useful, and everyone has some degree of 'sixth sense' which can be honed and trained with the right exercises - but be careful to check your psychic perceptions against other sources of information, to make sure you are well grounded in physical reality.

Mental health and Wicca

Some people have argued that people with mental health issues should not take part in Wicca, because the rituals are highly emotionally charged and involve a lot of magical practices which people feel might exacerbate mental health issues. I disagree – I think that the practice of Wicca can help people to integrate the psyche, which would be beneficial.

I think it is important to define terms at this point, as mental health and learning difficulties and learning disabilities are all different. None of them should be regarded as an automatic disqualification for taking part in Pagan or Wiccan rituals.

A learning difficulty is a learning or emotional problem that affects, sometimes substantially, a person's ability to learn, socialise, and follow social convention.

A learning disability is a significant, lifelong condition that starts before adulthood, affects development, and means that the person may need help to understand information, learn skills, and cope independently. [45]

A mental illness can affect the way you think, feel, or behave [46]. Many people have experienced common mental health problems, such as depression and anxiety, and there are rarer problems such as schizophrenia and bipolar disorder. Mental health conditions may be temporary (acute) or long-term (chronic).

Learning difficulties such as dyslexia can be an advantage in magic because dyslexia gives you a different perception of space and awareness of landscape and shape. Autism and Asperger's may also give you a different perspective (I have less knowledge & experience in that area). We can all learn from neuro-diverse and neurodivergent people. A learning difficulty does not affect cognitive ability in other areas, and people with learning difficulties can be very intelligent.

I cannot see why people with learning disabilities could not practice magic if they can understand the consequences of magical workings. The ability to understand depends on the level of disability, I guess. People with learning disabilities could certainly enjoy being in Nature and communing with Nature.

---

[45] Learning difficulty or Learning disability?
http://www.mindroom.org/index.php/learning_difficulties/w
hat_are_learning_difficulties/learning_difficulty_or_learning_dis
ability/
[46] MIND: *Mental health problems – an introduction.*
http://www.mind.org.uk/information-support/types-of-
mental-health-problems/mental-health-problems-introduction/

People with mental health issues can and do benefit from being involved in the Craft. Depression and anxiety can be helped by the experience of ritual. Anything involving manic phases or hallucinations might cause difficulties - but again, such conditions should never mean an automatic ban on participation. One of the finest high priestesses I know has bipolar disorder.

I think the best way forward (if it were possible) would be for the coven member, coven leaders, and psychiatrist or psychotherapist, to sit down together, discuss the kind of activities that happen in circle, and whether or how they might adversely affect the person with the mental health issue. As Wiccan practitioners are generally not professional psychiatrists, I do not think it is up to us to make these decisions. The problem is that most psychiatrists would just assume you were deluded if you started talking about deities and witchcraft — because most of them are not educated about Pagan traditions and witchcraft.

Ultimately, the best person to judge in these situations is the person with the mental health issue themselves. They know whether they can cope in a Wiccan circle, and can inform the coven leaders of any warning signs (such as being extra manic) which may mean they can no longer judge their own fitness to be in circle, and may need someone else to make that decision for them. (This last point was suggested by someone with bipolar disorder.) If the issue is severe enough to require medication, they do need to keep taking the medication, of course. And they certainly do not need to be told by well-meaning advocates of alternative medicine to throw their medication away.

In any case, many people develop mental health issues *after* they have become involved in Wicca (not as a consequence of being involved, more as a consequence of various stresses and strains in life, or perhaps from a previously dormant predisposition). In these cases, their covens are just going to have to learn how best to be supportive and sympathetic; so why would we exclude someone with a mental health issue that they know about and have reasonably well-controlled?

Several years ago, I experienced depression and anxiety because of a bout of seasonal affective disorder. The symptoms did not prevent me from taking part in rituals, and I found Wiccan rituals beneficial. During a period of doubt, uncertainty, and anxiety, Wicca was extremely helpful in keeping me balanced.

So why would we deny these beneficial effects to someone who has been diagnosed with a mental health issue?

Practices that may be risky

For some people with mental health issues, some spiritual practices may carry extra risk.

There is a growing body of evidence that mindfulness practices can make some people ill. There is a tendency in the West to assume that these practices are not life-changing and do not modify consciousness. However, they can be very effective — provided they are taught with the proper safeguards and that people do not go from zero meditation to ten-day silent retreats. These safeguards (developed by Buddhists over centuries of using these techniques) are often not passed on along with the practices.

An article by Dawn Foster in *The Guardian* (23 January 2016) asked "Is mindfulness making us ill?" It explored several case studies of people who had been made ill (or whose existing conditions had been made worse) by taking part in mindfulness sessions. Another article, by Matthew Jenkin in *The Guardian* (30 September 2015) suggests "Look out for your mental health before joining the mindfulness bandwagon". The article points out that the new mindfulness industry is not regulated and there are no minimum requirements for trainers in these techniques. People often set themselves up as trainers in these techniques without having the necessary experience and expertise. Similarly, an article by Robert Booth in *The Guardian* (25 August 2014) reports "Mindfulness therapy comes at a high price for some, say experts". The most extreme side-effects are rare but can include an experience known as "'depersonalisation', where people feel like they are watching themselves in a film". There is also an experience known as 'the dark night', where meditators relive traumatic memories. An expert from Oxford University's mindfulness centre stressed that people should be trained for at least a year before they deliver mindfulness training.

From my own experience, some magical and occult practices make me feel ill. I start to experience nausea, symptoms which seem to me to be like depersonalisation, and a sense of disorientation. I spent six months doing the Lesser Banishing Ritual of the Pentagram nearly every day, and it was like having my psyche scraped out with a rusty teaspoon. Since then, I have found that any meditation or visualisation that involves leaving the body (especially Hermetic-style visualisations which use a vehicle of light) brings on the same symptoms, and I need to leave the room.

If a magical or spiritual technique makes you feel ill or excessively disoriented, or exacerbates your existing symptoms, you would be well advised to stop and ground yourself. The last time this happened to me, I went outside and hugged a tree, and ate some food. Please be careful with magical and spiritual techniques. They have real effects on the psyche.

Discussion

Have there been times in your life when you have experienced a mental health issue (e.g. depression, anxiety, bipolar disorder, eating disorder, OCD, alcoholism)? How might Wiccan practice and ritual have helped you?

How could your coven or group support someone with a mental health issue? Are there limits to what you could cope with?

What 'safe space' measures and guidelines could you put in place to ensure that all members of the group are safe and supported (regardless of whether they have a diagnosed mental health issue)?

Are there any spiritual practices that make you feel ill or disoriented?

Yvonne Aburrow

Exercises

Read a book of traditional folk tales (such as the Brothers Grimm, Jewish folktales, or Italo Calvino's *Italian Folktales*). Is there a story that particularly speaks to you? Or perhaps you can remember a folktale from childhood that particularly resonated with you. Meditate on this folktale, draw pictures of it, write a poem or song about it, and see if you can work out why it spoke to you.

Draw images or write poetry of the various identities and archetypes you carry in your psyche. You can give them names if it helps.

Draw a mandala or doodle of your current mood, or of your psyche. This exercise can be repeated regularly, as it is interesting to observe the changes over time.

10. The night journey

The night journey was a very important feature of witchcraft accusations and confessions during the era of the witchcraft persecutions. The earliest recorded reference to the night journey appears in the writings of Abbot Regino in 899 CE. He wrote about women who believed that they follow Diana or Herodias on night journeys. They believed that they rode out on the backs of animals. Three hundred years later, in the 12th century, Ugo da San Vittore, an Italian abbot, described women who believed they went out at night riding on the backs of animals with "Erodiade," who he thought might be Diana or Minerva. Either these writers are copying each other (though it seems unlikely that the later writer would inveigh against these beliefs unless he himself had encountered them), or the legend of the night journey was remarkable widespread and persistent. But research by German historian Wolfgang Behringer shows that stories of night-flying societies, some of whom were said to be followers of Diana, were circulating in oral culture in the western Alps (a region that now includes parts of Germany, Switzerland and Italy) in the 16th century, and probably for a while before that.

Herodias was believed to be the daughter of Herod (actually Salome) who danced so well that her father offered her any favour she liked, and so her mother persuaded her to ask for the head of John the Baptist. After this had been granted, she was believed to have repented, and to have been blown up into the air by a wind coming from the dead saint's mouth. She was not good enough to get to Heaven, not bad enough for Hell, so ended up somewhere in between.

It is not clear whether the people themselves were conflating Herodias with Diana and Minerva, or whether the clerics were making a guess based on their knowledge of classical mythology. Both Herodias and Diana were associated with flying and with sexual wantonness, so that may be how they got conflated. Sabina Magliocco [47] explains that the goddess Diana was associated with witchcraft in early Classical Roman literature, and this carried over into later centuries.

Diana was often blended with Selene and Hecate, and all three goddesses were associated with the Moon, and known for helping witches. Hecate was the queen of the dead, manifesting at tombs and at the hearth, which was associated with ancestors. Hecate would appear at crossroads by night, leading her retinue of spirits through the air and accompanied by terrifying howling dogs.

Folklore about Diana's nocturnal rides may be a version of earlier tales about Hecate and her cavalcade of the unquiet dead, which were transmitted throughout Europe well into the medieval period. In northern Europe, these stories merged with the legend of the wild hunt.

During the 12th century, the faery folk began to be added to the legend-complex of Herodias / Aradia, Diana, and the night journey. The faery rade began to be associated

---

[47] Sabina Magliocco (2002), *Who Was Aradia? The History and Development of a Legend.*
http://www.stregheria.com/MaglioccoAradia.htm and
https://journals.equinoxpub.com/index.php/POM/article/view/14599

with the provision of abundant food and drink, the conferral of healing powers, the rewarding of cleanliness and tidiness, and riding out on horseback at night. In Germany, they were associated with goddesses like Berchta and Holde. In Italy, the goddess of these revels was called Bensoria, Diana or Herodiana (combining Herodias and Diana). In France, she was known as Satia and Dame Abonde.

It was at this time that these legends began to change and become entangled with ideas about malevolent witches who consorted with the Devil. Witch trials in the fourteenth century produced confessions of people consorting with Signora Oriente (the Lady of the East), also known as La Signora del Giuoco ("the lady of the game") who led gatherings where there was delicious food, music and dancing. La Signora could predict the future, reveal secrets, and resurrect the animals that had been eaten at the feast. In the morning, everything was restored to its former state.

By the sixteenth century, these night journeys were taking a more sinister turn, and began to include visions of cannibalistic feasts and sexual intercourse with the Devil. They also involved flights to the magic walnut-tree of Benevento (illustrated on the label of the popular Italian liqueur, Strega).

Some of the witches maintained that their experiences of the night journey were real; others insisted that they were dreams. It is possible that the witches were part of an actual secret society, which shared knowledge of herbs, ecstatic dances, and other folk magic. Or these experiences may have been hallucinatory fantasies, visions of abundant food and pleasure to compensate for the privations of peasant life. It is also possible that some people may have heard these stories as legends and then decided to enact them for themselves. This process is known as 'ostension' among folklorists.

Whatever the truth behind these experiences, the night journey remains a powerful symbol of the witches' Sabbat or *treguenda*. The idea of journeying in the spirit to an *omphalos* or spirit gateway in the landscape is found all around the Mediterranean and may be a very old legend.

In many ways, it is like the legend of the Wild Hunt, a cavalcade of spirits that was believed to ride on the wings of the storm, especially in winter. It was sometimes believed to be led by Hecate, sometimes by Odin, sometimes by legendary heroes of old, like Wild Edric in Shropshire, who was a Saxon lord who surrendered to the Normans too early, and so was condemned to guard the Welsh Marches for centuries; he was last seen just before the Crimean War in the mid-19th century [48].

The Wild Hunt travels along the spirit paths across the landscape, rather like witches flying to the Sabbat. Like Herodias, the hunters are believed to be souls who were not quite good enough for Heaven, not quite bad enough for Hell, or who (like Wild Edric) had unfinished business on Earth. The same is sometimes said of faeries, that they are the spirits of the dead, trapped between Heaven and Hell. The sound of their flight is said to be like the noise

---

[48] Richard 'Mogsy' Walker (1995), "Tales of Wild Edric". *White Dragon*. http://www.whitedragon.org.uk/articles/edric.htm

that geese make when flying, and so a flock of geese are sometimes called "Gabriel's Ratchet Hounds".

The night journey, with its attendant cavalcade of spirits and deities and spectral animals such as horses and dogs, is a particularly persistent and widespread motif in myth and legend. That suggests that it is ancient and significant, and a powerful tool for accessing the depths of the psyche.

Visualisation

You are sitting in a cottage by the fire. There are stone walls, with simple furniture, maybe some herbs and tinctures in jars and pots.

You open one of the jars, labelled 'FLYING OINTMENT' and dip your fingers into the fragrant green goo in the jar, and anoint yourself.

You dance naked on the hearth, astride a broomstick, making eerie shadows on the walls, chanting

> Horse and hattock! Horse and go!
> Horse and Pellatis, Ho Ho! [49]

---

[49] *"Horse and Hattock"* probably became associated with witches through Isobel Gowdie, a Scottish witch who was tried for witchcraft in 1662. In her confessions, she spoke of how she used the chants *"Horse and Hattock in the Devil's Name"* and *"Horse and Hattock, Horse and go, Horse and Pellatis, Ho Ho!"* in order to fly by mounting a broomstick. The faeries were also said to cry 'horse and hattock' when they wanted to return to Elfhame. [Source: Sarah Ann Lawless (2006), "Horse and Hattock", *Witchvox*.]

and begin to feel yourself getting lighter and more insubstantial. You fly up the chimney on your broomstick and start to fly over the moonlit landscape. The full moon shines brightly. The land seems blue and silver in the moonlight. There is mist in the hollows. You become aware of the roads glowing silver in the moonlight, only they are not roads, but spirit tracks. Fly above them, following them. You see people moving along them. Then you realise that all the tracks converge on a very high round hill. Other witches are coming from all directions, heading for the great round hill. It is a Sabbat, and there is dancing and feasting. Magpies and hares and cats weave in and out among the dancers. The great Horned God of the witches weaves in and out of the dance. Wild and ecstatic ululations and eerie cries echo about the mountain and the surrounding valleys. Towards dawn, retrace the route to the cottage.

Marginalia depicting Waldensians as witches in *Le champion des dames*, by Martin Le France, 1451 (Public Domain)

Part 2: Bringing it all back home

This section focuses on how we can use insights gained from the practice of witchcraft in everyday life. These include group dynamics and how they impact on the life of a coven; being a coven leader, and the process of teaching and learning in a coven, including learning styles and differentiation; the concepts of egregore, lineage, upline, and downline; followed by the uses and abuses of power and authority; the process of challenging oppression (racism, homophobia, transphobia, biphobia, sexism and misogyny), both within your own life and within the community; and how to evaluate your Craft and its impact on your life; the meaning and purpose of 'spirituality', religion, and magic; and the archetype of the witch and what it means.

11. Modes and types of ritual

There are several modes and types of ritual. Understanding the different types of ritual can be important for understanding how to craft your ritual to achieve the effects that you want. If you want to create a strong sense of presence, a ritual that builds slowly to a crescendo may be more effective than one with a lot of dancing and celebration. If you want to create something uplifting, then dance and song might be the way to achieve that. If you want something solemn and dignified, then a more ceremonial approach may be called for.

Modes of ritual

Ronald Grimes [50] identifies six different modes of ritual.

Ritualisation is simply the way that we tend to do some things the same way, or in the same order, every day, like having breakfast getting dressed, brushing teeth, brushing hair etc.

Rituals of **decorum** are those small gestures that ease social contact, such as shaking hands, saying hello and goodbye, please and thank you, and so on.

Ceremonial ritual is where power is on display, as in the state opening of parliament, or the crowning of a monarch, or the inauguration of a president.

Liturgy, which means 'the work of the people' generally involves waiting for power to manifest, but there is a dignity and solemnity in liturgical ritual which can be very

---

[50] Grimes, Ronald L. (1982) *Beginnings in Ritual Studies* Lanham & London : United Press of America

enjoyable, and if it is done well, it can bring power through just as much as a magical ritual does. I would like to see more of the liturgical mode in Pagan rituals. Liturgical rituals can include processions, ritual drama, singing and chanting, even dancing.

Magical rituals are intended to cause change and transformation, either in the inner states of the participants, or in the external world. These include rites of passage, whose function is to bridge the divide between one psychological state and another (for example, to manage the transition between childhood and adulthood); and healing rituals, whose function is to transform an ill person into a well person. Even seasonal festival celebrations could be said to be magical rituals because they manage the transition between one season and the next.

Magical rituals are much more focussed on symbolic transformation - the planting of seeds, the consecration of food and drink, the crossing of thresholds.

A magical ritual generally has a particular structure: the creation of sacred space as a container for the energies raised within it; the consecration of the participants and of the items to be used in the ritual; the performance of the ritual; and the closing of the sacred space. The build-up of magical energy in the sacred space is important, and so is the creation of the sacred space as a microcosm of the cosmos, according to the principle of "As above, so below" in order to aid in the performance of sympathetic or imitative magic.

According to David Wadsworth, a spell has four phases: the emanation of the energy from the source, the creation of the energy, the formation of the energy, and the action, when the energy is sent to do its work. These are based on the four worlds in Kabbalah (*Atzilut* or Emanation, *Beriah* or Creation, *Yetzirah* or Formation, and *Asiyah* or Action). These are also known, in the immortal words of David Wadsworth[51], as "Suck, squeeze, bang, blow", or the four stages of the four-stroke engine.

An invocation can also be said to have four phases: the desire for the deity to manifest, and the creation of the energy necessary to open the way for them; the sensing of their presence; their arrival; and their oracular utterance (see Chapter 7: *Evocation and invocation*).

Celebratory rituals can include birthday parties, but also parties to celebrate seasonal festivals. The aim of such a festivity is not to transform anything or manage a transition, but to let off steam. In the ancient world, carnivals inverted the normal social order and allowed everyone to let off steam, and then they returned to the normal social order when the festivities were over.

When writing rituals, you can deliberately make use of these different modes to create a different mood, depending on the purpose of your ritual. Sometimes a ritual can include more than one of these modes.

---

[51] David Wadsworth (1987/88), *Wicca & The Art of Motorcycle Maintenance*. (This article first appeared in *Children of Sekhmet*, May 1988.)
http://www.sacred-texts.com/bos/bos328.htm

Types of ritual

A rite of passage is a ritual designed to make sacred a life event or transition from one stage of life to another. We might also call these rituals 'sacraments'.

The Oxford English Dictionary defines a **sacrament** as "a thing of mysterious and sacred significance; a religious symbol". The word is used in Catholicism to refer to the seven sacraments of baptism, confirmation, the Eucharist, penance, anointing of the sick, ordination, and matrimony – which are mostly rites of passage; and in Protestant traditions, to baptism and the Eucharist. The etymology of the word is from Latin *sacramentum* 'solemn oath' (from *sacrare* 'to hallow', from *sacer* 'sacred').

An important element of rites of passage and sacraments is that they have a physical component, often linked to one or more of the classical four elements (earth, air, fire, water). Immersion in water is used in both Judaism and Christianity to signify entering a new phase, being consecrated (baptism) or re-consecrated (*mikveh*). Fire is used as a purifying medium in the Hindu ritual of *aarti*, which is both an offering and a purificatory ritual. Water is used for the Sikh baptism ceremony called Amrit Sanskar. The ancient druids are reported to have used sensory deprivation by requiring candidates for initiation to lie in darkness for several days and then thrusting them into the light, according to OBOD (the Order of Bards, Ovates, and Druids). All these rituals signify some sort of symbolic death and rebirth experience.

There is no standard list of sacraments for any contemporary Pagan tradition, but we can identify sacraments for most of them.

In Wicca, the sacraments could be said to be preparing the circle, cakes and wine, naming (sometimes called "Wiccaning"), initiation, handfasting, and croning.

In Druidry, the sacraments could be said to be preparing the circle, naming, initiation, and handfasting.

In Heathenry and Ásatrú, the sacraments could be said to be the blot, the *sumble* (or *symbel*), and the handfasting.

In *Religio Romana*, there are many rituals designed to connect the practitioner with the deities and sacralise life. These include libations, a prayer for ablutions (a ritual formula to purify oneself prior to the performance of other rituals), and various daily rituals at the *lararium* or home shrine.

Preparing sacred space

Most Pagan traditions have a preparation for ritual, as rituals are often held in spaces which also have other uses, such as a living room, a garden, or a park. Therefore, sacred spaces are temporary and must be reconsecrated. It is also necessary for the participants in a ritual to be prepared for ritual, to help us enter the right mindset. Preparation typically includes some form of consecration of both the space and the participants with the four elements (earth, air, fire, and water). Incense, water, salt, and other symbols of the four elements may be used to create sacred space.

Blot (Heathenry)

This ritual has three parts, the hallowing or consecrating of the offering, the sharing of the offering, and the libation. The offering, shared with the deities, is typically mead, beer, or juice.

Sumble / symbel / sumbel (Heathenry)

"The sumbel is actually quite simple. The guests are seated, (traditionally, in some formal fashion), and the host begins the sumbel with a short statement of greeting and intent, and by offering the first toast. The horn is then passed around the table and each person makes their toasts in turn. At the sumbel toasts are drunk to the Gods, as well as to a person's ancestors or personal heroes. Rather than a toast, a person might also offer a brag or some story, song, or poem that has significance. The importance is that at the end of the toast, story, or whatever, the person offering it drinks from the horn, and in doing so 'drinks in' what he spoke." [52]

Cakes and wine (Wicca)

In Wicca, cakes and wine are consecrated and shared. This happens at every circle. They are consecrated by a semi-invoked priestess. Usually a priest kneels and offers her the cakes and wine to be consecrated. In inclusive covens, these roles may be taken by a person of any gender.

---

[52] *The rituals of Asatru*
http://www.ravenkindred.com/RBRituals.html

Libations

These are offerings of mead or wine poured for the deities and spirits of place. The libation is important in *Religio Romana*, Heathenry, and Wicca. Some traditions perform the libation before the wine or mead is shared among the ritual participants; others do it afterwards. I like the idea of setting some wine aside for the gods before you start drinking. I also like the practice of saving a bit at the end. Some people practice 'reversion of offerings', where the wine is offered to a deity, left for a while, and then drunk by the practitioner.

Ritual drama

A ritual drama is a short play performed within a ritual, often for cathartic effect. Participants are invited to identify with the characters in the story, and let the archetypes interact with their own inner archetypes. If you allocate parts cunningly, it can be very healing and transformative for the participants. The performance of a ritual drama is often a great opportunity to explore a well-known story from a different angle. Many Wiccan rituals contain ritual dramas, sometimes scripted, sometimes extemporised. The drama may represent the myth associated with the seasonal festival being celebrated, or it may be something the group wishes to focus on for an esbat or full moon ritual.

Ritual games

A ritual game can be surprisingly moving and powerful. A game for a Lammas ritual is to divide the group into reapers, wheat, and a hare. (I did this by putting a lot of twigs into a bag. Twigs with bark on them were reapers;

twigs without bark were wheat; the hare was a twig wrapped in silver foil. Parts were allocated by people pulling twigs out of the bag.) The game is that the reapers must try to catch the hare, and the wheat must try to hide him (it's a bit like the game of Tag, or "It" as it was called in my childhood). This is based on the idea that the hare is the vegetation-spirit who hides in the last sheaf of wheat, and the reapers would always treat the last sheaf of wheat with special ritual. When the hare has been caught, all the reapers throw darts of grass at him, and he falls over, and is carried off with great lamentation.

Daily ritual

Many people perform daily ritual, which can be very effective. It may be the simple lighting of a candle, or a daily meditation or contemplative prayer session. It may be the yoga 'salute to the Sun'. Some Feri practitioners use the session to run the energy of the Iron or Pearl Pentacle. It provides a few moments each day to connect with the gods, Nature, the universe, the inner self, and to set an intention for the day. For some years, my daily ritual was noting 'small beauties' (a practice developed by Jacqueline Durban, where you note beautiful things that you have seen in a journal or diary).

Group ritual

Working with a group can be completely amazing, and it can also be utterly frustrating. Being in a group gives you someone to celebrate festivals with, and to learn from and bounce ideas off. Personally I love having a magical group, because it gives me the opportunity to do ritual with other people, to exchange ideas, and to have conversations about stuff that never normally gets talked about, and to experience those moments when all the energies of the group flow together and become more than the sum of their parts. Magical groups can create deep and lasting friendships.

Groups can be awesome if you find the right people to celebrate with; they can also be a bit dysfunctional. That is the nature of social interactions. Most groups go through phases of forming, storming, norming and conforming, so expect a bumpy ride. In the end, though, it will be worth it, because there is so much more that you can do in a group ritual than you can do on your own. It also decreases feelings of self-consciousness.

Solo ritual

Doing ritual on your own can be very useful, either as a supplement to group ritual, or as a substitute for it if you cannot find a group. It also means that you can express yourself and explore relationships with deities in your own personal way. I have had some amazing experiences in solo rituals and find them very refreshing now and again.

Indoor ritual and outdoor ritual

Indoor ritual is very different from outdoor ritual. Both have their advantages and disadvantages. An indoor ritual can have more props, and more elaborate ceremonial; it can have longer periods of meditation, silence, and visualisation; and you will not get rained on or disturbed by passers-by.

Outdoor ritual, on the other hand, means that you are very close to the elements, and out in Nature, among the tree spirits, wind spirits, and earth spirits. You can light a fire and dance around it (subject to fire safety regulations in dry areas of countryside); you can pour libations directly onto the earth; you can feel the wind in your hair. If you can find somewhere isolated enough to do outdoor ritual without being disturbed, it is a wonderful experience.

What do all these rituals have in common?

They all involve one or more of the four elements (earth, air, fire, and water). Earth may be represented by stone, salt, crystals, or soil. Air may be represented by blades, wands, feathers, or incense. Fire may be represented by a candle flame, a bonfire, incense, or wands. Water is represented by water, chalices, and cauldrons. Each element has a sacred direction, which can vary between different traditions.

Initiation ceremonies all include a section where the candidate is asked whether they wish to be there. In naming ceremonies, where the baby cannot be asked if it wishes to take part, a simple welcome to the wider community of humanity is all that takes place.

There is an assumption that things are already sacred because deities are immanent in the world, but sometimes we forget our connection with the divine, and need reconnecting.

They generally involve marking the transition from one phase to another – sometimes by crossing a threshold: stepping into the sacred space or leaping across a fire or a broomstick.

They generally involve deities or spirits being asked for their blessing and/or protection.

Discussion

What makes a ritual magical, celebratory, ceremonial, or liturgical?

Why are rites of passage important?

What are sacraments and why are they important?

Why do we need to prepare sacred space?

Exercises

Try creating rituals in different modes (liturgical, magical, celebratory)

Write a rite of passage for a significant life event. What elements do you need to include to make it meaningful?

Devise a new way of sharing food and drink sacramentally with your group. How can you make it even more meaningful?

12. Group dynamics

The subject of group dynamics is complex, but one way of observing group dynamics is to ask the simple question, "Where does the power go in the group?" In other words, who is wielding the power? Sometimes, it is not the designated leader, but the person who is most likely to veto new ideas.

In many groups, there is an elected or appointed leader. In most churches, the minister is officially the leader - but woe betide her or him if they upset the committee. In Wiccan covens, the leader is usually the high priestess. In a Druid grove or a Heathen hearth, there may be a small group of leaders, or a single leader. Quaker meetings usually have a group of elders.

In a small group, it can be an excellent idea to rotate the leadership role. Different members of the group take it in turns to write and facilitate a ritual. Most progressive and/or inclusive covens encourage their members to create and lead rituals.

Most people find that working in a group with a flat hierarchy is preferable to working in one with a very top-down hierarchy. Flat hierarchies are characterised by shared decision making and informal communication between team members.

Groups often go through a process of forming, storming, norming, and performing. First the group comes together (forming). Then there is a struggle to resolve the group's differences (storming). Once that has been resolved, the group's values, goals, and beliefs converge (norming).

Once that process is complete, the group is ready to perform. These stages can be a cycle rather than a linear process.

During the formation of the group and the convergence of its ideas, who is in the group, and who is outside the group, will become apparent. This is known as the in-group / out-group dynamic. The formation of the in-group can be a positive thing, in that it makes the group feel closer together, but it can be dangerous, because if the in-group projects its shadow onto the out-group, this can result in persecution of the out-group.

The projection of group members' shadows onto other people in the group can be a dangerous dynamic. If you are the leader of a group, this a thing to watch out for, as you do not want one person to be demonised or outcast by the rest of the group. The shadow is the aspect of our psyches that we have repressed because we do not like that aspect of ourselves, and we often project it onto other people, especially if they resemble the repressed aspect of personality.

If conflict arises, it may not be immediately apparent who has started the conflict. If you must pick a side, proceed with extreme caution, and try to get both sides of the story. The person who is making the most distressed noises may not actually be the victim.

A pattern that sometimes emerges is the Persecutor / Victim / Rescuer triangle. One person will see themselves as a victim and cast others in the role of persecutor and rescuer. They may even play the other roles themselves in some situations; or they may see the same person as both

Persecutor and Rescuer. People do not do this consciously, but it's a pattern to watch out for in conflict situations. People will often be stuck in these roles in every social situation, possibly because that was their role in their family dynamic, and now they find themselves playing this role in every social situation. The trick is to try to spot these patterns and interrupt them. [53]

One useful way to interrupt unhealthy patterns is the use of ritual and inviting people to identify with and internalise archetypes and characters who can show them how to play a different role in the social fabric. This is a slow process, and best accompanied by the person also working on this in a therapeutic setting, particularly if the pattern is very ingrained.

Group dynamics can be healing, or they can be retraumatising. That is why it is very important to spot conflict developing and try to nip it in the bud, by offering alternative roles for the participants in the social dynamic. Sometimes you just cannot fix the conflict, and then difficult decisions must be made. Either way, group interaction can be a beautiful experience or a traumatic one, but it has a massive impact on the inner work. This is because we carry around images of other people in our heads, consisting of the effect that they have on us and the archetypes we project onto them. Sometimes these images closely match reality, and sometimes they do not. The images can also change over time, especially your images of family members. The images you had of your parents

---

[53] Judith Lewis Herman, *Trauma and Recovery: The Aftermath of Violence - From Domestic Abuse to Political Terror.*

when you were a child is very different to the ones you have when you are an independent adult. We also slot new people into existing roles in our inner drama. This means it is a good idea to become aware of the dynamics of our inner drama, and our tendency to project the roles in it onto other people, so that we don't keep on falling into the same patterns.

People also fall into the roles of Parent, Child, and Adult in social interactions, as described in Transactional Analysis, a model of interpersonal psychology developed by Eric Berne in the 1960s. Berne had the insight that people give each other positive and negative reinforcement, or 'strokes', all the time, and that in these exchanges or transactions, they take on these roles.

The Parent role (rather like the superego in Freudian psychology) is the one who makes the rules and protects you and sets boundaries. They may be nurturing or controlling. Some people want the coven leaders to fulfil the Parent role. A "Parent to Child" interaction can often be controlling, and not necessarily healthy for adults to fall into.

An "Adult to Adult" interaction is working well because the participants are on an equal footing. The same applies to a "Child to Child" interaction, which is when people are playing and being creative together. There are several aspects to the Child role, however, some of which are less healthy. There's "Free Child" mode, which is the wild, carefree, and creative side of childhood. This is great to dip into and refresh one's spirits. The Free Child consists of two archetypes: the Natural Child who likes playing and is open and vulnerable and unselfconscious; and the Little

Professor who is curious and explorative, always trying out new things and asking why. The Adaptive Child reacts to the world around them, either conforming to or rebelling against restrictions. People may shift from one of these modes to another during a social interaction.

Another interesting dynamic in groups is 'somebody has to do it' syndrome. This is where one person takes on more responsibility than the others, and an expectation is created that they will always do the task that they have taken on. This might be always being the one who leads the visualisations, or always being the one who calls the quarters, or something else less obvious, like being the person who provides a ritual if no-one else is feeling inspired. The way to break out of this dynamic is for the person who always does the thing to let go of feeling responsible for it, and for the people who never do the thing to have a go at doing it. It also means breaking the ritual tasks down into small manageable chunks so that people who might find it daunting to take on the management of a whole ritual can build up gradually by doing a small piece at a time. Luckily, Wiccan ritual lends itself well to being broken down into manageable chunks.

It is a good idea if the locus of power in a group is visible. If it is not obvious who holds the power, then it will default to the person with the loudest voice or the most stubborn resistance to new ideas.

One way to ensure a fair and balanced approach within your group is to make the rules by consensus. In this exercise (preferably on the first session of the group), ask members to suggest what the rules should be. The purpose of the rules is to make sure that everyone has the power to ask questions, to feel safe in the group, to ensure confidentiality, and to prevent conflict.

The role of the leader of a coven is to empower others and enable them to develop as priestexes, priestesses or priests. This model is sometimes known as servant leadership or transformational leadership - because the leader is mindful that the group is not there to serve them; rather they are there to create safe space for the group, to hold the space, and to empower others to be creative in that space.

Discussion

Have you observed healthy or unhealthy dynamics arising in your group, coven, clan, hearth, grove?

How were the unhealthy ones dealt with? What was done to ensure a healthy group dynamic?

How did the dynamics impact on your inner life?

Exercises

Use the pebble game to explore your perceptions of the dynamics of the group. Get a bag of pebbles of all different colours and sizes. Place a pebble on the floor for each significant aspect of a situation, whether that is a person, a role, an archetype, a mood, someone's job, their parents, or other factors. When you are done, look at the patterns of relationship that you have made, and see if you can gain extra insights about them. You can do this alone, or with other people watching and asking questions.

Meditate on the archetypes you project onto other people. Do they fit? Are they replaying roles that are part of a familiar pattern?

Collaborate with your group to create a group covenant to express your values and maintain safe space.

Create a ritual to shift the group dynamic, using roles that complement or contradict the archetypes that people usually embody.

13. Being a coven leader

Leadership is a tricky business, especially if you are an anarchist like me, in a hierarchical culture that does not really understand consensual leadership styles, servant leadership, transformational leadership, facilitation, and how power dynamics in groups work. Most people's experience of leadership in the wider culture is one of hierarchical styles of leadership, although this is gradually changing as organisations realise that collaborative managers who act as facilitators cause less stress and get more work out of their teams.

People come to the circle with very different expectations and experiences around leadership. This means, I would suggest, that you need to think quite hard about what style of leadership you prefer (either as a leader or as a participant) and have a discussion about prior experiences and expectations fairly early on in the life of the coven.

I have found that even if you start a group with the intention of not having a leader, a leader or leaders will emerge, as the more powerful personalities come to the fore, or dig their heels in and refuse to co-operate. So, you might as well have the leadership role visible and negotiable.

So, before we get into a discussion of styles of leadership, it may be a good idea to take a moment to think about styles of leadership.

Think of a leader whom you admire (it can be in any context, work, the Pagan community, activism, but preferably someone you know well). Note down the qualities you admire about them. How do they handle conflict situations? How do they handle over-eager participants or team members? How do they handle people who do not pull their weight?

Think of a leader whose leadership style does not work for you (again, in any context, but someone you know quite well). What was it about their leadership style that rubbed you up the wrong way? How do they handle conflict situations? How do they handle over-eager participants or team members? How do they handle people who do not pull their weight?

From the two descriptions you have just written, can you identify any common features? **What do you think makes a good leader?**

Models of leadership

There are several models of leadership, and different styles will suit different people. Some people like a more hierarchical style; others prefer a more egalitarian and collaborative model. Fortunately, thanks to the concept of coven autonomy, different styles are available in different covens.

One popular model of leadership is the **servant leader**. The term was coined by Robert Greenleaf [54] in 1970 and refers to the idea that the leader puts the needs of the people they are leading before his or her own needs. Instead of being a leader to gratify some internal need for power, the servant leader wants to benefit those being led, to ensure that they

---

[54] Robert K Greenleaf Center for Servant Leadership (2016), *What is Servant Leadership?* https://www.greenleaf.org/what-is-servant-leadership/

can grow as people.

Greenleaf got the idea for the servant leader from reading Hermann Hesse's novel, *Journey to the East,* in which an expedition to the east is accompanied by a servant called Leo, who takes care of the travellers, prepares their meals, sings to them, and guides them. When he leaves the group, the travellers lose their sense of purpose and abandon the journey. They later discover that Leo was the head of the order that was sponsoring the journey. The insight that Greenleaf gained, on reading this story, was that in an age where everyone looks critically at authority, and is beginning to learn to work collaboratively and creatively, rather than coercively, the leaders will emerge by acclaim and consent of the group, rather than by being placed in positions of power and authority.

The group (either through consensus process or by the inspiration of the leader) needs to establish a common purpose or goal. The leader will then facilitate and nudge the group towards that goal or shared purpose. In this context, a goal is an outcome; a shared purpose is what is expected to emerge from every activity the group undertakes.

The group needs to trust the leader to guide them towards their goal. To ensure trust, the leader needs to have clear and transparent values, and good ethics.

The leader needs to be a good listener. Not just listening to what is said, but the intentions behind what is said. They need to be an active listener, and to repeat back to people what they said, to check that they have understood it correctly. They need to be able to empathise, and to take an interest in the members of the group, to care about their lives, both inner and outer. Sharing each other's joys and sorrows is part of the process of building a community. They also need to be accepting of imperfection. No-one is perfect.

The leader needs insight and intuition, an awareness of the undercurrents in the group and any obstacles in the journey ahead. They need to maintain a holistic picture of what is going on.

Another popular model of leadership is the **transformational leader**. This idea was developed by James McGregor Burns and Bernard M Bass[55]. This type of leader creates an inspiring vision, motivates people to engage with the vision and deliver it, manages how it is delivered, and builds strong and trusting relationships. The difference between this model and that of the servant leader, it seems to me, is that the servant leader puts the needs of the people first, while the transformational leader puts the achievement of a successful outcome first (whereas someone who just wants power puts their desire for power first). The transformational leadership model would work well in a business setting, where the goals and priorities are set at a very high level of the organisation, and then the sections of the organisation need to deliver the goals. For this to work in a coven setting, the group would need to agree the goals through some sort of consensus process, and then assent to the leader being the one to

---

[55] *Transformational Leadership.* MindTools.com
https://www.mindtools.com/pages/article/transformational-leadership.htm

guide them towards the goals, which is actually pretty similar to servant leadership.

There are many other models of leadership, some of which are not relevant to a coven setting, and some of which ought to be avoided.

One of these is the **charismatic leader**, who superficially resembles the transformational leader, in that they can inspire and motivate the team, but whereas a transformational leader does this to create change and improvement, the charismatic leader is only interested in increasing their own glory. In a coven setting, this would be the type of leader who acquires a lot of neophytes and followers but does not help them to develop leadership and magical skills of their own and keeps them as perpetual hangers-on.

Then there is the **transactional leader**, who operates on the principle that there is a contract between them and their team, and the team agreed to follow their orders when they signed up for the job. This tends to produce people who cannot think for themselves and who respond to unusual requests or creative suggestions with the response that it is not in their job description. These people tend to take the view that when you joined their coven, you accepted that they were the leader, so they can tell you what to do.

Then there are **bureaucratic leaders**, who are sticklers for the rules. This is great if you are in a high-risk situation, but not so useful elsewhere. These are the people who tend to spoon-feed their trainees, insist that they copy out the Book of Shadows, and refuse to do anything that is not in the Book of Shadows or the way they were taught the Craft.

In the 1930s, psychologist Kurt Lewin identified three typ of leaders: **democratic leaders** who consult the team on th way forward; **autocratic leaders** who make decisions without consulting their team; and **laissez-faire leaders** who give support where it is needed, but otherwise leave their team to get on with the job. Autocratic leaders are the types who rule their covens with a rod of iron and demand unquestioning allegiance; I hope that this style of leadership is becoming a thing of the past. Consulting the coven on the way forward is a good thing, especially if it involves inviting them to share skills and knowledge that they have acquired elsewhere. A laissez-faire style probably would not work in a coven setting, except when it comes to self-directed learning, because there needs to be teamwork and shared goals to create satisfying rituals that promote spiritual growth.

The goal and purpose of a coven

A coven has several different functions, and different covens will place differing degrees of emphasis on them. You might like to ask your coven to rank these in order of importance and see if you can arrive at a consensus on which are the most important for your coven, and why. You can also add anything to the list that you think I have missed out.

- To provide community and a sense of belonging.

- To provide a space where people can share their dreams, thoughts, feelings, hopes and fears, joys and sorrows.

- To create meaningful ritual.

- To facilitate transformative spiritual experiences.

- To worship the gods.

- To put us in touch with Nature and the Earth.

- To deepen the members' embodied spirituality.

- To learn spiritual and magical techniques.

Once these goals and functions have been identified and prioritised by the group, the leader is then tasked with facilitating the group in such a way as to ensure these goals can be achieved. It is also the responsibility of the members to contribute to achieving the goals of the group.

Creating and holding safe space

Witchcraft can have dramatic transformational effects on people, and at the very least, performing a part in a ritual can make people feel a bit awkward. So, it is very important that people feel safe in the coven and in the circle.

One way to make sure people feel safe is to create some ground-rules for how to behave in the group.

Another aspect of safety is keeping an eye on the energy in the circle, the undercurrents and dynamics that go on. Make sure everyone has grounded and centred effectively at the beginning of the circle, and that they have closed things down a bit at the end (this is usually achieved by the process of eating and drinking during the feast, but it's worth checking up on). If someone is invoked upon, make sure that they are fully present afterwards. Make sure that the circle has been properly cast and keep an eye on it to make sure it is still functioning adequately throughout the ritual.

On a physical level, make sure that fire risks are minimised, that there is a safe exit from the circle, that there are no trip hazards, and that the circle is well-ventilated and adequately but not excessively heated.

Make sure that everything that happens in the circle is consensual, and that people know they can withdraw consent for any activity at any time.

Apart from the actual concrete things you can do to make sure that people feel safe, there is the maintenance of a feeling of safety. This is somewhat difficult to describe, but it is about keeping the energies on an even keel and projecting a feeling of reassurance and safety. This is not enough on its own - the other factors must be present too - but it is part of the process.

Rules and guidelines

The single biggest thing you can do to ensure psychological safety in the circle is to collectively get your group to come up with a set of guidelines (see the exercises at the end of this chapter for a description of the process).

I have run three distinct initiatory covens, and each one had a different approach to coven guidelines. On founding the first one, I decided that we were all adults and know perfectly well how to behave decently, so there was no need to have explicit rules. That did not go very well, because a coven setting is different from everyday life.

With the second coven, I wrote a set of guidelines, which the three founder members worked through together and adjusted, and then we asked subsequent joiners to sign up to the rules. The problem with this approach was that the guidelines were too long-winded, and no-one could remember them; and because I had written them, no-one else felt ownership of them.

With the third coven, we all sat down together on the first occasion when we met, and all came up with a set of guidelines together, using the process described in the exercises at the end of this chapter. The advantage of this approach is that everyone feels they own the rules.

The advantage of having rules of any sort is that the coven leaders are not the ultimate authority in the group; instead, the rules are the ultimate authority, and if the rules were created by the group, then it is fairer. Of course, someone (usually the coven leaders) has to interpret the rules, and arbitrate any disputes that arise; but at least if there is a set of rules, people can have reasonable confidence that everyone in the coven is treated fairly and equitably.

Giving away power

If you are the visible leader of the group, people will tend to give you power. They will turn to you to check if they are doing something correctly; they will look to you to say when a particular activity should start or stop; they will expect you to arbitrate any disputes that arise. You will be the person who gets to write the ritual if no-one else wants to.

However, if your goal is to create an egalitarian coven, you might want to give away power to the group at these moments. If someone looks to you to check if they are doing something correctly, that may well be because you are the most experienced member of the group, so that's fine; but you don't necessarily want that to happen if another coven member is teaching the group a technique. If people expect you to be in charge of a ritual that is being led by another coven member, encourage the ritual leader to stand near the altar (as this is a symbolically more powerful position) and try to be inconspicuous. To avoid being the person who gets to write the ritual if no-one else feels like it, establish who will write the ritual well in advance, and encourage and support coveners in writing their own rituals. You will also need to establish from the outset that your goal is to have an egalitarian coven, because people may be used to a more hierarchical approach.

In the event of a dispute arising, encourage the disputants to share it with the rest of the coven as soon as possible, in a full open discussion or sharing circle with the rest of the coven, not individually (having secrets from the rest of the coven is a recipe for trouble, in any case).

One of the purposes of a training coven is usually to create competent and powerful ritual practitioners. They will not all want to become coven leaders, but they should be able to function as competent witches.

The lonely pinnacle of command [56]

Leadership is not easy, in part because our culture's expectations of how a leader should behave are currently changing and shifting. The key thing here is to have an open and honest conversation with your coven about what everyone's desires and expectations are, and how the

---

[56] I stole this heading from Douglas Adams. It's what the captain of the Golgafrincham 'B' Ark says whilst sitting in his bath.

whole group can work together to get to the desired outcome (whether that is an egalitarian group, or one where the coven leaders make most of the decisions). Consider what the goals and purpose of your coven are, and what kind of rules and guidelines you want, and how much power the coven leaders should have. Once you have had this discussion, at least everyone will be mostly on the same page.

Discussion

What are the goals, purpose, and functions of covens?

What are the goals, purpose, and functions of *your* coven?

What is the best style of leadership for covens?

What is the best style of leadership for *your* coven?

What is the best approach to developing rules and guidelines?

How do you create and maintain safe space?

What is the distribution of power in your group?

Exercises

Repeat the exercise at the beginning of this chapter. Has anything changed in your response now that you have learnt about different leadership styles? What was the closest leadership model to the person you admire? What was the closest model for the person who rubbed you up the wrong way?

Reflect on any past conflicts that you have had with coven leaders or coven members. What leadership style were you or they exhibiting? How could using a different leadership style have defused the tension or conflict?

With your coven, facilitate a consensus process to arrive at a set of guidelines for the group. Start by asking how they would want to be treated by the rest of the group. It is a good idea for you to start with a set of guidelines in mind (an example is offered in Appendix I), but the aim is for the coven to come up with as many of the guidelines as possible without your intervention. Put up a flip chart if you have one and write the guidelines on it as they are suggested. You can refine them as a group after the initial flurry of suggestions. The benefit of this approach is that people will feel they have created the guidelines themselves, and hence will feel ownership of them as a group and are more likely to adhere to them.

14. Teaching and learning in a coven

The process by which we pass on knowledge and wisdom is rarely examined or questioned. We tend to assume that it will happen somehow, and that knowledge will be passed on to the next generation of initiates. But the way that knowledge is passed on matters because it communicates the values of the tradition and of the teacher. If the teacher tells their students that things can only be done in one way, and that is the tradition, and it cannot be questioned, then they will make dull conformists and rigid traditionalists of their students. If, on the other hand, they encourage them to question and think for themselves and be creative, they will produce imaginative and creative initiates.

Every new generation of seekers has some obstacle put in their way. In the days before the internet, the obstacle was not enough information. Now the obstacle is too much information. There are loads of websites and would-be teachers out there offering you all kinds of advice.

Then one day, you decide to take the plunge and find a face-to-face teacher. This is generally a good thing, as in my experience, most humans learn better from personal interaction than they do from online interactions or books.

However, due to the prevalence of books and people claiming to be the ultimate authority, and the prevalence of the counterclaim that the only valid authority is the inner self, we have a situation where many people can neither learn nor teach because they are too convinced of their own rightness to actually consider new ideas from their teachers or their students.

An exchange of ideas

The theory of learning and teaching that I use in a coven setting is derived from Lev Vygotsky, who theorised the existence of a zone of proximal development. Vygotsky was a social constructivist; that is, he believed that learning was mediated through social interaction, and that our understanding of the world is socially constructed.

The zone of proximal development is the idea that there are some things the learner can do unaided (that they already know how to do); some things that they can do with guidance; and some that they cannot do. It also suggests that you need to build up from the things you can do, master the skills that you can do with help, and that this will provide the building blocks to access the next level (this idea was further developed by Jerome Bruner, David Wood, and Gail Ross with the concept of scaffolding).

The teacher and the student build a bridge between them so they can exchange ideas and knowledge and skills. But it is important to note that the teacher can also learn from the student.

This means that learning is a collaborative process between the teacher and the learner. It is not the case that the learner is an empty bucket that the teacher fills up with facts; rather, the teacher and the learner discover and elaborate the existing skills of the learner (and the learner may also be able to teach the teacher a thing or two). This is especially true of magical and ritual skills, which are often extensions of existing abilities.

So, if you are a seeker, find out from any potential teacher you meet what their methods are, and what they expect you to do. Do they expect you to ask questions? Do they welcome and celebrate your existing skills and knowledge? Do they recognise that you have a unique learning style? Do they invite you to bring prior experience to the table to enrich the learning process? Do they support students with dyslexia, dyspraxia, or other differences?

Many seekers seem to assume that all teachers are going to dictate a prescribed way of doing magic and ritual which will destroy the spontaneity and joy of it. Perhaps there are teachers out there who behave like that, but the majority are rather more flexible than that. If you do find a teacher who won't allow you to ask questions, who belittles your existing skills and prior experience, or who insists on doing everything in a set way, then run a mile – but don't assume that all teachers are like that.

The sharing circle

The method that I use for teaching conceptual ideas is the sharing circle. This is more accessible for people with dyslexia because it gives people time to formulate their thoughts. There is a set topic for each discussion (such as reincarnation, the nature of deities, the idea of the sacred, the four elements, etc) and we use a token to indicate who can speak at any one time. The token is passed around the circle, and everyone gets a chance to air their thoughts on the topic. Sometimes I use other tools such as mind mapping to enable people to tease out their ideas on a topic.

In the circle, when teaching magical techniques, I encourage people to try different techniques, to work out what feels right for them. Some people prefer one set of gestures for calling the quarters, cleansing the circle, and so on; others prefer a different set of gestures. These may stem from a different physical relationship with the energies, or from a different philosophical concept of what energies are and how we might relate to them. None of these different gestures and words is necessarily wrong. Obviously your tradition might have a specific way of doing these things, but my Book of Shadows offers a selection of different words and gestures for calling the quarters, casting the circle, and so on, and which ones you choose may be different, depending on different circumstances and choices.

I always encourage people to make a connection with the energy they are invoking or evoking first, and then to speak the words. After all, the energy is more important, surely? It can also be helpful to use analogies from physical experience to get people sensing subtle energies. I have also noticed that different people experience subtle energies differently – some people see them as colours; others experience them as heat, cold, or other physical sensations.

Another thing that I have noticed is that people are either overly reliant on books, and regard them as the ultimate authority on magical matters; or they dismiss books entirely and want to totally rely on their instincts. Surely there must be a happy medium between these two extremes. If something you read in a book does not agree with your experience, then examine why that might be the case, and either adjust your worldview, or discard what the book says. If the book is wrong in this instance, that does not invalidate either that book, or books in general. If the book happens to be right in this instance, that does not invalidate all personal experiences.

As with pretty much anything, it is all about finding the middle way between two extremes.

Differentiation and learning styles

Different people learn at different rates and have different ways of accessing and assimilating new concepts. Some people like to learn abstract concepts, and then 'flesh them out' with concrete examples; others prefer to get concrete examples and then work out the abstract principles they all have in common.

Personally, when I am learning something new, I like to get an overview of the topic (its history, what its aims and purpose are; the basic techniques associated with it), and then go into more detail as I get more experienced with it. That is one of the reasons why distance learning courses do not work for me, because they tend not to offer an overview of the topic to start with. The same applies to most books that attempt to teach you how to use a programming language.

Most people learn best in face-to-face settings or working side-by-side if they are learning a skill or craft. Humans have learnt things this way for thousands of years, so it is not surprising that most of us prefer it. That is the other reason I do not get on very well with distance-learning courses.

Some people prefer to learn from the outside in, others from the inside out. What I mean by that is that some people want to learn the outer form of a practice (dancing, calling a quarter, meditation, etc) and then they will experience the inward feelings that result from the practice. Others like to work out what they are feeling about something and then express that physically. This difference can sometimes be cultural as well as individual. Flamenco dancing, for example, is all about expressing your *duende*, your inner passion, and flamenco dancers are encouraged to express their feelings. Japanese dance, on the other hand, is all about getting the movements right, and the feelings will come after the dancer has got the movements correct.[57] So, although I often tell people to feel their way towards making a connection with the four elements, in the hope that they can then make an energetic connection with a quarter, this might not work for some people, and they might be better off doing the gesture and body movements and saying the words, in the hope of evoking the feeling within themselves. Most people probably do not know which of these methods they prefer, so it is probably best to try both.

Some people are kinaesthetic learners, who learn best by doing something in a physical space. Rather than being told about how to do something, they like to physically enact it with their bodies. They will learn how to do witchcraft by physically enacting ritual.

Others are aural learners, who retain things best when they have heard them. I am an aural learner, and I respond particularly well to things that are rhythmic or musical.

---

[57] Yolanda van Ede (2010), "Differing Roads to Grace: Spanish and Japanese Sensory Approaches to Dance." In: *Ritual Dynamics and the Science of Ritual*, Volume IV, edited by Geoffrey Samuel. Harrassowitz Verlag: Wiesbaden.

When I want to learn lines for a play or a ritual, I record them onto tape and play them back, and often end up learning all the other parts as well as my own.

The third category is visual learners. These people prefer visual things like diagrams, mind-maps, and written material.

It is possible that some people have a combination of two or more of these learning styles, so if you can, it is a good idea to offer learning experiences in all of these modes, to ensure that everyone can access them, and to assist with reinforcing the desired learning outcome. Luckily, witchcraft is a combination of the aural and the kinaesthetic in any case and has visual symbols which can act as mnemonics.

Some people have learning difficulties such as dyslexia and dyspraxia, so it is best not to have a one-size-fits-all model where everyone must copy out the Book of Shadows by hand, for example. Copying out the Book of Shadows by hand is very difficult for people with dyslexia. This is because dyslexia is not, as is commonly thought, a difficulty with reading, but a problem with transferring information from one medium to another. This is because the working memory of a person with dyslexia (the bit you use to remember a list of drinks to get from the bar, for example) has less capacity than most people's working memory. So, trying to remember the sentence you want to copy from one book to another is difficult for a person with dyslexia.

Differentiation is the art of managing all these different modes and styles of learning, and creating an environment where every learner can flourish, not just a group of people with a specific learning style. There are three different aspects to learning: the content of the lesson; how students process what they have learnt; and what they produce as a result.[58]

The content - *what* is being learned - can be presented aurally, visually, and kinaesthetically. For example, if your coven is learning to call the quarters, get them to move through the process, stop and feel the energies, do a dance to help them connect with the element.

The process of learning will be different for different people. Those who learn from the outside in, and the kinaesthetic learners, will be focusing on the movements. Those who learn from the inside out will be focusing on their feelings and inner processes. Those who learn visually will be noticing the patterns and shapes that the whole process makes. And those who learn aurally will be noticing the sounds and the rhythms.

The product - the desired outcome - will be reached in different ways by different people, and it may look different. Visual learners might want to choreograph the whole process or produce a diagram. Aural learners may want to record the words on a tape to help them learn. Kinaesthetic learners will want to do the physical movements in the ritual space.

---

[58] John McCarthy (2014), *3 Ways to Plan for Diverse Learners: What Teachers Do*. Edutopia.
https://www.edutopia.org/blog/differentiated-instruction-ways-to-plan-john-mccarthy

So, it is a good idea to provide different ways of accessing the content, different ways of processing it, and different ways of getting to the outcome (the 'product'). Luckily, because witchcraft rituals generally involve different modes of learning, most coven training will be very easy to modify to ensure that it is accessible to different learning styles.

Discussion

What are the predominant learning styles of members of your coven?

What barriers exist that prevent them from learning new things?

Does anyone in your coven have a learning difficulty? What barriers exist for them?

Are there areas of knowledge that your coven neglects because of the learning styles and preferences of members of your coven? (e.g. if you are all visual learners, you might be neglecting dance, gesture, and movement)

Exercises

Try learning a new technique or piece of ritual poetry. Try different methods of learning it. What works best for you?

Try learning something outside your comfort zone. What feelings arise for you when you are trying to learn it?

Try starting the circle with a talking stick session or sharing circle. How did it change the energy? Did it make it easier for people to share ideas, thoughts, feelings, experiences?

15. Egregore, current, lineage, upline, downline

Group dynamics are complicated by the magical energies generated by inter-group dynamics, energies being passed by initiation, and the extension of group mind beyond the individual coven. Different practices develop in different groups, and practice evolves from one group to another. The meaning of a practice is lost or changed, and so people adapt things to fit their own understanding of how magic and spirituality work. This is a normal and natural part of the evolution of a religious tradition. What we do not need to do is get our knickers in a knot about it and declare one way of doing things "the true Craft" and dismiss all the rest.

However, due to this process, it is possible for things to get lost, watered down, or misunderstood. So, it is a good idea to check back to some key magical concepts now and again, to try and prevent the loss of magical awareness by dilution from mainstream ideas.

Wicca (and several other witchcraft traditions) is an initiatory tradition. I shall primarily talk about Wicca, specifically Gardnerian Wicca, because that is what I understand best - but I think that these ideas are applicable to other witchcraft and magical traditions. If it fits your paradigm, great; if not, adopt, adapt, or ignore as you see fit.

Lineage

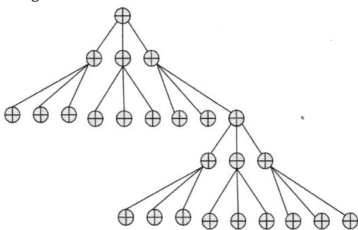

A lineage is all the initiatory descendants of a witch. So, the Gardnerian tradition is everyone who can trace descent back to Gerald Gardner and does Wicca in a recognisably Gardnerian way. There is enormous variation in Gardnerian practice, but there are still recognisable elements and an ethos that can be described as Gardnerian. Within the Gardnerian tradition, there are specific lineages, with their own egregore, distinct ethos, and distinct set of practices. Even within these, there is variation in practice. A lineage looks like a fan, or a family tree, and has many branches spreading out from witches who have initiated other witches. In these various branches, differences in practice, ethos, and understanding of magical concepts will inevitably vary. Different people are drawn to different ways of doing ritual, different mythology and symbolism, and different deities. In the diagram on the right, every initiate (represented by a node) is part of the lineage.

Upline

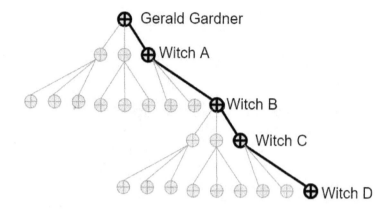

Your upline is your personal line of descent from the
founding witch of the tradition or lineage. For example,
Gerald Gardner initiated Witch A, who initiated Witch B,
who initiated Witch C, who initiated Witch D, who
initiated me. An upline is a single line of descent traced
through a family tree (a bit like the list of who begat whom
in the Bible). The diagram on the right shows Witch D's
upline. Magical current has been passed along this line to
Witch D.

Current

Current is the magical energy that gets passed from one
initiate to another. In my opinion, current is passed from
one person to another. An upline has a current, but a
lineage (the wider tradition) has an egregore. A current is
quite focused and consists of the cumulative energy of the
all the witches in the upline (Gerald + Witch A + Witch B +
Witch C + Witch D + me).

Downline

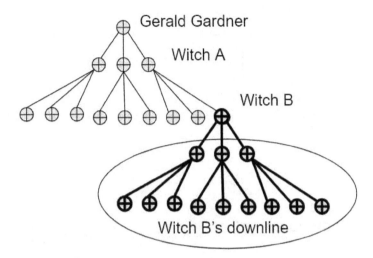

Gerald Gardner

Witch A

Witch B

Witch B's downline

Your downline fans out from you, and consists of everyone you initiate, and everyone they initiate. If your ritual style and coven ethos are particularly distinctive, it may one day be regarded as a lineage. Otherwise, it remains part of the wider tradition and lineage, but perhaps with your own local variations. The more downline you have, the more likely it is to develop its own distinct egregore and become a lineage.

Egregore

Every group has an egregore. It is a group mind or collective thought-form that is created when a group comes together for a common purpose. The word appears to be derived from "*ex*" (in the sense of 'from' or 'out of') plus "*gregor*" (a flock, herd, crowd, or group), so the egregore emerges from the crowd or group. Examples of egregores can be the group minds of political parties, factions within political parties, covens, witchcraft traditions, rock groups, orchestras, and so on.

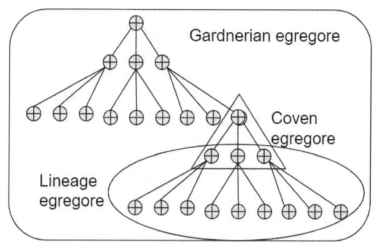

Egregores can be loose, fluid, and very fuzzy, or very tight-knit and focused. An egregore is a distinct identity, not a discrete entity. An egregore can be composed of many smaller egregores - for example, many covens making up a lineage, and several lineages making up a tradition. A lineage has an egregore. A lineage does not have a current - the group mind or energy of a lineage is far too fuzzy to be described as a current, and in any case there are many currents running through it, transmitted through the various lines within the wider lineage. In this diagram, the lozenge around the whole family tree represents the Gardnerian egregore; the triangle represents a coven's egregore; and the oval represents a lineage's egregore.

Initiation

When you are initiated, you are brought into the egregore of your coven, your lineage, and your tradition. You do not become part of the egregore just by being initiated; it is a gradual process of mutual adjustment, learning, and building of trust. The transmission of magical current is a separate process that happens later, at the discretion of the coven leaders.

An initiation is an experience of inner transformation, personal encounter with the deities, and entering on the path of Wicca. Once you have been initiated (at first, second, and third degree), you shouldn't need to be initiated again, unless the initiation didn't "take" (in other words, it had no effect for some reason - like failing to light a damp firework), or if you had a massive falling-out with your initiators and want to make a fresh start.

Reculing and withdrawing a vouch

In the USA, some covens have a practice of "reculing" - declaring an initiation null and void. If an initiation "took" (had an effect), then I cannot see how it can be declared null and void.

In the UK, the practice is to cease to vouch for someone as a person who is worthy to be in a Wiccan circle. The withdrawal of a vouch is only done in extreme cases, such as if a person persistently makes unwanted sexual overtures and will not take no for an answer, or similar.

Moving from one group to another

If you move to another coven that is part of a different lineage, it ought to be sufficient to have an adoption ritual, where you are welcomed into the egregore of that group. You have already been initiated into Wicca, so there is no need to be re-initiated if you move from Lineage A to Lineage B. Adoption should be enough.

In Britain, Gardnerian and Alexandrian initiations are considered interchangeable, and the initiations of different Gardnerian lineages are considered interchangeable. If someone moved to a different coven or lineage, or from an Alexandrian coven to a Gardnerian coven, there would most likely be an adoption ritual, but not a re-initiation. There are also dual-heritage covens, who can trace their descent from both Alexandrian and Gardnerian lineages.

The reason that there is no need for a re-initiation when moving from one coven or lineage or tradition to another is that current is transmitted along your upline, which remains the same, and is unique to every individual. What you are doing when you move to a different coven, lineage, or tradition is moving to another egregore.

Why is this important?

The whole issue of egregore, lineage, current, upline, downline, and so on has become important because a practice of re-initiating people every time they move to a different lineage has developed in the USA. To most British witches, this practice seems divisive, and likely to fragment the Craft into ever-smaller divisions.

When I named the particular ethos and set of practices that I and others have developed "inclusive Wicca", or when the founders of progressive Wicca (Karin Rainbird, Tam Campbell, and David Rankine) named their practices "progressive", we were very clear that we were *not* founding a new tradition, but rather offering an expansion or a clarification of existing practices which could be adopted and adapted (wholesale or piecemeal) by other witches and covens.

What I consider to be my tradition is the set of practices and values that I inherited from my high priestess, and the ideas and practices that I have added to those. She in turn inherited a set of practices and values from her high priestess and added ideas and practices. Taken together, all these practices form a coherent ethos and style of witchcraft, which is our tradition.

Discussion

Do you agree with the descriptions of egregore, lineage, upline, downline, and current in this chapter? If not, how would you define them?

What makes an initiation 'proper' – is it the exchange of energies, the passing-on of a lineage, the active participation of the deities, using the correct words, or all of these?

What are justifiable grounds for reculing someone or withdrawing a vouch?

16. Power and authority

Does the Pagan movement need leaders? What is a good model of leadership? The best kind of leaders are those who empower, nurture, and teach others. We neither want nor need the kind of leaders who block others' access to the numinous, and fleece them of large amounts of money – but frankly they would not get very far in the Pagan community anyway: Pagans are generally independent-minded. Even those paid leaders who work hard and serve others do not make a lot of money.

We might have a lot of leaders, but I do not see a lot of followers. Pagans are not sheep, we are goats. We do not really have congregations (which is basically Latin for "flock"); we are more like tribes or perhaps friendship networks. There are many people who serve the Pagan community in an administrative or representative capacity. There are many people who share their thoughts on blogs and in books. There are some leaders who want power, admiration, and followers (fortunately these are fairly few and far between).

Personally, I have a small team of people with instructions to kick me up the backside if ever I start exhibiting the symptoms of a Big Name Pagan with a lot of perpetual neophytes in tow. This is unlikely, however, as I am far too lazy to organise my own life, let alone anyone else's.

My approach to leadership is to seek to empower others and enable them to write and facilitate ritual and learn new skills. However, not everyone who joins a coven wants to write and facilitate rituals, and that is alright. They may have other abilities which could be nurtured.

In Gardnerian and Alexandrian Wicca, every initiated Wiccan is a priestess or priest. However, a first degree is a priestess or priest unto themselves; a second degree can be a priestess or priest to others; and a third degree to the rest of the community. This is not a hard and fast rule – it is just that the degrees are not *expected* to take on being a priestess or priest for others until they attain the higher degrees. It is also worth remembering that in Wicca, witches are held to be 'the hidden children of the Goddess' – in other words, we do our public service covertly, not necessarily advertising that we are witches. If someone asks me for help, they do so because I have a sympathetic manner, not necessarily because they know that I am a witch. We do not need to wear a special hat – if we are any good, people will recognise the qualities of witchiness in us, and seek our help. I do not hide the fact that I am a Wiccan, but I do not advertise either. (There is also the problem that if we did wear pointy hats, they would not fit under most door frames.)

In OBOD Druidry, there are also three grades – Bard, Ovate, and Druid. The Bard is a storyteller and uses words to enchant. The Ovate is more shamanic and prophetic. The Druid is more of an all-round magical practitioner.

In Heathenry, there are goði and gyðja (priests and priestesses) who are generally selected by acclaim of their group, because of their experience, or end up leading rituals because they are the most experienced.

In Religio Romana, priestesses and priests are expected to have a sincere calling to the deity for whom they wish to be a priestess or priest, and to carry out research on their chosen deity, and to worship the chosen deity in their home.

In my experience, even if some leaders of Pagan groups let it go to their head for a while, they soon learn that they are leader by consent of the group, and if they do not care for the needs of all the members of the group, and nurture and empower their members, people will leave.

The best Pagan leaders are those who listen – both to the promptings of spirit, and to their group members. A Pagan leader should not regard their community as serving them but feel that they are serving the community (which includes other-than-human beings). Those who think they are elders are probably not elders; one gets that title by being acclaimed by others (and not just by virtue of being old, either, but by having wisdom and experience). People who think they have an innate right to lead and to be looked up to by others are frankly dangerous and should have a long hard think about privilege.

In return, the community should value those who serve. They should not be expected to cover their expenses from their own pocket; if they spend time preparing a day or weekend workshop, and travelling long distance to deliver it, then they should be remunerated for their time, skill, and expenses. I do not think people should ever pay for coven training in Wicca, but I do think leaders of public workshops should be adequately remunerated.

As high priestess [59] of my coven, I am in that role because I am the most experienced member of the group. As high

---

[59] Although I am nonbinary and genderqueer, I like the term priestess because it feels entirely Pagan to me.

priestess, I encourage members of my coven to develop their skills in ritual and magic, so that they can also design and facilitate rituals. If a new member wants to join, every member of the group must agree that they can join (it is not just on my say-so).

What makes you a priest/ess/ex?

If you feel a calling to be one, then you probably are one, even if you are on the beginner slopes.

My working definition of a priest or priestess is a person who can facilitate contact between the other-than-human and the human, and/or who can create meaning, community, and a sense of connectedness for others. Note that this definition includes atheists and animists.

The role of mediator

Traditionally a priestess, priest, or priestex is a person who makes contact between the divine realm and the human. The divine realm can include deities, spirits, and the numinous in general. From an animist perspective, deities and spirits include genii loci, tree spirits, rock spirits, water spirits, and so on. The priestess, priest, priestex, or shaman is a specialist in communication between the human and the other-than-human, using trance, spirit travel, invocation, evocation, and other techniques. They create a sense of connectedness for others.

Creating community

One of my tests of who is a priestess, priest, or priestex is, can you produce an atmosphere of calm and safety in a roomful of distraught or agitated people. If you can, you are a priestess, priest, or priestex.

203

A priestess, priest, or priestex builds community, creates safe spaces, resolves conflicts. They serve the community, and in exchange, the community values their efforts.

Creating meaning

The priestess, priest, or priestex is also a storyteller and lore-keeper for the community. They keep track of traditions, stories, rituals, lore, and the history of the community, lineage, or tradition. They interpret the cosmology and symbolism of the tradition for others. In short, they help to create meaning.

Of course, meaning is co-created by the whole community, but the priestess, priest, or priestex keeps track of the changing lore and rituals and offers expert input.

What makes a priestess, priest, or priestex?

Probably the most important aspect of the making of a priestess, priest, or priestex is the person experiencing a vocation or call to be a priest/ess. Without that call, you would not set foot on the path towards being a priestess, priest, or priestex.

A formal initiation can be valuable for the creation or formation of a priestess, priest, or priestex, but it is neither necessary nor sufficient. The inner transformation must occur for it to "take", and that is an alchemical mystery. An initiation can trigger that transformation, but it can be triggered by an encounter with a deity, or with the numinous, or a sense of the awesomeness of Nature.

There are three levels of Wiccan initiation. The first-degree initiation is generally held to make you a priestess, priest, or priestex unto yourself. The second degree makes you a priestess, priest, or priestex to others in your coven. The third makes you a priestess, priest, or priestex for the wider community.

Druidry also has a system of three levels: Bard, Ovate, and Druid. The Bard creates meaning by creating stories and songs. The Ovate communicates with spirits and deities. The Druid is more community-based (I think). The Ovate incorporates the functions of the Bard. The Druid incorporates the functions of the other two.

Each of these levels is conferred by your ability and calling. The initiation may just be a recognition that you have already achieved that level.

Obviously, real priests and priestesses exist outside of formal systems of recognition and training, but within those systems, you are not going to be recognized as a priestess, priest, or priestex of that system without going through the required training and initiations. That is not a comment on your general competence or priestly status, only about your validity within that specific system.

There are many different types and modes of being a priestess, priest, or priestex, and this section is a general description of all of them. Some people focus on a specific path within the general set of priestly functions described here. They are still valid as a priestess, priest, or priestex.

Not everyone wants to be the leader or ritual facilitator, and there are many other valuable roles available within a group.

Being an elder

The first rule of being an elder is not to talk about being an elder. Do not even *think* about being an elder. And do not proclaim from the rooftops that you are one. If you think you are one, you probably are not. However, if you are in a position of leadership, then you need to hold yourself accountable - you have been given power, so use it responsibly and mindfully. My favourite elders are the people who do not even know that they are elders. Very few of them are famous, and they just get on with serving the community and being themselves.

Obviously, if you are older and have experience, then people are likely to look up to you, ask your advice, and regard you as wise. But never forget that you can learn from others too, and do not let that prestige go to your head.

Honour and Humility

Behave honourably and with humility. If you screw up, admit that you screwed up. If you screwed up in public, admit publicly that you screwed up. If you caused damage, seek to repair it.

Be aware that you do not know everything. There is always something new to be learnt. For example, the things you learnt about gender, sexuality, and consent when you were younger may need revising in the light of new experiences and new understanding. Being old is no excuse for being a massive transphobe or a homophobe, for example.

One of my favourite elders (who is not famous, but is awesome) once said to me, "The more you know, the more you realise that you don't know." Now that is a wise attitude.

Power and Compassion

If you have power, own it. Acknowledge that you have it and wield it responsibly and with compassion. You will also need discernment. Remember that power is given to you by other people; it is not an inherent quality that you possess. If you do not wield your power with compassion and discernment, then you will lose it.

You *may* have been chosen by the gods for your leadership role - but you had better not act as if that was the case. If you do, the gods can certainly choose someone else instead of you. An arm clothed in white samite did not offer you the sword Excalibur from the lake - and you do not get to wield supreme executive power without the consent of the governed. It is more likely that you got your role because you were a willing and useful person who was in the right place at the right time. So yes, you have skills and knowledge, and that should be celebrated and is worthy of respect (but not servility). But you are not infallible.

Combine your power with compassion and discernment. If someone comes to you with a story of abuse, do not dismiss it or try to brush it under the carpet. They have taken a risk by talking about it: the risk of ridicule or of not being believed. However, it is a good idea to seek confirmation or corroboration of their claims. 99% of the time, it is probably true: but occasionally, it is paranoia or hearsay. Hence the need for discernment.

Strength and Beauty

Be graceful and skilful. Acknowledge and cultivate your strengths and your good qualities - but be aware of your shadow side and seek to channel its energies appropriately. If you are generally an angry person, then you need to keep that under control, but it is not an entirely negative trait: sometimes anger can be righteous anger, but you need the wisdom to know the difference between projecting your shadow on to someone else, and calling out injustice and bad behaviour.

Mirth and Reverence

Always be prepared to take the piss out of yourself and your delusions of grandeur. Therefore, kings would license a fool or jester: so that when they were about to do something stupid, there was one person who was not afraid to tell them it was stupid.

Be aware that there is something greater than yourself, and that you are in service to it (whether that is the Craft, the gods, your community, truth, love, or what you will). The transformational leader knows that they are there to empower others and create safe space for them to grow in.

How to have healthy elders

It seems to be a tendency in much of contemporary culture, including the Pagan movement, to put people on pedestals and hero-worship them, and when we discover that they are flawed human beings like the rest of us, to knock them off their pedestal and dismiss every good thing they ever did.

Sure, a genuinely wise elder is a pleasure to learn from and to be around, but that does not mean the rest of us should put them on a pedestal and assume that they can never do anything bad. This encourages them to avoid seeing their own issues and to assume that they can do no wrong. That is dangerous because then they have too much power, and also means that when they do something wrong, it is hard for anyone to challenge it, knowing that the person will be completely knocked off their pedestal, instead of just taken down a peg or two. It means that people are less willing to believe that a community leader could have done something bad.

It means that calling someone out for a bad thing they did whilst acknowledging the good stuff they did becomes harder and harder to do. The more we think in this binary either/or way, the harder it becomes to see nuance and put things in perspective. But, to progress as a movement (and for society in general to progress), we need to be able to challenge bad behaviour, and to set boundaries to prevent it, without dismissing the person completely. Obviously, some behaviours are so terrible that they are grounds for ejection from the community. I am talking about one-off instances of bad behaviour, not a string of repeat offences. When someone repeatedly behaves badly, then it is time to call them out, but 'calling in' is preferable, when possible.

Surely the answer, then, is to be more realistic in the way we treat elders. Loved and respected for their wisdom and/or their contributions to the community, yes. Put up on a pedestal and assumed never to do anything wrong, and therefore not held accountable for their actions, no. Ejected into the outer darkness for the slightest transgression, no. The higher we put them on those pedestals, the harder they fall. The answer? Do not put them up so high in the first place.

The only reason that people get to be leaders in the first place is because others give them power, and because they have some quality that makes them leadership material - knowledge, or wisdom, or charisma, or the ability to make others feel safe. All of those are worthwhile and valuable qualities, and a good leader or teacher or elder has those qualities: that does not mean that he or she should be ruling their group with a rod of iron. A good teacher empowers others to develop those qualities.

It is also noticeable that many Pagan leaders have ended up suffering from spiritual burnout from taking on far too much work. This is perhaps because people have seen the high cost of leadership (the flak that leaders get for sticking their head above the parapet) and do not want to go there. I think that a shift to a less binary way of looking at leaders and elders would help with this issue too.

We are generally quite an egalitarian movement - but the shadow side of that is wanting to knock people off their pedestals if we think they have got too big for their boots. But if we remembered that they are just flawed human beings like us, and did not elevate them so high, then they would not fall so hard.

Power and authority in religious traditions

There are different kinds of power, as famously identified by Starhawk (and others before her): power-over, power-from-within, and power-with-others. Authority comes in at least two flavours: being an authority on a topic (that's why writers of books are called authors) and having authority over others. All of these are conferred by others to a greater or lesser extent (even power-from-within occurs when the pressure from inside is greater than or equal to the pressure from outside).

Some people have a problem with any authority whatsoever; but sometimes this is for very good reasons. We all mistake authority-on-a-topic for authority-over-others. Many writers have the experience of getting the comment "You can't tell me what to do" when the authorial tone of their article was intended to be authority-on-a-topic and not telling others what to do. This is frustrating (but sometimes people get the authorial tone of their writing wrong, including me).

But there are those who quite blatantly *want* to have power and authority over others and use their powers of manipulation and persuasion and their apparent deep knowledge of a topic to gain power over others. They use the confusion over what is legitimate power and authority to create a mini-kingdom for themselves. These are the people and power-structures we *should* be resisting. As soon as one person or group claims sole access to meaning, then they have usurped the production of meaning as their sole preserve and are in pursuit of power and authority over others.

The Buddha made a very sensible disclaimer about his teachings – that if they make sense to you, follow them, and if they do not make sense to you, do not follow them.

If someone says a thing that makes sense to you, then you would be well-advised to follow it. If it does not make sense to you, do not follow it – but do think about why it does not make sense to you. Is it because you have an issue that is getting in the way, or is it because you have genuine solid objections to it?

Power and authority in groups

I have observed several different religious groups with different ways of dealing with power.

The Quakers make their structure as flat as possible, with elders and various committees. Sometimes the elders have too much power, but this is presumably balanced by the committees, and by the strong Quaker discernment processes. They also strongly recommend that people attend their classes on being a Quaker – so presumably those would also teach you about how to complain if somebody "forcefully eldered" you. I think we can learn a lot from how the Quakers do things. They also have regional Yearly Meetings in which all the Quaker meetings come together to discuss things, again using Quaker process. The disadvantage of this system is that the power is not out in the open where people can see it.

In Wicca, there is no formal power structure beyond the immediate coven. Covens have autonomy, and this is an important principle to most Wiccans. (Some groups have leaders who are referred to as Lord and Lady – but this is a North American innovation and is not done in Wicca in Britain, where we have quite enough aristocracy already, thank you. As far as I can tell, in most groups it is an honorary title only.) The system of coven autonomy has its pros and cons – it means that there can be very dodgy behaviour in a coven, and they can get away with it – but it does prevent hierarchy forming above and beyond that.

OBOD Druid groves generally have leaders, but different people are encouraged to lead rituals. They also have sub-groups for the different grades (bard, ovate, druid) and these could develop some odd power dynamics, but I have not observed any groups beyond the bardic grade, so I could not say for sure. There is also the rather odd idea of the chosen chief of the order (who chose him? I did not vote for him...) but this seems largely ceremonial, as far as I can tell.

In Unitarianism, they have ministers and committees. In fact, they have a lot of committees for such a small group. They also have an annual General Assembly (like the Quaker Yearly Meetings). The power of the minister and the committee generally balance each other. (Sometimes one has too much power, sometimes the other.) Congregations have autonomy, and there are also the important principles of the freedom of the pulpit (the freedom to state your truth in the pulpit) and the freedom of the pew (the freedom to believe your truth and disagree with what is said from the pulpit).

Authority (use of power legitimated by the structure) in the Quakers, Unitarians, and OBOD is well-distributed in a system of checks and balances between the national body and the local regions and congregations. Wicca does not have a national body, but we do get together to discuss things and we have a shared body of practices, as well as freedom to be creative. None of these systems are perfect, but they are pretty good. There is always someone with a

big ego trying to gain power, but most of the time they are
balanced by the structures that exist to regulate power and
authority. It is perhaps inevitable that some people will
seek power and control. That means we must create the
structures, the checks and balances, that will prevent them
from gaining too much power.

Freedom of belief, freedom of conscience

All the above groups have freedom of belief: you can be an
atheist, a pantheist, a duotheist, a monotheist, a polytheist,
and so on. In practice there are not that many polytheists in
the Unitarians and Quakers in Britain, but there are some,
and both groups include atheists. The same is true of Wicca
and most Pagan traditions. What is important in all these
groups is your values, including a willingness to play
nicely with others. They do share a worldview, an ethos,
and these should inform their lived values.[60]

It is also worth noting that these groups are mostly stable.
Of course there are arguments about what it means to be a
Unitarian or a Quaker or a Wiccan (and probably a Druid
too, but I don't know) but as every group has a variety of
different preferences within it, I expect these arguments
will never be definitely settled by a schism. Instead, there
are affinity groups of Unitarian Pagans, Unitarian
Christians, Quaker Pagans, Christian Quakers, and so on
and so forth. And in terms of *values*, these groups generally
have more agreement with each other than disagreement.

---

[60] Caelesti (2015), *Belief vs. Worldview*, Pagan Left,
https://paganleft.wordpress.com/2015/01/20/belief-vs-worldview/

What is oathbound?

There is much talk in initiatory Wicca of things being "oathbound". However, a piece of knowledge cannot be oathbound. Oaths and vows are binding on those who swear them, not on the things they swear to protect or keep secret. A person is oathbound, not an item of knowledge.

The oaths sworn can vary slightly from one lineage to another, but they pretty much all focus on not revealing certain things to those who have not sworn the same oath and undergone the same initiation.

The purpose of oaths

The reason that oaths and secrecy are important is threefold:

To protect the Craft from arseholes: fraudsters, abusers, and other nasty types.

To hedge the true Mysteries (that which cannot be spoken) around with secrets (that which must not be spoken).

To protect the unprepared from accessing experiences that they are not ready for.

Being a witch is cool; people want in without doing the work or preparing themselves properly or learning in advance or having to go with any tedious prior definitions of what a Wiccan is. (A similar situation exists *vis à vis* the Indigenous spiritualities and life ways of North America.) It sometimes happens that someone has a lapse of judgement and initiates a person with destructive tendencies; but the goal is still to protect the Craft from such people.

215

The purpose of the oath is to protect the wanna-blessed-be types who don't want to put in any work from real magic, and the Mysteries from the wanna-blessed-bes; and innocent bystanders from the havoc wrought by inept use of magic.

The purpose of the oath is not to protect some writings which may or may not give access to the Mysteries. Only a proper initiation and a profound encounter with the numinous can do that. Reading a Book of Shadows probably would not give access to the Mysteries.

Of course, I would prefer that Wiccan rituals were not published online, but I do think that we are unduly focused on protecting the text, to the detriment of passing on and sharing knowledge with other witches and Wiccans.

We need to protect the Mysteries from the profane, but for the most part, we do not need to protect them from each other. And let us not conflate the text of a Book of Shadows with the experience of the Mysteries, which is ineffable and non-verbal.

The witch's pyramid

When performing magic, many witches follow the magical dictum known as the witch's pyramid: "To know, to dare, to will, to keep silent". This has relevance to the concept of being bound by oath. We know things that others do not; we dare to use that knowledge; we work magic to bring about our will; but we must keep silent about the workings of the spell, otherwise its power will be dissipated (as every child knows, when you make a wish whilst blowing out the candles on your birthday cake, you have to keep the wish secret, or it doesn't work). The reason we must keep silent about the secrets that hedge the Mysteries is that you must approach the Mysteries in the right way, or you can get hurt; and it can dissipate the effect if the Mysteries are discussed.

Fraud, and why it matters

What is a fraud? In the context of witchcraft, it is someone who deliberately and knowingly seeks to deceive others about the origins and nature of their tradition or claims that they were initiated by a genuine practitioner of a tradition, but they were not. In other words, they lie about their origins to make themselves seem more authentic.

Examples include claims that a tradition calling itself Wicca, or possessing a Gardnerian book of shadows, is older than Gardner, or used the word Wicca before Gardner; these should be treated with extreme caution. (There are witchcraft traditions that are pre-Gardner, but they mostly do not call themselves Wicca; see *Appendix IV: Witchcraft Traditions*.) Claims that a tradition has an unbroken initiatory lineage back to ancient pagan times are also fraudulent. Claims to an unbroken initiatory lineage stretching back any earlier than 1900 should also be treated with extreme caution.

Why does this matter?

If you are going to trust someone enough to engage in transformative and powerful ritual with them, you want to be able to take them at their word. You want to be sure that they know what they are doing, that they have been taught a tried and trusted set of techniques, and that you are not going to be asked to do something that is massively outside your comfort zone.

If someone lies about something as simple as where they got their initiation from, or the origins of their tradition, how can you trust their word about anything else?

It has been observed that fraudulent claims about origins, and fraudulent claims of initiation, are often accompanied by abusive behaviour. I do not think an implausible origin story should automatically be viewed as a sign of potential abuse, unless it is accompanied by other warning signs of abusive behaviour.

It is advisable to seek external confirmation that someone's story (either about their initiation, or about the origins of their tradition) is true. Get a vouch from other Wiccans.

Honest traditions

Any tradition or group that does not lie about its origins is honest, genuine, and valid.

A tradition that cannot trace its initiatory lineage to Gardner or Sanders, but does not claim to, is honest, genuine, and valid. There are many Wiccan and witchcraft traditions, particularly in North America, that do not claim lineage back to Gardner or Sanders but do call themselves Wicca. That is perfectly fine. Wicca is a useful term for 'softening' the word witchcraft in areas where fundamentalism is rife. It is honest to call yourself a Wiccan if you do not have a Gardnerian or Alexandrian lineage – provided that you do not lie about your origins, lineage, or initiations.

Some Gardnerians and Alexandrians object to anything outside their traditions being known as Wicca. That is a different argument and should not be confused with fraudulent origin stories.

A person who has been lied to by their initiators, but believed the story, and repeats it in good faith, believing it to be true, is not fraudulent. A bit gullible perhaps, but not deliberately lying about their origins.

A tradition that possesses a Gardnerian book of shadows, and thereby believes itself to be Gardnerian, but doesn't have a lineage back to Gardner, and does not claim to – not fraudulent; not actually Gardnerian by the standard definition of the term Gardnerian, either; but not actually fraudulent, because it is not lying about its origins.

Witchcraft traditions that are honest, genuine, and valid include (but are not limited to) Reclaiming witchcraft, Feri witchcraft, Bread and Roses, 1734 witchcraft, Clan of Tubal Cain witchcraft, Central Valley Wicca, Georgian Wicca, Wiccan Church of Canada, Blue Star Wicca, Odyssean Wicca, Mohsian Wicca, Kingstone Wicca, Protean Wicca, Algard Wicca, to cite some well-known examples. None of these traditions claim to be much older than Gardnerian Wicca; they have clearly traceable origin stories, and do not claim a lineage that does not exist.

There are clearly some traditions of folk witchcraft that do pre-date Gerald Gardner, but not by more than fifty years, as far as I am aware. Claims of origins back in the mists of time should be treated with extreme caution.

Some groups are not entirely sure of their early history. In these cases, an honest answer to a question about origins would be, "We don't really know for certain, but to the best of our knowledge and belief, what happened was this..." If new evidence comes to light which refutes the origin story, the members of the tradition accept the new historical information. For example, if contemporary Alexandrians and Gardnerians discover that Sanders or Gardner made something up, we admit it, and do not seek to cover it up.

Once Ronald Hutton had traced the historical origins of Wicca (in *The Triumph of the Moon: a history of modern Pagan witchcraft*), the vast majority of Gardnerian and Alexandrian Wiccans accepted the new information and stopped claiming older origins for Wicca. Subsequent research by Philip Heselton has shown that Gardner's story that he was initiated into an existing coven was true (and they sincerely believed themselves to be reincarnations of nineteenth century witches). I believe that Gardner sincerely believed he had stumbled upon something genuinely old, whose fragmentary nature he sought to supplement based on his reading of Margaret Murray's work and The Key of Solomon.

A fraud is someone who deliberately and knowingly seeks to deceive others. If you cannot trust their word, it would be inadvisable to trust them about anything else.

Conclusion

Power (like most things) is always better when it is shared. It is a good idea to have checks and balances in an organisation to prevent one person wielding too much power. I recommend having the leadership role out in the open where everyone can see it, otherwise the power in the group tends to devolve to the grumpy naysayers.

Leaders should bear in mind that they serve their community; it does not serve them. A good leader seeks to empower and inspire others, not to rule over them and put them down.

Discussion

Does the Pagan movement need leaders?

What is a good model of leadership?

Where does the power go in your group?

Is there a tendency to scapegoat anyone?

Who makes most of the decisions?

Can your leaders be elected / re-elected?

Exercises

Meditate on the eight Wiccan virtues (or the equivalent in your tradition). When you are in a position of power, how do these virtues come into play?

Invite every member of your coven to produce a ritual for a Sabbat and/or an esbat. If there are any barriers for them, make sure they have the resources to overcome the barriers.

Meditate on any conflicts or power struggles you have had with others. At what point did your or their shadow side come into play in the process? Were you projecting shadow aspects onto each other?

17. Challenging oppression

Every time an advance is made in people respecting and accommodating others' bodily autonomy, gender identity, disability, sexual orientation, or other difference, you are sure to hear the cry "it's political correctness gone mad!". A similar cry, of "Alphabet Soup!", goes up whenever a new letter is added to the LGBT+ acronym, or LGBTQ2SIA. The latest right-wing catchphrase is "cancel culture" to describe the practice of no-platforming.

The point of refusing to share a platform with a far-right speaker, and trying to prevent them speaking, is that allowing racists and fascists to speak (particularly if they speak unopposed or in a university setting) lends an aura of respectability to their ideas, and there is documented evidence that incidents of racist violence increase in areas where fascists and racists hold events.

What you are hearing is the sound of the privileged complaining about a loss of privilege (otherwise known as 'playing the game of life on a lower difficulty setting than other people',[61] or 'getting away with stuff that minority groups would not get away with').

Examples of advances in respect for others include the word cisgender being added to the *Oxford English Dictionary*, having gender-neutral toilets, labelling food for allergens, providing food for people with special requirements (halal, kosher, vegan, vegetarian, coeliac, etc), providing electricity for disabled people to recharge their

---

[61] http://whatever.scalzi.com/2012/05/15/straight-white-male-the-lowest-difficulty-setting-there-is/

wheelchairs, implementing consent policies at Pagan events... the list goes on. You name it, someone will probably have exclaimed "it's political correctness gone mad!" (or something very similar) in response to every social advance that has ever been made, right back to that dangerously radical innovation of giving the vote to women, or perhaps even further back than that.

Where does this insidious phrase come from? Its history is quite convoluted, but it has often been used as a pejorative term and was rather obscure (and a left-wing in-joke) until it was taken up by conservatives who were opposed to progressive educational policies. After George Bush Senior used it at a commencement ceremony at the University of Michigan in 1991, its use became widespread among conservatives to refer to anything they regarded as an "imposition of liberal orthodoxy". Its use rapidly spread to the UK, where it is used every time someone wants to do something inclusive and someone else perceives that their privilege will be eroded by being more inclusive.

One example of privilege is that non-disabled Pagans don't have to worry about wheelchair access to venues, and expect public Pagan events to be low-cost or free, so when event organisers book a venue, they are constrained by these expectations to look for lower-cost venues, which often don't have wheelchair access. When it is suggested that all public Pagan events should be wheelchair-accessible, even if it costs more, you are sure to hear cries of "it's political correctness gone mad" – despite the fact that accessibility is actually a legal requirement for public events.

Similarly, inclusive Wicca advocates an expanded understanding of concepts like polarity, and a few tweaks to Wiccan rituals, to accommodate a more up-to-date concept of gender and sexuality. To hear the howls of protest from some quarters, you would have thought that inclusive Wiccans had advocated abolishing the whole of Wiccan liturgy, or something. (Meanwhile, many people outside Wicca are baffled that we are still having a conversation about this in the early 21st century - especially other witchcraft traditions which are more queer-friendly.)

As Neil Gaiman [62] pointed out, however, 'political correctness' is just another name for

> 'treating other people with respect'. He goes on to suggest that people should try replacing the phrase "politically correct" wherever we can with "treating other people with respect". And now, thanks to a New Zealander called Byron Clark, there's actually a Google Chrome extension that does exactly that.[63]

The latest version of "it's political correctness gone mad" has emerged from some sections of polytheism: the accusation of "putting politics before gods". It is particularly insidious because it implies that those of us who care about respecting the rights of our fellow humans (and of other animals) are somehow impious.

The central tenet of my religion is "only connect": connect with other beings, respect their autonomy, honour their

---

[62] http://neil-gaiman.tumblr.com/post/43087620460/i-was-reading-a-book-about-interjections-oddly

[63] http://www.huffingtonpost.com/entry/this-google-chrome-extension-replaces-political-correctness-with-something-more-accurate_us_55c82605e4b0923c12bd4a91

dreams and aspirations, and recognise the divinity within them.

I believe that divinity is immanent in everything; every being has the seeds of godhood within them. Some choose to trample on the seed, others choose to nurture it towards growth – but divinity is everywhere, however dimly reflected.

If I deny the divinity immanent in my fellow beings, then I am also denying the divinity of gods, who are expressions of the same divinity.

Therefore, in my world, treating other people with respect *is* honouring the gods. The ancient stories of gods and angels visiting humans disguised as mortals are metaphors to express this idea. You never know whether the stranger to whom you showed hospitality and respect was a god in disguise – so you may as well behave as if everyone you meet is a god in disguise. Because really, they are.

The question of which comes first, gods or politics, is for me rather like the question of the chicken and the egg. The one exists in the context of the other, and they are inextricable. The deities we choose to worship (and even the deities who choose us to work with them) are influenced by our politics, because why would they choose to have a relationship with a human whose values and goals differed from theirs, and why would we choose to have a relationship with a deity whose values and goals differ from ours?

Let us take a step back and talk about definitions.

What is a deity?

A deity is a powerful entity or identity who has emerged from the complexity of the universe, and is shaped by social interactions (with humans, animals, their environment, other deities, and other spirit entities) just as humans are. Deities have agency, or at least they seem to. Often that agency involves influencing people to do their work for them. That is what I believe anyway; you may have a different idea. It is worth thinking, too, about what kind of person a deity might be. If they are advanced beings of great virtue, then one would expect that they have ethical values that are similar to the highest values we can imagine (unless they possess information about how the universe works that is simply unavailable to our finite perceptions, in which case they might have a different concept of what is ethical). But nevertheless, any ideas they come up with must work on the physical plane and be comprehensible to our finite perspective.

What is politics?

Politics is any situation where a conflict of interest or a difference of power is resolved by negotiation (which could be a large-scale vote or a small-scale consensus process) instead of war. It has even been said that war is a continuation of politics by other means (which is true, as when negotiation breaks down, either the status quo or an outbreak of physical violence will follow).

Conflicts of values

If you believe that the gods come before politics (by which I mean the way humans negotiate living in community), what would you do if a deity commanded you to do something that was against your ethics? I imagine that, at the very least, you would do some practice of discernment (such as divination) to check that you had heard their message correctly and were not just deluding yourself. You might even refuse outright to do the task they have requested. In that case, you have (rightly in my view) put politics before gods.

If you are a person with a marginalised identity who wants to honour Pagan deities in community with others, and something about the way Pagan rituals are constructed excludes you from those rituals, then there is a conflict of interest (the existing members want to keep doing their rituals a certain way, but you want to join the group, which requires change). There is also a power differential, in that the existing members of the group hold the power to change their rituals or practices to be more inclusive (or not). So that's politics, right there.

So, if a disabled person, person of colour, or LGBTQIA+ person is structurally excluded from your rituals but they were chosen by a deity you honour – then your political decision to exclude them dishonours that deity and you have (wrongly in my view) put your exclusive politics before gods. Especially if your rituals are the only ones in town.

If your chosen deities command hospitality towards the stranger, but your politics and values demand that you turn refugees and migrants and the disabled and LGBTQIA+ and People of Colour away... then you have (wrongly in my view) put politics before gods.

Many Pagan deities command hospitality, honour, and the exchange of gifts (reciprocity).

The politics of the gods

I think the deities are part of Pagan society, not separate from it, and therefore even the way we negotiate our relationships with deities is political. They may want one thing; we may want something else (a conflict of interest). They may have a different perspective; they also have greater – possibly infinite – power in a specific sphere of influence. They are part of a complex web of relationships which involves differences of power, conflicts of interest, and negotiations about how to resolve those conflicts. So, your relationship with a deity is political, just as the personal and the interpersonal are political.

And rather than politics being a sphere that is separate from deities, it is the complex web of relationships between human and human, human and other-than-human, humans and deities, spirits and deities, spirits and spirits, deities and deities. So, you cannot put one before the other – politics is the very stuff of our relationships with gods, the context in which those relationships happen.

I became a Pagan, a witch, and a polytheist because I believe that all life is interconnected, interwoven, interpermeable. My values informed my choice of religion and theology, and my values are political because they are about how I relate to other beings. It is impossible to consider the gods (or any other entities) outside of that context of interrelationship – and therefore, politics.

There is a view of life in which events are not perceived as connected, people are viewed as separate entities, mere expendable units to be crushed under the wheels of the great machine known as 'progress'. It was this view that prevailed during the Irish Potato Famine in the nineteenth century, when full grain ships were allowed to leave Irish ports because 'market forces' meant that their contents could be sold elsewhere rather than being used to feed the starving farm workers.

In his great novel, *Howard's End*, E. M. Forster presented an extended critique of this view. Two middle class sisters befriend a young working-class man, who ends up dying. The husband of one of the sisters cannot see that he is in any way responsible for the young man's death, even though it is intimately bound up with all the other events of the novel. The novel is an extended illustration of its epigraph, "Only connect".

> ...she might yet be able to help him to the building of the rainbow bridge that should connect the prose in us with the passion. Without it we are meaningless fragments, half monks, half beasts, unconnected arches that have never joined into a man. With it love is born, and alights on the highest curve, glowing against the grey, sober against the fire. Happy the man who sees from either aspect the glory of these outspread wings. The roads of his soul lie clear, and he and his friends shall find easy-going.... It did not seem so difficult. She need trouble him with no gift of her own. She would only point out the salvation that was latent in his own soul, and in the soul of every man. Only connect! That was the whole of her sermon. Only connect the prose and the passion, and both will be exalted, and

human love will be seen at its height. Live in
fragments no longer. Only connect and the beast
and the monk, robbed of the isolation that is life to
either, will die.

E. M. Forster, Howard's End, chapter XXII

But the novel is not simply about *making* the connection
between the inner and the outer, the beast and the angel in
us, but also *seeing* the connections between different aspects
of life, and different circumstances. The young working-
class man is crushed by the middle-class man's inability to
connect, to see the lights and shadows. He is crushed by
the whole social system in which the characters are
trapped. E. M. Forster, himself a socialist and a friend of the
great radical pioneer the late nineteenth century, Edward
Carpenter (a gay Pagan socialist vegetarian anarchist), was
trying – ever so gently – to point out that the whole
capitalist and hierarchical system was built to destroy life,
love, and pleasure.

Once we start to see the connections between one
circumstance and another, they cannot be unseen. If you
look at the whole system of property, capital, profit, race,
class, and kyriarchal oppression, and start to trace it back to
its roots, you can see that the parts of the system are not
independent of each other, but developed together. This
makes the system of oppression hard to unravel if you only
try to tackle it piecemeal, and do not see the connections
between the different parts.

If you look at the alternative ways of living that people
have tried to create over the last few centuries, you can see
that they are also a set of interconnected ideas and

practices. Different co-operative, p/Pagan, spiritual,
Dissenting, anarchist, socialist, and communitarian groups
evolved out of each other, shared ideas, and built similar
alternative structures. In trying to create a vision of an
alternative society, we do not have to reinvent the wheel, as
the effort to create something different has been building
momentum for a while.

The interconnected kyriarchy

The kyriarchy – the hierarchical view of human relations,
built on power over others, and regarding those others as
lesser beings, perhaps not even human, has been with us
for more than two millennia. In *Truth or dare*, Starhawk[64]
put forward the idea that it came about because of farming.
As hunter-gatherers settled down and started to farm the
land, they started to regard the land as belonging to them.
The population got larger. They also needed to irrigate the
land, and this led to over-salination. As more and more
fields became unworkable, land became scarce, and this
gave rise to war. War meant that warriors, who were
usually male, were now the most valued members of
society. To be able to kill another human being, warriors
needed to see them as other, as less than human. In this
way, the whole system of hierarchy, war, kings, and
power-over came about. The new system also meant that
because men were the most valued members of society,
inheritance passed through the male line, which meant that
women's sexuality had to be controlled. This kyriarchal
view of existence fed into the Roman Empire, which co-

[64] Starhawk (1988), *Truth or Dare: Encounters with Power, Authority and Mystery*. (San Francisco, Harper San Francisco).
http://starhawk.org/writing/books/truth-or-dare/

opted Christianity around the time of the Council of Nicaea (325 CE).

By 500 CE, the lack of connection between the spiritual and the physical had reached such a pitch that there was a highly toxic and misogynist view of all things fleshly, especially women. Every time a small group of people tried to build a radical communitarian way of life, whether on political or religious grounds, or both, they were crushed, but another group rose from the ruins and carried on.

In England, after the Norman invasion, the land rights of the local population were taken away. It has taken centuries of struggle, and we still have not entirely recovered them. There were the appropriation of Saxon lands, especially forest, by the new Norman overlords; the Acts of Enclosure, which took away common land, so memorably bemoaned by the poet John Clare; the regulation of rights to forage, and the imposition of heavy fines and penalties for any infringement. In Scotland, the Highland Clearances involved much the same kind of theft of lands and livelihoods of ordinary people. The excellent travelling show and website[65] *Three Acres and a Cow*, performed by Robin Grey (who shot to fame as the busker who suggested that David Cameron should 'fuck off back to Eton') and Rachel Rose Reid, documents the history of resistance to the theft of land by the ruling classes, from the Norman Conquest, via the Peasants' Revolt, to the Enclosures and the Highland Clearances, and links these with today's issues of housing shortages, fracking, and food.

---

[65] http://threeacresandacow.co.uk/

In North America, lands and livelihood, labour and the fruits of labour, were stolen from Indigenous people, and from enslaved people. Just for a moment it looked as if Thomas Morton would set up an alternative community at Merry Mount, but it too was crushed.

All these thefts and appropriations stem from the view that some people are inherently worth more than others, by 'virtue' of their ability to crush dissent, subdue others, and get more money and power. They stem from the idea that land can be property and is not held in common for the benefit of all. This hierarchical and commodified view of the worth of people and land (instead of viewing them as intrinsically sacred) gave rise to war, enslavement, rape, and torture. All these horrors are made possible by viewing the victim as worth less than the perpetrator; othering them and devaluing them.

This hierarchical and commodified view of value was made much worse by capitalism, which disconnected the workers from the work of their hands, and alienated them, by introducing mass production. By valuing the profits due to the investors and shareholders over giving a living wage to the workers, workers were stripped of their humanity and became mere cogs in the machine.

The Whig interpretation of history would have you believe that the ruling classes came to their senses by themselves and distributed resources more evenly. However, even just looking at the last decade in the UK, we can see that this is not true, because the ruling classes and the rich have grabbed more money and power – in the form of the privatisation of education, prisons, and the health service, pay-outs to bankers, tax evasion, and vastly inflated salaries (in the UK, several University Vice-Chancellors get paid more than the Prime Minister, for example). At the same time, they have imposed vicious grinding austerity on the poorest and most vulnerable, in the form of benefit cuts, benefit sanctions, and the removal or erosion of the social safety net such as council housing and the National Health Service. All of this has led to a massive widening of the gap between rich and poor.

The web of life

Fortunately, there has always been resistance to the hierarchical and commodified view of humans and the natural world. There was the Peasants' Revolt, protest marches against Enclosures, the Diggers and Levellers, who tried to create a more equal and just society. There were the Reform Riots against mass starvation in the 1830s; the rally in London in protest against the deportation of the Tolpuddle Martyrs; the Chartist uprising. There was the mass trespass on Kinder Scout in 1933, where the factory workers of Manchester surged onto the surrounding moors, which had previously been reserved for the landowners who used them for shooting wildlife. There were rent strikes against extortionate rents; there was the co-operative movement which aimed to build an alternative economy. There was the struggle for liberation from slavery, and the women's rights movement. The struggle for women's rights arose out of the successful organising of women who campaigned against slavery. We can learn something from both the successes and failures of each of these movements: the horrific oppression they struggled against; the seeming insurmountability of the obstacles, and their eventual victory, however partial.

The Unitarian movement arose out of a radical religious group – the late 15th century humanists of North Italy, who fled first to Poland, and then to Transylvania. While they were in Poland, they had their own printing press and sent radical pamphlets to England, which fuelled a fresh wave of radical dissent. Eventually the Unitarians gave rise to Transcendentalism, which included such luminaries as Ralph Waldo Emerson, Theodore Parker, Nathaniel Hawthorne, and Walt Whitman, who corresponded with Edward Carpenter. Transcendentalism [66] was one of the strands that led into the Pagan revival. Many Unitarians and Transcendentalists were socialists, campaigners for the abolition of slavery, and at the forefront of women's rights. Two Unitarians, James Reeb and Viola Liuzzo, died after being attacked by racist thugs at Selma. In 2008, two Unitarian Universalists, Linda Kraeger and Greg McKendry, were killed in a shooter attack on Tennessee Valley UU, a church that actively supports LGBTQIA+ rights.

In England, the Labour movement was born out of many strands of resistance, including Chartists, trade unions, the co-operative movement, socialists, feminists, and anarchists. The Arts and Crafts movement was founded by socialists, who sought to restore dignity and beauty to craftsmanship, and reforge the connection between the maker and the made, which had been so brutally severed by the alienation caused by mass production, where an

---

[66] Chas S. Clifton (2006), *Her Hidden Children: The Rise of Wicca and Paganism in America (Pagan Studies Series)*, Altamira Press

artefact was no longer the work of one person, but the anonymous and uniform production of several workers.

One of the key figures in the early Labour movement was Edward Carpenter, who had links with both anarchists and socialists, and who wrote movingly on the restoration of the connection between people and Nature. He could be regarded as one of the founders of the Pagan revival, as he wrote extensively on the joys of Paganism, and made the connection between the Pagan revelry of May Day and the celebration of workers' rights. Sadly, he is largely forgotten today by both Pagans and socialists, perhaps because he was gay and was side-lined during the excessively homophobic period of the 1950s, but his ideas are enjoying a revival amongst gay men, and he has never been forgotten in his adopted city of Sheffield.

A study of the all the different radical movements of the last 400 years would reveal a fascinating web of connections between the people and ideas involved in them.

The excellent film *Pride* (2014) revealed the connection between the miners' strike in the mid-1980s and LGBT+ rights in the UK. Lesbians and gay men formed a support group to raise funds for the miners during the darkest days of the strike, and in return, the unions who represent the miners voted *en bloc* for Labour policies supporting LGBT+ rights (such as the repeal of section 28, the lowering of the age of consent for same-sex partners to the same age as for opposite-sex partners, and the introduction of same-sex marriage).

The ability to connect with someone else's struggle, even in the midst of your own struggle, can give rise to unexpected results. After the abolition of slavery, many Black abolitionists supported the cause of women's rights, just as women had campaigned for the abolition of slavery. The solidarity of trade unionists around the world has led to many victories for freedom and democracy and human rights. The ability to connect your own experience of oppression with someone else's experience of oppression is the key to radical transformation.

The power of the internet to enable rapid communication between movements resisting hegemonic oppression and capitalist exploitation around the world has been a key lever in helping them to build connections. Irish activists resisting Shell in Ireland have linked up with Nigerian activists doing the same in the Niger delta. Recently I have attended two demonstrations about the UK's racist immigration policy, both of which were mobilised via the internet. Groups resisting capitalism and racism can make and maintain connections, both over the internet, and at May Day rallies and other events. I was pleased to see that the trades union banner at the 2015 May Day Rally in Oxford, UK, expressed solidarity with Baltimore and the Black Lives Matter campaign.

In the last decade, with the re-election of a Conservative government in the UK, and the election of a far-right demagogue in the USA, the resurgence of far right and populist movements, and the seemingly relentless systemic racism in white colonialist countries, it seems as if there is no hope of change. However, the people of Greece have sent a resounding anti-austerity message by voting in a left-wing government. In 2020, the coronavirus pandemic has made people rethink society's priorities, and may even bring an end to neoliberalism and austerity. The tide is turning. People are beginning to see that there must be another way to live than greed, consumption, and exploitation.

People are beginning to make the connection between the sacredness of the Earth, the waters, the animals, the birds, and the people.

People are beginning to reconnect with the gods and spirits of the land, recognising that returning to right relationship with the land, making deep connections with place and community, making loving connections with others, is the key to harmony and indeed survival, both physical and spiritual.

By recognising the sacredness of the land, the idea that no-one can own it, and that it must be held in common for the benefit of all beings, we radically reaffirm our connection to nature.

By recognising the sacredness of the body and of pleasure, we reconnect to our very instincts, and the gods-given pleasures of the flesh.

By connecting our present predicament with the threads of oppression and resistance woven for us by our ancestors, we can begin to unravel destructive ways of being, and begin to weave new possibilities, drawing on the bright threads of dissent and revolutionary ways of being from the past.

By connecting our own hopes and dreams with those of others around the world who are reaching for new ways of being, we can learn from each other and strengthen our own visions, and correct our cultural biases by seeing with multiple perspectives from different cultures.

By connecting with the struggles of others, we reaffirm our humanity.

With our thoughts we make the world

Paganisms are countercultural, like most religions. They present a critique of the status quo, and some alternative visions of how the world might be if it was re-enchanted; and they offer a variety of methods for bringing about the desired change. There are several overlapping, and sometimes conflicting, visions available from the Pagan dream factory. Some are benign, involving ways to cope with climate change, and promotion of social and environmental justice. Others are retrogressive, wanting to take us back to a (somewhat mythical) earlier era.

Religious and spiritual ideas do not exist in a vacuum. They are intimately connected with politics. What you believe about how your religious group should be organised, and how ideas and information are verified and validated, and who gets to have authority and why, inevitably spill over into your ideas about how society as a whole should be organised. Ideas about culture and society are what is known as metapolitics [67], which is a way of

---

[67] Gods & Radicals (2016), *Weekly Update: No Pasaran.* http://godsandradicals.org/2016/03/25/no-pasaran-weekly-update-25-march/

pursuing political goals through cultural, spiritual, and social change, rather than through overt political means.

If you think about it, most religions are a form of metapolitics: their goal is exactly to transform society and individuals (which is the purpose of politics) through cultural and spiritual means. (Christianity's goal is and has always been to transform society, for example.) Pagan religions are no different: we also desire the transformation of society, but our visions of a transformed society are rather different from theirs.

The key thing about metapolitical processes and shifts is that they prepare the ground for political change. If you consider the changes wrought by feminism, LGBT+ liberation, and the civil rights movement, it takes about fifty years of preparation and social change before any legal rights are gained. Take feminism for example: the first attempt to bring a bill before the UK Parliament to give women the right to vote was greeted with derision and laughter. It took fifty years to win the vote for women. It took forty years from the decriminalisation of homosexuality to get same-sex marriage in the UK. And there has been a massive shift in attitudes towards women and LGBT+ people that prepared the ground for those political changes. Retrograde steps (such as placing limits on immigration, threatening to deport Muslims, etc) also require metapolitical changes, such as an increase in xenophobia, in order to create the political momentum to successfully bring in legislation.

In an article I wrote about a decade ago, *News from Nowhere*,[68] I noted the links between science fiction and Pagan thought. Both offer alternative visions of society, both utopian and dystopian; and both include egalitarian and hierarchical possible futures or alternatives. In that essay, I glossed over some of the more right-wing science fiction writers such as Robert Heinlein, who has also had a significant influence on the Pagan revival, and focused more on left-wing writers and their visions. But science fiction and fantasy, by presenting plausible visions of different societies, are important drivers of social change, and they present alternative societies that might appeal to all parts of the political spectrum. Fantasy in particular enables the leap of imagination required to re-enchant the world. As John Halstead writes [69], "A work of fiction may open a person up to having a very real experience to which they were not open before."

The metapolitics of Pagan traditions

We must guard against retrogressive ideas becoming unexamined norms within Pagan traditions. It is worth mentioning that just because someone's ideas overlap with those of the New Right, does not mean they are necessarily an adherent of the crypto-fascist ideas of that movement. But it does suggest that it would be a good idea to carefully examine where their ideas might lead if carried to their

---

[68] http://pagantheologies.pbworks.com/w/page/13622155/News%20from%20Nowhere
[69] John Halstead (2016), "*American Gods* and the Growth of Devotional Polytheism". *Allergic Pagan.* http://www.patheos.com/blogs/allergicpagan/2016/03/19/american-gods-and-the-growth-of-devotional-polytheism/

logical conclusion, precisely because these ideas prepare the ground for political and social change.

With that in mind, let us examine some of the ideas that are popular in some corners of Pagan and polytheist communities.

Apparently, some people are rather fascinated by kingship and aristocracy. I think I can safely say that such notions are not very popular in England, where we still experience the inequalities of the class system, the monarchy that sits on top of the pinnacle like the visible part of a pimple, and where a study of our history reveals the disastrous instability introduced by the vagaries of succession in a hereditary monarchy (I am referring to the war of Stephen and Maud, the Wars of the Roses, the English Civil War, the "Glorious Revolution", and so on). That is why you do not get Wiccans in the UK adopting titles like Lord this and Lady that.

The failures of hereditary monarchies should be completely obvious to anyone who has studied the history of monarchy wherever it has been tried. The only time monarchy worked was when the king was elected (and nowadays we call that office a president). The only way that an absolute ruler can maintain their authority is through fear, as Machiavelli pointed out.

It is possible to have a leader whose position is sacred, and even one who is referred to as a monarch, provided that their style of leadership is not authoritarian and absolutist (see chapter 16, *Power and authority*, for an extended discussion of this).

Another popular concept is direct communication from deities. You received a message from a deity. Great. That is nice for you. But how do I know whether it was really a message from a deity, or just another aspect of your psyche trying to shore up your fragile ego? I would evaluate a purported revelation from a deity the way I would evaluate a purported message from anyone else, by asking questions:

- Is it consistent with what I know of reality?

- Is it consistent with what I know of that person/deity?

- Is it consistent with my ethics?

If the answer to any of these is no, then either I will not believe that the message came from the deity, or I will not believe that the message was intended for me.

"A deity told me to do it" is never a sufficient justification for any action. If a deity tells a group of people to slaughter another group of people, we rightly regard that deity as deeply immoral (or alternatively, we deny that the commandment came from that deity). All communications from deities must be evaluated against common standards of ethical behaviour.

That is not to say that no-one ever receives valid and interesting messages from deities: certainly they do. It just means that we need to be aware that messages from deities might just be our own ego talking, rather than a genuine divine communication.

Another disturbing tendency that has been rearing its head of late is the view that you can only work within your own culture, worshipping the gods of your ancestors. This 'folkish' view is being used to exclude People of Colour from traditions based on European culture. It takes a monolithic and essentialist view of culture, regarding cultural themes as being predetermined by genetics. For those of us who are of mixed descent (which is most people these days, especially in North America), this approach literally makes no sense. I am an English person with some Cornish ancestry, and as I grew up in Hampshire, probably Saxon ancestry too – maybe even some Norman. Should my Paganism consist of Cornish practices, Saxon practices, or Norse practices according to this view?

This folkish/genetic essentialism uses the concept of cultural appropriation to justify its racist discourse, which is ironic as they are appropriating the real struggles of Indigenous Peoples to defend their culture and lifeways against the depredations of colonialism. But resisting cultural appropriation is about resisting oppressive colonialism; it is not about keeping culture 'pure'. Cultures and traditions are not monolithic and unchanging silos: they are discourses. You cannot just lift a practice from one culture to another in a superficial way without radically changing its meaning; but this does not mean that no-one can ever do anything inspired by another culture.

The problem with folkish views is that they assume that races and cultures are monolithic, unchanging, never influence each other, and that people from different ethnicities never intermarry. Folkish views construct different cultures as different races, which in my book is basically racist.

If you desire to create a society where conflict is the norm and the weakest go to the wall, then your interim goals and methods need to be consistent with that goal. And creating hierarchical structures where outsiders are scapegoated and disagreement cannot be tolerated, will take you a long way towards that goal. Fetishizing power-over and symbols of power-over will also lead you towards that goal.

If your goal is to create a sustainable, egalitarian, peaceful society, then your interim goals and methods need to be consistent with that goal. As A J Muste wrote, "There is no way to peace. Peace is the way". The structures we need to create to realise this goal should be democratic, egalitarian, and non-hierarchical, and there should be room for differences of opinion and for diversity.

If you are creating a new religious movement that is characterised by fear of difference, distrust of outsiders, the crushing of dissent, the insistence on only one right way to do things, then you will sow the seeds of perpetual conflict and division.

That is why I am happy that atheist Pagans are part of Paganism: because I welcome a diversity of views, and I want my ideas to be challenged and tested. The only way that theories are strengthened is if they are tested against other theories.

That is why I am delighted by the ideas of Rhyd Wildermuth about worlding the gods[70], because the way

---

[70] Rhyd Wildermuth (2016), "Worlding the Gods", *Paganarch*, http://paganarch.com/2016/02/18/worlding-the-gods/

we world the gods into the earth reflects the sort of society we want to create:

> "The gods exist as independent beings from us regardless of our belief in them. But it is we who actually world them into the earth, and how we world them is dependent upon what we do, who we are, and the sort of world we create around us."

I want the Pagan movement to be diverse and inclusive, because a diverse and inclusive movement is stronger, more interesting, and more viable. I want to create a world where it is safe to be me. A theocracy run by people who want power over others might be fine for the people at the top (as long as they succeeded in staying at the top) but it wouldn't be very pleasant for anyone else.

That is why the only viable vision of a sustainable and just future is one where social and environmental justice prevails. One where the rapacious greed and overconsumption promoted by capitalism has been replaced by a more sustainable and equal distribution of wealth. One that values the gods as the consciousnesses of the natural world, not as beings who desire to lord it over humanity. One that does not appropriate other cultures' practices but does not treat cultures as monolithic silos either.

As the Buddha once said, with our thoughts we make the world. We are all co-creating the future of the Pagan movement now. Let us be careful to lay the foundations of a world that those who come after us can be happy and fulfilled in.

Unlearning racism and colonialism

How do we unlearn the racism, white supremacism, and colonialism that runs through the whole culture like a poison? The first step is to become aware that it is present, and systemic. The next step is to examine our privilege, and our unexamined assumptions about Black people, People of Colour, Indigenous Peoples, and colonised peoples.

Racism and colonialism are insidious and widespread and affect many (if not most) interactions between ethnic groups. We are all immersed in the racist discourse and systemic racism that is endemic in our society. Even the most progressive people occasionally come out with some crass comment (I have done it myself). Even the most progressive people are, however unwillingly, complicit in the way society denies basic rights to BIPOC people – Black, Indigenous, People of Colour. [71]

A white supremacist society is one that is predicated on the assumption that white people should be in charge, that white ideas and behaviours and culture are the norm, and that is organised in such a way that it benefits white people and disadvantages BIPOC people. Such societies were often founded by people with overtly white supremacist ideas, but they do not have to be composed of extremists to be systemically biased against BIPOC people. Once the

---

[71] Preferred terminology varies between the UK and the US and elsewhere. In the UK, people tend to use BAME, or Black, Asian, and Minority Ethnic; in Canada, the term BIPOC is frequently used (Black, Indigenous, People of Colour), and in the USA, the term PoC (People of Color) is used.

systemic oppression has become embedded in the culture, it gains momentum, becoming seemingly unstoppable.

There are different levels or degrees of racism, but if you are white, you have white privilege, and are benefitting from it. If you accept the legitimacy of colonial and racist systems, you are complicit in them, and are upholding white supremacy, however unwillingly.

There are people actively working to unlearn racism. These are the people who show up in support of Black Lives Matter, campaign against deportation and immigrant detention centres, read Michelle Alexander and Ta-Nehisi Coates, and generally seek to amplify Black, Asian, and Indigenous voices.

Then there are people who believe they are not racist because they do not say certain words, but they are propping up systemic racism by their denial. These are the people who just want Black people to be quiet and not rock the boat.

There are people who deny that racism exists because race is a social construct. Well yes, race is a social construct, but that does not mean it does not have massively harmful consequences.

Then there are people who actively express racist ideas and stereotypes but would deny being racist. They uncritically absorb the racist narratives and stereotypes peddled by right-wing media and repeat them in conversation and on social media.

Then there are unashamedly racist people, who think that the "white race is being persecuted", and actively promote racism and racist ideology. At one time, the term racism meant a belief in the idea that races were biologically distinct. Now it means "power plus prejudice" (the power is conferred by the weight of systemic oppression).

And then there are those who are avowedly white supremacist, who believe that the white race is superior and all that sort of rubbish. These are the kind of people who join extreme white supremacist groups and far right political parties.

There is a spectrum from the least racist to the most racist types, and of course they are all unhelpful, but some are actively harmful.

Often, if a white person, or the white system, gets called out for racism, they immediately think they are being labelled as a Big Bad Racist, whereas they may be unwittingly upholding white supremacism.

People also get very confused between racism on an interpersonal level, and systemic racism, which is the entire system of oppression throughout social structures such as the courts, the police, the schools, the prison system, and so on.

It is not enough to be 'not racist', we must be actively anti-racist, seeking to undo the bias and assumptions of ourselves and others, and challenging systems of oppression.

Eco-fascism

"Gaia's revenge" or "Gaia's vengeance" is a trope where our planet is a sentient being, or at least a coherent system, which is willing to destroy humanity to save all the other species and ecosystems on Earth. The problem with this view is that it is not humanity as a whole that is destroying wildlife habitats, disrupting ecosystems and the climate, and causing mass extinctions: at the time of writing, just 100 companies are responsible for 71% of the world's carbon emissions [72], while the poorest 50% of the world's population are responsible for only 10% of those carbon emissions [73]. The problem is capitalism, industry, and consumerism, not humans.

The emergence of pandemics and viruses is related to our disregard for nature and wildlife and ecosystems, and we should treat pandemics as a wake-up call. But the problem that causes pandemics is our failure to co-operate with Nature, not our mere existence. There are many viruses out there in the forests and the populations of wild animals. As industry cuts down more and more forests[74], the forests get smaller; wildlife is forced into smaller areas, and the viruses become more virulent. People get hungry because of economic inequalities and then eat wildlife; this can cause viruses (such as HIV, Ebola, SARS, MERS, and COVID-19) to cross into human populations with little or

---

[72] https://www.theguardian.com/sustainable-business/2017/jul/10/100-fossil-fuel-companies-investors-responsible-71-global-emissions-cdp-study-climate-change
[73]
https://www.theguardian.com/environment/2015/dec/02/worlds-richest-10-produce-half-of-global-carbon-emissions-says-oxfam
[74]
https://www.theguardian.com/environment/2020/mar/18/tip-of-the-iceberg-is-our-destruction-of-nature-responsible-for-covid-19-aoe

no immunity to them. Nature *is* sending us a message[75], but it is that we must stop industry and capitalism from destroying the planet.

What I mean by capitalism here is the idea that a group of investors sink some capital into a venture or a company, which then returns them profits: this idea was one of the major drivers of colonialism, as some of the earliest venture capitalists founded companies to exploit the resource of the Americas. The reason this becomes a problem and a huge drain on resources is that profits become more important than anything else. I do not mean mercantilism, which is small traders exchanging goods for money.

George Monbiot points out that Western culture has become complacent[76], believing ourselves to be outside of or above Nature, able to use technology to get us out of the consequences of pollution, destruction, and climate change, or relying on exporting the problem to the southern hemisphere.

The occurrence of a pandemic has massive implications for what we prioritize as a species, as communities and nations. Do we prioritize economic growth, or quality of life, or taking care of everyone? What kind of a civilization do we want to be?

75

https://www.theguardian.com/world/2020/mar/25/coronavir us-nature-is-sending-us-a-message-says-un-environment-chief
76

https://www.theguardian.com/commentisfree/2020/mar/25/c ovid-19-is-natures-wake-up-call-to-complacent-civilisation

Some people are all too willing to sacrifice civil liberty and bring in mass surveillance and policing in response to people being irresponsible and not practising physical distancing and self-isolation in a pandemic. However, this has terrifying implications for a future where not only your movements but even your body temperature could be used to gather data about what you are doing and thinking[77].

The "New Deal for Nature" and eco-fascism

One "solution" to climate change and ecosystem destruction that has been proposed, and is gaining momentum, is the idea of the "New Deal for Nature". This is being promoted by several prominent environmental campaigners, and the World-Wide Fund for Nature (WWF). The idea is to give a third of the planet over to wildlife, with no humans inhabiting it. The problem with this is threefold: it would involve huge displacement of Indigenous Peoples; it seeks to put a monetary value on Nature, as if it could be commodified; and it perpetuates the notion that humans are not part of Nature.

The World-Wide Fund for Nature has been complicit in, or actively encouraged, the torture and illegal imprisonment of people living in conservation areas[78]. They also actively promote the idea of the empty wilderness[79], which has

---

[77] https://www.ft.com/content/19d90308-6858-11ea-a3c9-1fe6fedcca75
[78] https://www.buzzfeednews.com/article/tomwarren/wwf-world-wide-fund-nature-parks-torture-death
[79] https://www.survivalinternational.org/articles/3456-killing-conservation-lethal-cult-of-the-empty-wild

been used as an excuse to persecute and displace
Indigenous Peoples.

The idea of removing humans from tracts of land set aside
for nature has a long and murky history. Some of the
earliest proponents of national parks wanted to remove
villages of Indigenous people from the area designated as a
national park[80]. Ecofascist ideas are undergoing a revival
among the extreme right[81], and gaining traction in
mainstream discourse.

The "New Deal for Nature", like its predecessors, the
National Parks, would involve displacing large numbers of
Indigenous Peoples. This is a terrible idea, because it is
utterly racist and would be a massive act of genocide, and
because Indigenous Peoples manage the land they live on
and promote and support biodiversity. For example, in
California, the Yurok, a local Indigenous People, had done
controlled burning in the forest for generations [82], until
they were stopped by the Parks Service. Their controlled
burning managed the undergrowth and prevented large
forest fires by clearing out the dry underbrush.
Presumably, it also let in more light for a more diverse
range of plants to grow. They are now permitted to do their
traditional controlled burning in some counties, but this
did not include the area which suffered the worst from
wildfires last summer.

---

[80] www.theguardian.com/environment/2019/aug/15/anti
[81] www.theguardian.com/world/commentisfree/2019/mar/20/
eco-fascism-is-undergoing-a-revival-in-the-fetid-culture-of-the-
extreme-right
[82] https://www.theguardian.com/us-news/2019/nov/21/
wildfire-prescribed-burns-california-native-americans

Rhetoric like "humans are a virus" is the start of a slippery slope that leads very rapidly in the direction of eco-fascism. Another variation on this is the idea of overpopulation. It's true that, given the destruction of ecosystems, rising temperatures, rising sea levels, and so on, that we are likely to see famines and wars – but these will be caused by the unsustainable way of life of the richest 10% of people; not so much by overpopulation.

Indigenous responses

Indigenous activists and allies are rightly speaking out against the "New Deal for Nature" and eco-fascism. Not only are Indigenous lifeways more sustainable, but it has been shown that 80% of the biodiversity on Earth is in environments managed by Indigenous Peoples[83].

Indigenous Peoples are on the front lines of the battle with fossil fuel companies, mining companies, fracking, pipelines, and still struggling with the consequences of genocide, missing and murdered Indigenous women, residential schools, and being forced onto ever smaller parcels of land; but they are having a resurgence of their languages and cultures right now, and we should do everything we can to support them, both because of our shared humanity and because their way of life is the most sustainable and their knowledge of taking care of the Earth is important.

Sadly, over the last year or so, I have also seen Indigenous people having to argue with vegans online, who are

---

[83] https://blogs.scientificamerican.com/observations/
Indigenous-knowledge-can-help-solve-the-biodiversity-crisis/

persecuting them for hunting. The massive food insecurity in the Arctic and the North generally means it is necessary for the Inuit and other First Nations to hunt to supplement their diet; and it is not their respectful, traditional, sustainable hunting that is the problem, but the industrial-scale slaughter of wild animals that made them scarce in the first place.

Pagan responses to disasters

Over the last few years, I have observed an increase in Pagan responses to disaster that focus on community-building and community service; this is a heartening sign. It shows the strength of the Pagan community, and the increasing depth of our theology.

In the past, people have often responded to disasters with the idea that Mother Nature is getting tired of humans cluttering up the Earth. This idea is about as sensible as those right-wing Christians who claim that hurricanes and floods are caused by God wanting to smite the gays.

Instead, we have realised that compassion and community-building is the way forward and found uniquely Pagan ways to put that into practice. We have started to build the world we want to live in.

We need to emphasize the interconnectedness of everything – how pandemics emerge from the destruction of forests and habitats by industry and mining; how we and all other species are involved in a complex web of life, which we rupture at our peril; how we need to embrace Indigenous ways of thinking and being, and tread gently on the Earth. As we start a virtuous cycle of action, we will find that other unexpected benefits will emerge.

Let us choose social justice, climate justice, learning from Indigenous Peoples, and caring for Mother Earth. Resist increased surveillance and authoritarianism; promote science that emphasizes interconnectedness and a sense of wonder; keep building community.

Views of racism in the Pagan community

In the Pagan community, there is a wide spectrum of views about race and racism. I am proud that so many people in the Pagan community have stepped up to support Black Lives Matter, Indigenous rights, and migrant rights. But there are still people who just do not get it, who think that it's all "political correctness gone mad", who do not agree that there is a systemic problem in both the Pagan community and in our wider society.

We urgently need to engage with those who still cannot see the weight of oppression that is crushing minority communities, who cannot see the connection between oppression, poverty, and the sheer desperation that gives rise to crime in marginalised communities.

If you are one of the people who cannot see those connections, I recommend reading *Like Water* by T Thorn Coyle. As well as being a great insight into systemic racism, it is one of the most uplifting books I have ever read. It is an exploration of human nature and building loving and beloved community as much as an evocation of a life and the ripples of love and connection that someone leaves behind them.

I would also highly recommend reading *Bringing Race to the Table: Exploring Racism in the Pagan Community*, edited by Crystal Blanton, Taylor Ellwood, and Brandy Williams. It has chapters by several well-respected Pagan authors, exploring racism and responses to racism.

Understanding systemic racism

Understanding how systemic racism and oppression works is key to beginning the process of dismantling it, both on a personal level and on a societal level. We need to stop seeing a specific group of people as being of less worth than other people. We need to stop being frightened of people who dress differently, walk differently, or talk differently. Instead of trying to force people into a dehumanised mass of work units, we need to see every human being as having inherent worth and dignity.

I have written this section mainly from a white point of view. This is partly because I am white, but also because most People of Colour are fully aware of the effects of systemic racism and colonialism; it is usually white people who try to deny that it exists. People of colour are forced to do the work of resisting racism just to survive; it is long past time that white people started to dismantle our own privilege.

Christian supremacism

As Pagans, we need to examine the links between Christianity and white supremacism, between anti-Paganism and anti-Indigeneity. The strongest evidence that Christianity has been used to justify the theft of lands

occupied by non-Christians is the Doctrine of Terra
Nullius, also known as the Doctrine of Discovery [84].

The Doctrine of Discovery is the collective name for several
Papal Bulls issued in the 1400s. This pernicious doctrine
was used to justify the gradual takeover of Indigenous
lands, based on the alleged racial, cultural, and religious
superiority of Europeans and of Christianity. This is not
ancient history: the same view that was used to justify the
theft of Indigenous lands is used to justify the settler-
colonial states that continue to occupy those lands, and
commit genocidal acts against Indigenous Peoples.

Prior to the discovery of Turtle Island (North America),
Christian countries had already used a similar principle to
dispossess ancient Pagan peoples of their lands.

The entire Pagan population of Old Prussia was
slaughtered and replaced with Teutonic Knights and their
vassals. In some cases, they even claimed that the local
Christian population was still Pagan and used that as a
justification for stealing their land. This is known as the
Prussian Crusade [85]. During this crusade, the Teutonic
Knights led armies against the pagan Old Prussians,
crushing their language, their culture, and their pagan
religion. Polish Christian Kings had previously tried to
crush Old Prussian pagans, and invited the Teutonic
Knights to continue with the campaign in 1230. By the end

---

[84] The Assembly of First Nations, *Dismantling the Doctrine of
Discovery*, https://www.afn.ca/wp-
content/uploads/2018/02/18-01-22-Dismantling-the-Doctrine-
of-Discovery-EN.pdf
[85] https://en.wikipedia.org/wiki/Prussian_Crusade

of the 1200s, after quelling several uprisings, the Teutonic Knights had established control over Prussia, and attacked the Lithuanians and the Samogitians. Some Prussians took refuge in neighboring Lithuania.

Similarly, the Northern Crusades, also known as the Baltic Crusades, between 1198 and 1290, were the violent overthrow, colonization, and Christianization of the Baltic states [86] by Catholic kingdoms and military orders. They attacked the pagan Baltic, Finnic, and West Slavic peoples on the southern and eastern shores of the Baltic Sea, but they also attacked Orthodox Christian Slavs.

The military campaigns against the Baltic pagans were also authorized by a Papal Bull, *Non parum animus noster*, in 1171 or 1172.

So the Catholic Church already had a long tradition behind it of declaring an area to be available for colonization because it was occupied by Pagans, and this tradition was continued when they encountered the Indigenous Peoples of the "New World", Africa, and Australia.

Even after the Reformation, Protestants continued to use the Doctrine of Discovery as justification for taking over and colonizing the lands of non-Christian peoples. Several settler-colonial states have not repudiated the Doctrine of Discovery, nor endorsed the United Nations Declaration of the Rights of Indigenous Peoples [87] (UNDRIP). The Canadian government spent several years claiming that

---

[86] https://en.wikipedia.org/wiki/Northern_Crusades
[87] https://www.un.org/development/desa/Indigenouspeoples/declaration-on-the-rights-of-Indigenous-peoples.html

UNDRIP could not be incorporated into Canadian law, then claimed they would implement it in Canada, but they have produced a watered-down version of it.

In North America (Turtle Island), we are on the traditional territories of Indigenous Peoples, many of them unceded. Indigenous Peoples frequently did not receive payments or restitution for lands covered by treaties, and those treaties were almost all reneged upon by colonial governments.

The destructive exploitation of Indigenous lands by corporations and governments, and the prevalence of violence against Indigenous women, girls, and two-spirit people, is perpetuated by capitalism in the form of projects like the Coastal Gas Link and Trans Mountain pipelines. Many development projects have promised jobs and other economic benefits to Indigenous Peoples who have consented to them, but the promised benefits frequently did not materialize.

Indigenous Peoples have been in North America (Turtle Island) for thousands and thousands of years, and have unique and sacred relationships with the land, and the waters, and with Mother Earth. Lands managed by Indigenous Peoples have 80% of the biodiversity on Earth.

The aim of Indigenous protests, blockades, and strikes is to disrupt business-as-usual. That is what makes them effective. The small inconvenience caused by blockades and protests is negligible compared to the genocidal policies inflicted on Indigenous Peoples over the last 400 years. Other First Nations, environmental groups, land defenders,

Yvonne Aburrow

and other protesters have a right to protest in solidarity with them.

Missionaries

Another example of Christian supremacism is the efforts of the various Christian churches to convert people of other religions to their religion. The Orthodox Christians generally aim to preserve as much of the culture of converted peoples as they can. The policy of the Catholic Church has varied dramatically on the preservation of culture. The approach of Protestant missionaries has generally been to try to inculcate their converts with Western culture. (Honorable exceptions to this being the Unitarians, who did not send out missionaries, and the Quakers, who sought to strengthen and preserve Seneca culture.)

It is generally racist to assume that your faith and culture is better than someone else's faith and culture, and often these missionaries assumed that they were racially and culturally superior to their converts. The more destructive of culture, language, and sacred traditions these missionary efforts were (and are), the more they amount to cultural genocide.

When there were outbreaks of smallpox in Canada[88], the Jesuits inoculated converted Indigenous people, but those who had not converted to Christianity viewed the vaccinations with suspicion, so rather than trying to convince them, the Jesuits often just dismissed it as an act of God. The Hodinöhsö:ni' (the "Iroquois") and the Hurons

---

[88] www.thecanadianencyclopedia.ca/en/article/smallpox

often viewed baptism as some sort of sorcery that caused people's deaths, because the missionaries would baptize people just before they died.

Residential Schools / Indian Boarding Schools

Residential schools [89] (known as Indian Boarding Schools in the USA) were the continuation of cultural genocide by other means, and in both the USA and Canada, were sponsored by the state and run by the churches. These schools were also used to break the connection between Indigenous people and their cultures and languages in Scandinavia and Australia.

In Canada, the residential school system was at its height in the early 1930s, and there were 80 of these schools across Canada. The Roman Catholic Church ran 48 of them, the Anglican Church ran 20 of them, and the remaining ones were run by the United Churches. Prior to 1925, the Methodists and Presbyterians ran schools, but these became United Church schools when these two churches merged.

Indigenous children were forced to attend these schools and were dragged there by the Royal Canadian Mounted Police (RCMP). The painful history of the RCMP's role in the destruction of Indigenous cultures makes them particularly unsuited to any policing activities on Indigenous lands.

---

[89] www.thecanadianencyclopedia.ca/en/article/residential-schools

The residential schools were a deliberate attempt to force Indigenous children to forget their Indigenous language and culture, indoctrinate them with Christianity, and train them in industrial skills. Many of the children at these schools died of tuberculosis or malnutrition. The schools experimented on many of the children, and they were often sexually abused. In the USA, these schools were known as Indian Boarding Schools [90]. The social, cultural, and economic repercussions of this disastrous and monstrous attempt to destroy Indigenous cultures is still being felt. It is one of the reasons why there is such a shortage of Indigenous elders who can pass along Indigenous languages and cultures, and why many Indigenous languages are endangered.

Indigenous resurgence

Thankfully, Indigenous Peoples are currently engaged in a process of resurgence – reclaiming their lands, cultures, languages, and religious traditions. They have established powwows, cultural programs, language teaching, and protests to protect the lands and waters from pipelines, dams, and other destructive and exploitative projects. However, they still have control over only 0.2% of land in Canada, and they need much more than that in order to regain their sovereignty and independence.

Anti-Pagan, Anti-Indigenous

The forced conversion of Indigenous Peoples to Christianity, and the theft of their lands, was a direct continuation of the policy of exterminating Pagans and

---

[90] https://en.wikipedia.org/wiki/American_Indian_boarding_schools

stealing their lands that had existed in the 13th and 14th centuries, just prior to the European invasion of the Americas. Even today, many Christians still do not accept that Paganism is a valid religion, nor do they view Indigenous religions as valid. They are still sending missionaries to uncontacted tribes, often with disastrous results, as they risk infecting them with European diseases.

As Pagans, we should repudiate the Doctrine of Discovery or Terra Nullius, and we should support the efforts of Indigenous Peoples to get their land back. Find out whose land you live on [91] and acknowledge this in meaningful ways [92].

The creation of racial categories

The concept of 'whiteness' as a social category began as a justification for the transatlantic slave trade. The slave traders and their supporters tried to defend their utterly inhumane and indefensible actions by claiming that Africans were inferior, a different species or biological race, and did not fully count as persons. Similar arguments were used to deny Chinese people citizenship in America and Canada, or to justify the colonisation of large swathes of Africa and Asia, or the attempted extermination of Indigenous people in America, Canada, Australia, Africa, and elsewhere, and the widespread attempts to assimilate them by force.

When people from Ireland or Southern and Eastern Europe first moved to North America, they didn't count as white,

---

[91] https://native-land.ca/
[92] https://native-land.ca/territory-acknowledgement/

and were excluded from white privileges (such as being able to vote, being able to live where you wanted, get loans, and be treated fairly in the courts and prison system). Gradually, Jewish, Irish, Eastern European, and Southern European people have been assimilated into the category of 'white' and now mostly enjoy the same privileges as other 'white' people. This process of assimilation, and the accompanying sense of superiority, manifest destiny, and privilege is known as the construction of whiteness.

The systemic impoverishment and oppression of Black and Indigenous people in North America is well-documented. Ta-Nehisi Coates and others have written extensively and in detail about exactly how the system operates to keep People of Colour down. Black and Indigenous people are systematically discriminated against in housing, schooling, and employment, from preschool onwards. Black and Indigenous children are more likely to be suspended from school, punished more harshly for misdemeanours, and regarded as less innocent than white children. African American job candidates are less likely to be hired on the assumption that "they do drugs", and more likely to be arrested on suspicion of drug possession, despite the fact that white people take more drugs than Black people. Black and Indigenous people are more likely to be arrested and incarcerated, and more harshly treated by the system than white people.

Combine that with routinely giving guns to the police, and the authoritarian and white supremacist attitudes of many police officers, and it is hardly surprising that so many Black men and women are getting killed, just for "walking while Black". Even in the United Kingdom, where access to guns for the general population is far more restricted and the police do not routinely carry guns, more Black and minority ethnic people get arrested or stopped and searched than white people [93]. And there are still shootings of Black and minority ethnic people: Mark Duggan, Jean Charles de Menezes.

Many white people seemingly cannot understand the legitimate anger and frustration of Black people. Try to imagine being afraid just to walk down the street in case you get arrested and killed. Try to imagine being afraid just to send your son to school in case his walking out the door in the morning is the last time you see him alive. Try to imagine being turned down for employment just because of the colour of your skin. Try to imagine people asking where you are from, and not accepting the answer of a place in the same country, because you must be from somewhere else, right? Try to imagine being someone's token Black friend. Read about the experiences of Black people in being confronted with systemic racism, ingrained in the very institutions that we take for granted will treat us as equals. Read about the ways in which inequality was maintained and reinforced.

In the USA, such practices included segregation (where separate facilities were created for Black people and white people); redlining (made illegal in 1968, this was the practice of creating districts where only white people would get houses sold to them); sundowner towns (where Black people were not allowed to remain after dark); lynching (the hanging, and sometimes burning, of a Black

---

[93] http://www.bbc.co.uk/news/uk-24902389

person by a mob of white people); preventing Black people from registering to vote; and Jim Crow laws – the legal enforcement of these oppressive restrictions.

In Canada, segregation of Black people was not legally enforced, but there was racism towards Indigenous, Jewish, and Black people, and other ethnic minorities such as Eastern Europeans. The most shameful thing, however, was the treatment of Indigenous Peoples. John A Macdonald, a 19th century prime minister of Canada, encouraged the systematic starvation of thousands of Plains tribes; he also refused citizenship to Chinese immigrants. Indigenous people were forced to remain on their reservations, and their children were sent to residential schools to assimilate them. These schools were very brutal and inhumane, and the last one did not close until 1996.

In the UK, after England had colonised and brutalised Scotland, Wales, and Ireland, the English and Scots went on to colonise much of India and Africa and the Caribbean. The UK may have been the first country to make slavery illegal, but it was also the country that began the slave trade. Brutal repression followed, especially in Burma, Kenya, and much of India, where uprisings against the colonial regime were put down with vicious slaughter. Then, in the 1940s and 1950s, when immigration from the former colonies occurred in greater numbers than before, people started complaining about the influx of people from other cultures - despite the fact that many of them had fought in the Empire's wars and much of their wealth had been expropriated to Britain.

Similar stories can be told about the colonial exploits of other European countries. The amount of wealth acquired by Europeans from other parts of the world is staggering. In order to begin to face up to this horrific legacy and stop it from shaping how we relate to people of other cultures, we need to become aware of it, and make some sort of reparation for the brutality, genocide, and stolen resources.

We can derive some comfort from the fact that not every one of our ancestors subscribed to the racist and colonialist worldview, and many resisted it by helping the struggle against slavery, and supporting anti-colonial movements; but let's not use the decent people who tried to do something as an excuse to ignore or sugar-coat the atrocities. Nor should we be convinced that these liberation movements were led by white people; on the contrary, the first impetus towards freedom and resistance came from enslaved and colonised people. Instead, let us use their example and methods to inspire us to rise up against the oppression of People of Colour that is happening now.

One form of oppression that is happening now is institutional and systemic racism, which is the assumption by police and other authority figures that a Black person is more likely to be a criminal, that the expensive car they are driving must be stolen, that they are involved in a gang, or shoplifting, or that they have a gun or a knife.

The Macpherson Report[94] defines institutional racism as:

---

[94] The Macpherson Report was the report on the collective, institutional and systemic failure to respond adequately and fairly to the murder of Stephen Lawrence, a Black teenager.

The collective failure of an organisation to provide an appropriate and professional service to people because of their colour, culture, or ethnic origin. It can be seen or detected in processes, attitudes and behaviour which amount to discrimination through unwitting prejudice, ignorance, thoughtlessness and racist stereotyping which disadvantage minority ethnic people.

Systemic racism is a similar concept to institutional racism, but it occurs when the way a society is structured systematically ends up giving advantages to some and disadvantages to others. Individual racists are a problem, but it is when the system gives them a free pass to act out their violent supremacist views that we have a systemic problem.

The other aspect of racism experienced by People of Colour is the constant barrage of microaggressions - the ways in which white people act towards them which are driven by racist assumptions, but are not severe or overt enough to challenge - things like a woman clutching her handbag more tightly on the bus, or commenting on a Black person's hair, or making assumptions about how People of Colour live, or what they believe. If they only happened occasionally, microaggressions might be bearable, but a person of colour may have to endure hundreds of these slights every day.

---

https://www.gov.uk/government/uploads/system/uploads/attachment_data/file/277111/4262.pdf

Then there is the tendency of white people to downplay any racist incident, try to find another explanation other than racism for what happened, and to dismiss and belittle the hurt feelings of the person of colour who has experienced the incident. This is known as whitesplaining.

When I first encountered the concept of 'white tears', I thought it referred to white people crying tears of empathy at the suffering inflicted on Black people, but not actually doing anything to help dismantle systemic racism. I was really shocked when I found out that it refers to white people bursting into tears when a Black person tells them about the constant barrage of oppression they experience, because the white person is upset, not at the oppression, but at the thought that their Black friend actually really hates them. How utterly selfish.

There is another version of white tears, which refers to the use of bursting into tears as a weapon (usually used by white women) to get Black people (usually Black men) into trouble. There have been numerous documented instances of this, some of which led to lynchings. In at least one instance it led to the destruction of an entire Black village.

A related concept is white fragility, or the inability of white people to hear any criticism of their racist behaviour. I have experienced such moments myself, when I found another unexamined attitude lurking about in my subconscious, but you need to push past them and think 'this is not about me'. Sometimes this is hard. No-one wants to be thought of as a racist, because racists are bad and scary - but we must dismantle our own racist attitudes as part of the effort to dismantle systemic racism. Sometimes it is not obvious that an attitude you thought was positive and helpful is actually stereotyping and exoticizing People of Colour (like the idea that all Indigenous people are in touch with the Earth and Nature – how romantic, how noble, how instinctual... how stereotypical).

The roots of much of the inequality and oppression experienced by People of Colour can be traced back to the aggressive period of colonial expansion from the late sixteenth century to the mid twentieth century. We are still living with the consequences of that period of colonial expansion, and many colonialist attitudes are still entrenched in western culture. Some of the more egregious and disgusting examples, such as the 'doctrine of manifest destiny' (the idea that it was the destiny of white people to colonise and enslave Indigenous Peoples) or the 'white man's burden' (the idea that because white people were 'more civilised', it was their duty to civilise the other 'races'), have been largely withdrawn from, but their legacy persists. There are still people who go around claiming that white people are 'cleverer' than People of Colour, because we had an industrial revolution and they did not. The simple answer to that is, look at all the environmental destruction wreaked by industrialisation and rampant capitalism, and compare it with the way that Indigenous Peoples traditionally lived in sustainable ways, working with nature instead of against it. So which group is cleverer now?

Colonialism is, at root, the consequence of the process of primitive accumulation. This was based on the notion that land can be owned, and that resources are there to be plundered. This requires the reclassification of whole groups of people as 'less than', as resources to exploited, whether they are European peasants or enslaved and/or colonised populations. The logical next step is the expansion of humanity onto other planets - and that is worrying, because one can just imagine the negative attitude of some humans towards aliens.

But mineral resources here on Earth are finite and not renewable, so we will have to readjust the way we live so that it works within the parameters of what we have. That means the rapacious greed of capitalism and consumerism must stop, and people will need to learn to co-operate with each other and live sustainably. Environmental and social justice are intertwined: the adverse effects of climate change, which is occurring at a far more rapid rate than is natural because of the carbon emissions of industry, will affect more people in the third world, and in low-lying countries such as Bangladesh, than in Europe.

Because of the destructive impacts of racism, colonialism, consumerism, capitalism, and primitive accumulation on people and planet, we must address systemic racism, colonialism, and capitalism.

One way to do this is to become aware of the history of where you live. If you live on colonised land, find out the history of the people who lived there originally. Find out what they called the places, how they related to the land, how they lived, how they were displaced (if they were displaced). Find out about, and get involved in, the struggles of Indigenous people and People of Colour (Black Lives Matter, Idle No More, Standing Rock, Land Back, and related movements).

If you live in a country that colonised other countries, find out about the struggle for land rights in your country, and how colonialism shaped the history of your country. What resources were plundered from elsewhere to enrich your country? Were the poor and landless peasants displaced to colonised lands to make room for land grabs by the aristocracy?

If you have anthropomorphic depictions of deities, are they all white and/or blond and/or blue-eyed? Do you make a concerted effort to examine racist assumptions and challenge microaggressions? Would your group or coven be a safe place for a person of colour to be?

Check your assumptions and attitudes towards People of Colour. Do you regard them as "exotic" or "primitive"? Do you regard them as having a culture, but do not recognise that you are part of a culture? Do you assume that they are only "authentic" if they are living in the way their ancestors lived? Do you regard individuals as being somehow representative of their entire culture? Do you assume that they are the experts on some aspect of their culture (hairstyles, clothing, food, religion)? Conversely, do you assume that you know better than they do about their own culture?

Learn about other religions and cultures but try to avoid appropriating them or assuming that you are now an 'expert' on that culture.

Being anti-racist involves rooting out a lot of ingrained assumptions about culture, the concept of civilisation, individuality, othering, and stereotypes. It is more difficult than it first appears because we are embedded in a culture that constantly reinforces racist stereotypes.

It is not the responsibility of People of Colour to educate white people about racism and its effects. We need to work on educating ourselves. Fortunately, there are many excellent resources and support groups available, and many articles on the internet written by People of Colour explaining the effects of racism and colonialism on their lives.

Cultural appropriation

Cultural appropriation cannot be properly understood unless you look at it in the context of colonialism, power, money, exploitation, and capitalism. Although Pagan religions are not part of the dominant paradigm of Western culture (which is predominantly Christian with an overlay of Enlightenment rationalism and a big dollop of capitalism), and are often relegated by the dominant discourse to the realms of the "primitive" – white practitioners of Pagan religions still benefit from being members of the dominant social group much of the time. Cultural appropriation is usually done from the dominant position in any encounter between two cultures. So, if you are not in the dominant position in the encounter, it will be difficult to appropriate the culture of the other.

Ritual techniques and practices are not universal, and it is difficult to lift them from one context to another; doing so without consideration for their original meaning and context is disrespectful; and it is often a continuation of colonialism, capitalism, and commodification.

Here is a suggested list of what defines **cultural appropriation:**

- taking someone else's practice without permission or proper handing-on of the tradition and making money out of it (especially if the originators of the practice have a tradition of teaching it to people for free)

- taking someone else's practice and doing it in a completely different context where it does not fit

- taking someone else's rituals, practices, or stories and pretending they are your own

- taking someone else's ritual and then excluding them from it

doing someone else's practice and pretending that you are authorised by the people whose practice it is

- claiming a fake identity as an Indigenous practitioner

- doing others' spiritual practices and changing the meaning, and/or failing to build in the appropriate safeguards, and/or failing to acknowledge that you have changed the meaning in the new context

- failing to acknowledge the history of oppression suffered by the people whose practice is being copied

- doing something which has nothing to do with a culture and dressing it up and claiming it as part of that culture when you are not a member of that culture.

- all this adds to a culture that misrepresents ('noble savage' discourse for example) and mythologises Indigenous Peoples and makes their real struggles invisible

- wearing an item of clothing that expresses someone else's identity and sacred traditions as a fashion statement or a joke

In my view, cultural appropriation is a form or outgrowth of racism, because it continues the oppression and marginalisation of People of Colour.

It is an extension of colonialism. First the colonisers stole land and natural resources, and persecuted the colonised and enslaved, trying to prevent them from continuing with their cultural practices and lifeways; and then, having destroyed and commercialised our own cultural icons, their descendants plunder the remnants of Indigenous cultures for meaning. Obvious examples here are the destruction of Native American / First Nations culture, and the way that whites tried to prevent slaves from having any kind of family life by splitting them up.

It exoticizes other cultures, regarding them as inscrutable, mysterious, alluring, and barbaric. Take for example the Chinoiserie craze in 18th century England, or Orientalism in the late 19th century. Neither of those was particularly respectful towards the cultures being commodified; it was the exotic and strange that people were attracted to.

It commodifies other cultures, regarding them as a resource to be plundered, and a marketable product to be repackaged and sold.

It erases the complexity of other cultures. The idea that "all cultures are the same really" erases centuries, possibly millennia, of subtle and complex thought. Examples here include the Perennial Philosophy (the idea that all cultures have the same central core idea), and New Agers who make this claim. The idea that "yoga could have been discovered by anyone" erases the genuine achievement of Indians in inventing it (*not* discovering it). The idea that you can understand Eastern traditions well enough to teach their spiritual practices without proper study, and without learning about them in depth, is another manifestation of this erasure of complexity.

It trivialises other cultures. Dressing up in a bastardised version of someone else's sacred garb or painting your face in a parody of their skin tone, is offensive.

It is arrogant. It assumes that everyone has a right to everyone else's cultural forms. There is an idea floating around that all culture is public property, and everyone should have access to it. Several spiritual traditions with initiations and gradual revelation of mysteries beg to differ. And where one culture has a history of violently persecuting another culture, it is downright insulting to steal their rituals on top of that.

It rides roughshod over the feelings of People of Colour. It denies the agency and the feelings of oppressed and marginalised people. It says, "I don't care if this thing is sacred to you, I want it, so it's mine."

Many people do not understand what is and is not cultural appropriation because they assume that practices and techniques can be easily transplanted from one context to another, but this does not take into account the issues around the particularity of traditions to their culture, place, and history, and it does not recognise the impact of colonialism and the commodification and commercialisation of Indigenous traditions.

Take for example the practice of calling the quarters. This is based on several assumptions: that circular space is the most sacred; that there are four cardinal directions, and four elements with a meaning that is embedded in a particular cultural context (the Western Mystery Tradition, or of several Native American traditions), and that making a connection with the four elements and the four sacred directions helps you to become more connected to Nature, or the universe, because we are the microcosm of the universe (an idea found in Neo-Platonism, Kabbalah, and Swedenborgianism). If the practice of calling the quarters is transplanted to another tradition which does not have these assumptions, myths, and symbols, it will only be a shallow version of the practice, and will probably not even make sense in the context to which it has been transplanted.

People who charge money for the practices of others, without respect for their situatedness in a particular culture, history, tradition, and totally failing to notice the power relations involved in the colonialism of the very recent past, and the continued assertion by the West of the superiority of capitalism, consumerism, and the rationalist enlightenment is a big ethical issue. Spiritual traditions are not and cannot be divorced from context, and they are not automatically the property of all humanity. We need to approach other traditions with mindfulness and respect, and not assuming that everything is ours for the taking.

Spiritual traditions are rich with meaning, both mythological and historical, and taking a practice or a ritual out of the context within which it was created strips it of the rich associations that it had in its original context. If you take practices out of context, you are very likely to end up doing them superficially. Respectful engagement with other traditions requires a reasonably in-depth engagement with them, and a certain amount of immersion, not just a brief encounter.

However, say you have encountered a practice that really speaks to you, or that will significantly improve your health, and you want to borrow it respectfully. What should you do? Is it enough to ask someone who might be considered an authority in the tradition you want to borrow it from? The problem here is that there are many different people within a given tradition, and they do not all speak with one voice. So, what should be the criteria for whether a person can be considered the keeper of a tradition? Is it strength of belief? Is that they are a priest or recognised holy person? Many people would argue that the laity should have just as much say in the matter as the priesthood. Or should the criterion be the consensus view of many members of the tradition?

However, the construction of an argument around strength of belief as a possible criterion for being the keeper of a tradition, or the idea of a holy person as no more worthy than a secular person, is all grounded in a particularly Western and rationalist and Protestant view of how religion works. My argument has nothing to do with strength of belief, keepers of tradition, or any inherent ownership of ideas: it is about the historical and cultural context in which something arose, and (in the case of Native American spirituality in particular) the colonialist appropriation of ideas, artefacts, rituals, and the commodification of them. Cultures whose spiritual traditions have been appropriated are complaining about the commodification of their ideas, and the way they have been packaged and sold and marketed by fake gurus and shamans in the West.

A priest or shaman has been trained in the technique and the safeguards that go with it. Many popularisers of various meditation techniques forget to tell you the safeguards. The shaman or priest is steeped in the culture and the context and the meaning of the practice. A populariser (whether a lay person from the same culture, or someone from another culture) is not necessarily aware of the context, meaning, safeguards, etc. The people who don't want their practices taken out of context are not doing it to protect the practice as a commodity which they could package and sell – as far as most of them are concerned, their practices are not for sale. They are very likely to be trying to protect us from bad, shallow, and poorly understood versions of the practices. Because without the safeguards and correct techniques, and an understanding of the context, some practices are dangerous. The people doing the commodifying are the appropriators, who often want to make a fast buck out of repackaging the practice for a Western audience, usually stripped of its sacred context and meaning.

All of this does not mean that you can *never* borrow a practice or a ritual from another culture – but it does mean that shallow engagement with it is not enough. You need to examine whether the practice fits within your own tradition, by looking at the religious, spiritual, and cultural assumptions which have gone into its construction.

There have been many fruitful and successful moments of syncretisation of different traditions, and some failed ones. The most successful ones seem to be when the two traditions met as equals and engaged in genuine dialogue and exchange (as when Buddhism met Taoism and created Zen Buddhism, or when Buddhism met Shinto and created Ryobu Shinto). When an imperial and colonising tradition moved in, the Indigenous religion was often either crushed (like when Christianity met ancient paganisms) or subsumed (like when Buddhism and Eastern Orthodox Christianity met Indigenous religions).

Anyone studying the history of encounters between religions and cultures can easily see that cultures are not monolithic, intact, or impermeable. In fact, cultures are always exchanging ideas, inventions, material goods, books, food, recipes. There is clearly a lot of healthy and respectful cultural exchange. Therefore, I would make a distinction between cultural exchange and cultural appropriation.

Appropriation means claiming that you own something or have a right to it. Exchange means acknowledging that the other party owns it and offering something of equal worth in exchange. They are not synonymous. Exchange can be respectful. Appropriation is disrespectful. The trick is learning the difference. However, if a person from another culture says, hands off, you cannot access this without going through the proper process – then proceeding to take it without their approval is theft.

If the culture which you were born into goes around colonising other countries (both by conquest and via economic power) and you then come along and steal their spiritual traditions, despite them saying no: that makes you part of the colonisers.

If on the other hand you acknowledge them as the ones with expertise, and learn from them, and acknowledge their sovereignty, and they decide to give freely: that is respectful.

The key feature of cultural appropriation is the power differential. People forget that we are living in a postcolonial world, where non-European cultures are still routinely dismissed as "primitive", "backward", reactionary, and hidebound by tradition, and European culture is presented as the norm, and an ideal to live up to, despite its over-consumption, cycle of boom and bust, and exploitation of other parts of the world in order to maintain the expensive western lifestyle.

In countries with a majority white, western, Christian population, European cultural norms prevail. The rituals, clothing, and even hairstyles of other cultures are viewed as outside the norm, "exotic", and "primitive".

Being regarded as exotic makes the products of other cultures ripe for commodification and packaging up as a consumer good. Consider the late 18th century and early 19th century craze for Chinoiserie. Lots of people made a lot of money out of that one. But it did not help actual Chinese people trying to survive in Western culture – they were labelled strange, weird, foreign, the "Yellow Peril".

Being regarded as primitive makes the products of other cultures seem taboo. This means that countercultures within the European cultural sphere want to adopt them. However, whilst such countercultures have less economic and cultural leverage than the mainstream, they still have more leverage than the culture being borrowed from.

Either way, the economic power, social power, and cultural prestige of the European hegemony massively dominates the world in terms of what is seen as "normal". In the religious sphere, Christianity is seen as the norm, and everything else (including Pagan religions) is seen as exotic and/or primitive. In the economic sphere, capitalism and commodification are viewed as the norm, and other systems of exchange are viewed as exotic and/or primitive.

This situation creates a massive imbalance where the products of other cultures are trivialised, fetishized, and repackaged as consumer goods for the amusement of Europeans.

Consider the way in which Hallowe'en has been commercialised, commodified, and trivialised, and you can imagine how people from other cultures feel when their treasured traditions, clothing styles, and rituals are repackaged as consumer items.

"But I don't mind the commercialisation of Hallowe'en", I hear you cry. Fine – now imagine that it is on top of your land being taken away, your ancestors being enslaved and murdered, your economic, employment, and housing chances being severely limited by systemic racism – are you angry yet? (Oh wait, many of our pagan ancestors were forcibly converted, or killed for their beliefs – albeit a long time ago – so we ought to have empathy for peoples who have suffered the same oppression.)

So, if a person from another culture adopts a European practice or personal adornment style, they may be doing so in an attempt to gain some of the economic and cultural leverage that they lack; whereas if a European-ancestry person adopts a non-European practice or cultural adornment style, they may well be doing so because they want the "exotic" or "primitive" glamour conferred by it, which is why it is often disrespectful and erasing of the other culture, because it contributes to the "othering" of that culture.

This unequal power dynamic is why a white person painting their face black is considered inflammatory, whereas a black person painting their face white is not. In vaudeville theatre, the black-and-white minstrel shows presented a caricature of Black people which is deeply offensive.

In Morris dancing, the origins of black face paint may be because Morris dancing was originally an imitation of Moorish people brought back from the crusades; or it may be because the dancers wished to disguise themselves, and using soot to 'black up' their faces was effective as a disguise; or it may have been an imitation of miners and/or chimney sweeps, whose faces were black because of coal dust; or it may have been copied from vaudeville blackface; or it may have been a combination of all of these. It does seem likely that the introduction of black-and-white minstrel shows to England gave fresh impetus to Morris blackface. Therefore, many Morris sides have modified their face-paint so that it does not resemble vaudeville blackface quite as much; or they explain the miners / chimneysweeps / disguise theory before they begin their performance.

This unequal power dynamic does not mean that we can never do anything associated with another culture; it does mean that we should approach other cultures with sensitivity and tact, and if we are told to back off, we should back off.

I do not think that worshipping a deity from another culture is wrong – deities have migrated from one culture to another for millennia. I do think that it is disrespectful to take someone else's ritual to that deity, or any ritual, rip it out of its original cultural context, and plug it into your own cultural context without regard for the differences between the contexts.

The same applies to clothing styles, hairstyles, and artefacts which may have specific meanings and be associated with specific identities, especially if those identities have been crafted in resistance to European cultural hegemony, or are expressions of the sacred in a particular context. When the artefact, clothing, or hairstyle is ripped out of its context, the original meaning can be lost, diluted, trivialised, or erased. That does not mean you can never wear an item of clothing made by another culture, especially if it was sold to you by a member of that culture; but it does mean that you shouldn't wear their clothing as a costume, or as a caricature of their traditional style.

If there is no power differential between the appropriating culture and the appropriated one, then it is not cultural appropriation. If I start wearing a *dirndl* and practicing Austrian folk dancing, that's not cultural appropriation: my culture has not oppressed the Austrians or threatened to erase their existence or frequently belittled their beer-drinking and yodelling.

I read a great story recently where a guy moved to the Amazon rainforest, married the daughter of the tribe's healer, learnt their practices and traditions, and is going to be the next tribal healer. Now that is respectful engagement with a tradition.

Racists will try to tell you that anyone who does not have Viking or Celtic blood in their veins cannot do Norse or Celtic spirituality. Well, the Vikings intermarried with people of other cultures all the time, and the "Celts" (apart from being a label imposed by the Greeks) were a vast range of people from Galatia in Turkey, Galicia in Spain, Wales, Brittany, parts of Austria, and were united not by genetics but by shared culture, related languages, and similar art styles. So even based on what we know of history and lore, that claim is utterly spurious.

If the culture being revived or recreated or reconstructed is a "dead" culture, and there are people reviving it who are not genetic descendants of the people who created the original culture, that's not cultural appropriation. Culture has nothing to do with genetics. **Culture is transmitted through word of mouth, stories, practices, and being immersed in it; it is not transmitted genetically.** If I moved to another country and became immersed in their culture (or if I decided to become a Taoist), the fact that I am probably not closely genetically related to anyone from that culture is completely and utterly irrelevant.

The Romans oppressed the Indigenous people of Britain and assimilated their deities into a cultural fusion that we now refer to as Romano-British (and thereby preserved those deities' stories by writing them down). But both the ancient Britons and the ancient Romans are dead and gone, so we are not perpetuating that oppression by reconstructing Romano-British culture and religion.

If you go and live in another country, it behoves you to learn their customs and culture and stories and traditions, so you can appreciate their local culture and be a good guest. That is not cultural appropriation. "When in Rome, do as the Romans do", as the saying goes.

If a deity from another living culture calls to you, that's not cultural appropriation - but it is a good idea to seek advice from the people of that culture if it happens, especially if their religious tradition and access to their deities are 'closed' (i.e. only available through specific lineaged initiations). If you lift the rituals of that other culture out of context and offer them to the deity without fully understanding how they work and what they mean, then that would probably be cultural appropriation. You do not have to be genetically related to the culture that originally named the deity to work with or honour that deity. It helps if you can understand and relate to the deity's cultural context, but that has nothing to do with genetics.

Many people have taken the idea of cultural appropriation to mean that you can never do any practice that comes from another culture. That is not what cultural appropriation is about at all – but racists want you to believe that that is what it is about. They believe that each "race" is unique, has essential characteristics that are genetically transmitted, and that these characteristics are immutable – and that, in their view, is why people of Asian or African descent cannot participate in European spirituality. The racists also try to claim that the Native Americans told them to seek their own heritage, which somehow justifies their völkisch views. Yes, they told people of European cultural background to seek our own *cultural* heritage – I very much doubt that they meant that it was somehow genetically encoded in our DNA.

The view that you can only do the spirituality associated with your genetic background is clearly racist and deserves to be called out wherever it appears.

This also means that we need to be really clear about what cultural appropriation means, and to push back against people who claim (either sincerely or in order to derail a conversation about it) that cultural appropriation means no-one can ever do anything from another culture.

We also need to be clear about what "race" and racism are. Race is a social construct, but one that has been used to oppress people, and therefore it is a social construct with real effects. However, there is only one "race", the human race. Some people have tried to use the non-existence of separate races to deny the existence of racism, but that is clearly a specious argument.

If you engage respectfully with the other culture, seek to learn from it, make sure that you are learning from the real sources (or people who have learnt the practice from a genuine lineage or tradition) and not from somebody who has made up their own version of something and stuck an "exotic" label on it – then that is respectful engagement with another culture, and definitely to be encouraged.

What about cities where many different cultures come together and create a unique fusion of concepts? That is great – they are probably all on an equal footing in the city, and they can create vibrant and exciting fusions of ideas. And probably the original culture is flourishing perfectly well in its home environment, so everything will be just fine. This cultural fusion and exchange is how new cultural forms and traditions arise. But just because this kind of creative fusion exists and is good, does not mean that cultural appropriation is not an issue. In situations of cultural fusion and exchange, there is little or no power differential between the two cultures; there is probably no history of oppression (because they're probably both formerly colonised cultures); and there is no loss of meaning, but mutual enrichment. As to making money out of it, if both sides are making the same amount of money out of it, all will be well.

The blues is an interesting example – sometimes the performance of blues by people who aren't Black is respectful cultural exchange (e.g. when musicians from different backgrounds perform it together), and sometimes it is cultural appropriation (as when all-white radio stations would only play blues music performed by white musicians, and prior to that, the blues, and rock'n'roll, were dismissed and denigrated by white people).

It matters because if you accept the watered-down, stolen, distorted, or culturally appropriated version of the ritual or tradition as being somehow real, the meaning and value of the original and genuine practice is in danger of being lost, and it endangers the culture, and therefore the well-being, of the people whose ritual or practice or symbol it is.

Much recent research has shown that loss of cultural traditions and stories and language underlines and destroys traditional cultures. By eroding, erasing, and distorting those cultures' precious cultural heritage, cultural appropriation threatens the wellbeing of those cultures.

And it must be remembered that there is a long and continuing history of oppression which leaves painful emotional scars in the memory of the oppressed group.

Many people would like there to be a single easy-to-work-out formula to identify when something is cultural appropriation and when it is not. But I think you must do the work of examining each and every situation to work out whether it is cultural appropriation or respectful cultural exchange. You can use my suggested criteria to help you decide (is there a continuing history of oppression? is there still a difference in power between the two groups? is there a loss of meaning when the ritual or symbol is transplanted? is there financial exploitation involved?) but even then, there will be differences of opinion.

Homophobia, biphobia, transphobia

Unlearning homophobia, biphobia, and transphobia is another necessary process if we are to achieve full equality for LGBTQIA+ people.

There is systemic oppression of queer people, and this is compounded by other types of oppression. Queer People of Colour are much more likely to be attacked and killed. LGBTQIA+ people experience discrimination in housing, education, employment, the prison system, and healthcare. This particularly severely impacts transgender people, and queer disabled people.

Many types of witchcraft are inherently liberatory for queer people, but Wicca (with its focus on heterocentric symbolism) really needs to work at unlearning heterocentric and cis-centric attitudes. As with racism, there is a spectrum of different attitudes towards LGBTQIA+ people, ranging from heterocentric symbolism and rituals, all the way to full-on homophobic and transphobic violence. Very few witches are at the extreme end of the spectrum. Most Wiccans are welcoming to LGBTQIA+ people, but a bit baffled by ideas like transgender, cisgender, agender, genderqueer, non-binary, and so on, and tend to enjoy heterocentric rituals. Feri, Reclaiming, and folkloric witchcraft are much more inclusive and queerer by design.

There are numerous examples of how to adjust Wiccan ritual and symbolism to be more inclusive to LGBTQIA+ people throughout this book, and in my previous book, *All Acts of Love and Pleasure: inclusive Wicca.*

Adjusting your internalised social norms to be more welcoming and inclusive might start with examining your assumptions about gender and sexuality. Familiarise yourself with the terminology and concepts that other people use. Be aware of the specific oppressions that they may experience on account of their orientation or identity.

Examine your attitudes for heterocentric, homophobic, ciscentric, or transphobic views. One such trope that particularly irritates me is whenever a Christian bishop makes a pronouncement on LGBTQIA+ issues, someone is sure to mention that bishops are 'men in dresses'. Have they no idea how queerphobic that remark is?

If you are heterosexual, when did you first realise that you were attracted to the other sex? Did you ever wonder if you were not heterosexual?

If you are lesbian, gay, or bisexual, when did you realise that you were attracted to the same sex, or to both sexes? Was your coming-out a gradual process, or was there a moment that really stands out for you? Did you have to overcome internalised homophobia or biphobia?

If you are asexual or demisexual, when did you realise that you do not experience sexual attraction in the same way as other people? How do you experience romantic attraction, if at all? Did you have to overcome societal messages about how we must all experience sexual pleasure?

If you are transgender and/or genderqueer, how young were you when you first experienced feelings of being a different gender than the one you were assigned at birth? Was coming-out a gradual process or a big event?

If you are cisgender, have you ever considered how you grew into the gender identity you were assigned at birth? Were there moments when you felt that you had to suppress thoughts and feelings, or drop activities, that were deemed 'unmanly' or 'unfeminine'?

For many LGBTQIA+ people, internalised homophobia and transphobia can be an issue. It is hard, when society tells us we are too camp or butch or femme, not to internalise the criticism. The name-calling starts when we are children - sometimes before we ourselves are aware of our sexual orientation - and these barbs get embedded in the psyche. That is why tackling homophobic and transphobic bullying in schools is important.

Bisexual people (especially those of us in a monogamous relationship with a person of another sex) often feel 'not queer enough', and that our identity and existence is erased by both heterosexual people, and lesbians and gays. Fortunately, there are now well-organised bisexual activist groups, where we can affirm our bisexual identities.

Some pansexual people have criticised the concept of bisexuality for being 'too binary'. In my experience, bisexual people are mostly pansexual, and will happily date transgender and cisgender people and genderqueer people. It is just that when I first came out, the term pansexual had not yet been invented.

My preferred metaphor for gender is a scatterplot (not a spectrum). If a person's assigned gender is at one point on the graph but their actual gender is at a different point, then they need to express their actual gender, rather than their assigned gender. If another person's actual gender is at a point near their assigned gender, then that person is cisgender.

If we model gender as a spectrum, it suggests that male and female are at opposite ends of the spectrum, and supports the gender binary, hence positioning genderqueer, nonbinary, and gender fluid people somewhere on that spectrum, whereas they might be outside it. A line is a one-dimensional model. We have more dimensions available to us than that. Perhaps we could reimagine gender as a landscape [95], or an ocean [96].

Focusing on being your fabulous and unique self, and hanging out with other LGBTQIA+ people, is often the best cure for internalised homophobia and transphobia. Honouring queer deities and queer ancestors is also important in overcoming negativity.

Disability

The social model of disability describes how disabled people are chiefly disadvantaged by society's negative attitudes towards them, and failure to accommodate their needs. For instance, many architects add disabled access to buildings as an afterthought, rather than centering it in the design from the outset. Pathways, doors, and toilets are badly designed or inaccessible, and routes for disabled people are often blocked or inadequate. People organising events often fail to consider the needs of disabled people, particularly those who are neurodivergent.

As with other groups who experience oppression, the key here is listening and inclusion. What do disabled people need to be fully included in your event or activity? A motto of the disabled community is 'nothing about us without us', so when designing an event or ritual, it is best to

---

[95] https://dowsingfordivinity.com/2018/02/10/the-landscape-of-gender/
[96] Wrycrow, *Gender is an Ocean*, https://wrycrow.com/2019/02/14/gender-is-an-ocean/

include disabled people in the organising team from the outset.

Another aspect of the oppression of disabled people is negative attitudes towards disability. These can be particularly insidious in Pagan and New Age settings. Attitudes such as assuming that you could be cured by alternative medicine, or spending more time in Nature, are not helpful. These things might be helpful and therapeutic, but the disabled person may need their medication to manage chronic pain, and simply to stay alive. Another unhelpful idea is the assumption that the best kind of revolutionary activity is protesting in the street. But declining to participate in the culture of capitalism and consumerism by staying in bed can also be a revolutionary act.

Non-disabled people frequently harbour negative attitudes about disabled people unconsciously. The first step towards being inclusive of disabled people is to examine and dismantle these attitudes.

Misogyny and sexism

The repression of women has been going on, to a greater or lesser degree, for centuries. There have been occasional times when things started looking up for women, followed by a setback. Women in ancient Northern European societies (Norse and Celtic) had independence and respect. The arrival of Christianity was, in most respects, quite a setback for women, as it brought the patriarchal attitudes of the Romans with it. The age of chivalry and courtly love signalled the beginning of a change in attitudes, but things were pretty bad until the 14th century, when women could learn Latin, own their own property, and run their own businesses. This was probably because of the Black Death, which caused considerable improvements in the lot of the peasantry. Sadly, the Reformation, by removing the quasi-divine status of the Virgin Mary, destabilising property, and beginning the rise of capitalism and the acceleration of the process of primitive accumulation, caused a big setback for women's rights.

Things began to improve for women in the eighteenth century, with the publication of Mary Wollstonecraft's *A Vindication of the Rights of Woman*, and an increase in the number of women receiving a proper education. By the late nineteenth century, there were women preachers in dissenting churches, who became ministers in the early 20th century, there were women agitating for the vote, and there were campaigners for women's property rights. Women first learnt to organise as part of the anti-slavery movement (boycotting cotton and sugar from slave plantations) and many anti-slavery campaigners such as Frederick Douglass turned their attention to women's rights after emancipation from slavery.

The first wave of feminism focused on getting legal rights for women: the vote, the right to own property, the right to have a profession and an education.

The second wave of feminism was broadly about valuing women and qualities traditionally associated with femaleness, which had previously been undervalued or regarded as lesser. Many queer women protested the gender essentialism that this sometimes entailed.

The third wave of feminism is about the intersection of women's rights with other forms of oppression: race, class, sexual orientation, gender identity, disability. Some people have claimed that there is a fourth wave, but it seems to me to be talking about the same issues as the third wave.

Sadly, there is a misogynist backlash against feminism going on right now, with rape culture continuing to be promulgated, and young white men being given very light sentences for rape, and senior Republicans in the USA spouting horrible misogynistic and transphobic concepts.

Some women have ceased to identify as feminists, in part because of stereotypes about feminism promulgated in the media, and in part because of the gender essentialism and sex-negative attitudes of many prominent second-wave feminists.

There is also, sadly, a move to exclude trans women from feminism, which is sad and wrong, because they also experience misogyny and anti-femme attitudes. The problem in our society is not the devaluing of cisgender women, but the devaluing of all women and femme-presenting people, whether they are transgender, genderqueer, or cisgender. Therefore, transgender women should be included in feminism.

How can we ensure that we are not suffering from internalised misogyny and femme-phobia, or reinforcing ideas of toxic masculinity?

One way is to look at breaking down gender stereotypes; examine your assumptions that certain activities or movements or postures are 'unfeminine' or 'unmanly'. What does a positive expression of masculinity, femininity, or genderfluidity look like to you? Can you think of counterexamples that do not fit your ideas?

Try to come up with rituals where a person of any gender can have the role of a warrior, a healer, a hunter, a gatherer, and so on. Do not reinforce gender stereotypes with your choice of symbolism and mythology.

Why unlearn internalised oppression?

The reason we want to unlearn all these stereotypes and oppressive ideas is to help with transforming society to a place which will be welcoming, inclusive, and safe for everyone, not just for the privileged few. Everyone deserves to have their gender identity and expression supported, validated, and welcomed, whatever that looks like. Transforming society begins with each one of us being ready to change, and to challenge each other to do better.

Even those of us who are playing the game of life on one of the easier settings (bisexual genderqueer middle-class white woman with passing cis-het privilege, in my case), can benefit from the dismantling of systemic racism, misogyny, homophobia, and transphobia.

Straight white men (the lowest difficulty setting in the game of life), for example, would benefit from the removal of expectations that they will never burst into tears, always be able to do home improvements and fix the car, always be the breadwinner, and so on. They will no longer have to crush the feminine and sensual sides of their personalities.

White people could certainly benefit from dismantling white privilege and making reparations for the horrors of colonialism, slavery, segregation, and so on. We could stop being assholes.

The removal of systemic oppression would also mean that instead of having to spend huge amounts of their time resisting racism, misogyny, and homophobia, oppressed groups could engage in other activities like science and history and art. Many prominent Black activists gave up a career in science or the arts to focus full-time on campaigning for civil rights, for example.

Oppressed groups would obviously benefit from the dismantling of systemic oppression. Disabled people would benefit from having public spaces designed with them in mind from the outset, instead of regarding them as an afterthought and a 'burden'. Black people would be able to exist without constant microaggressions, risk of arrest or murder by police, and general reduction of their life chances through being denied jobs, equal treatment in education, and so on.

Discussion

Can you identify instances of systemic oppression of women, Black people, Indigenous Peoples, People of Colour, and LGBTQIA+ people that are not described in this chapter? How has systemic oppression impacted on your life or the lives of people you know?

Can you identify aspects of witchcraft, Wicca, and other Pagan traditions that exclude People of Colour and LGBTQIA+ people, or perpetuate gender and racial stereotypes? How can these be changed?

Exercises

Practice challenging racist, homophobic, transphobic, and misogynist remarks. There is an excellent workshop on civil courage from *United Against Racism*.[97]

Find out more about someone who inspires you - a suffragette, an anti-racist, an LGBTQIA+ activist. Build a small shrine to them in your house, and/or create a ritual about them. What can you learn from their example?

Create or find an image of a Black or queer deity. Add the image to your personal altar or shrine. Meditate on the deity. However, avoid deities from 'closed' systems like Lukumi and Voudun, as these deities have expressly communicated that they only want to be approached through the proper rituals and initiatory channels of these religions.

---

[97] http://www.inclusivewicca.org/p/leaflet-no.html and http://www.unitedagainstracism.org/archive/pages/info30.ht m

18. Evaluating your Craft

There is a great deal of discussion in every religion and spiritual tradition about what constitutes the core beliefs and practices of that tradition. Sometimes these discussions turn into violent persecutions of those who take a dissenting view from the majority. History is littered with examples of horrible tortures inflicted on heretics and dissenters. We do not want to go down that road again.

Religions consist of beliefs, practices, festivals, values, written texts, and oral lore. You cannot separate these from each other, nor claim that one is more authentic than the others. Religions are embedded and entangled in the culture and history of their locale. Cultures and religions influence each other, and it is often hard to say where culture ends and religion begins. Quite often, practices which come from a specific culture get entangled in a religion and validated by its practitioners, even though they did not originate with that religion, but pre-date it.

Every religion seems to bear the hallmarks of the time and place in which it originated. The Pagan Revival has more than a whiff of the swinging sixties about it, and some of the more negative aspects of that era too.

Gaining some historical and anthropological insight into the development of religions shows that religions do change and evolve over time, in response to social conditions, in the light of new information. Consider the changes wrought upon Christianity by the knowledge of evolution and the Higher Criticism. The awareness of evolution gave rise to a more liberal movement of Christians who tended to view their mythology as metaphorical more than literal; and the Higher Criticism (which was the application of the techniques of literary criticism and historiography to the Bible) made Christians realise that the Bible was not a book dictated by God, but a book written by people who were inspired to write by their encounters with the Divine. Alongside these more liberal tendencies within Christianity, there was also a rise in fundamentalism, which was started in the 1890s by people who felt threatened by the new knowledge and wanted a more literal Christianity.

There are also distinct tendencies within Wicca, although they have yet to crystallise out into separate sects or movements. There are those who prefer to stick to the heterocentric mores of the 1950s and 60s, and those who seek to expand their magical knowledge to include queer perspectives on sexuality and gender.

Given that Wicca and witchcraft are in flux, and always have been, and given that different people place different emphasis on what is important and a core part of the tradition, and what is not, how do we evaluate changes we wish to make to our practices to make sure that they are not merely whims caused by the ego's resistance to something which might actually be of spiritual benefit?

Many people appeal to tradition as the ultimate arbiter of these questions - either saying "you have to do this because it is traditional" or "you can't do that because it is not traditional". But the tradition only goes back as far as the 1950s, and we know full well that the founders of the tradition were flawed human beings influenced by the cultural milieu in which they grew up, and were not demigods from the far past. So, we can't necessarily rely on tradition as a guide to what is good.

What is tradition?

Tradition is something that grows and evolves. It is not set in stone, but is more like a discourse; if you start with a particular set of premises, ideas and values, you will get further ideas and practices that are consistent with the initial set of ideas. Religious traditions evolve according to social, cultural, and political circumstances. For example, a Catholic community in India had the tradition of having a procession in honour of the Virgin Mary. It was a special honour to carry a special flag in the procession, and to raise and lower the flag on a special flagpole. This meant that more people wanted to have the honour than could be accommodated by a single flag and a single raising of the flag. More flags were added to the procession, and more occasions of raising and lowering the flag were added, till over the years, the original custom was elaborated by considerable additional flags and flag-raising. There is an example of a tradition evolving.

Some people think that tradition is rigid and unchanging (or that it ought to be so), but this is not the case. Other people think that saying "because it's traditional" is sufficient reason for doing a thing. But because tradition evolves in response to circumstances, and because customs can sometimes be harmful, saying "because we've always done it that way" is not a sufficient reason for doing something. First, we need to consider why it was done that way in the first place. If the reason for doing it that way is still valid, then that is not a problem. But if there is a new group of people to be taken into consideration (who were not considered when the custom was first devised), then we may need to adapt or drop the custom to accommodate them.

Folklorists pay attention to the **transmission** and **context** of a tradition, as well as to its content. The means of transmission is also important in Pagan traditions. In Wicca, the validity of an initiation is important (it must be done by someone who is already initiated, and it must be done according to certain criteria).

In reconstructionist and polytheist traditions, many people derive the legitimacy of their practice from ancient texts about their religion, mythology, and deities. Before a new insight (an Unverified Personal Gnosis) can be more widely adopted by practitioners, it needs to be compared to textual evidence, and/or substantiated by comparison with insights from other contemporary practitioners. It then becomes a substantiated personal gnosis.

In Native American religions, the transmission and context of tradition is incredibly important. They argue that you cannot take their traditions out of the context of people, language, and land where they arose. When such traditions are taken out of context and borrowed indiscriminately, with little understanding of what they mean, it is cultural appropriation, which erases the identity of the keepers of the original tradition and can be actively harmful.

That is not to say that you can never adopt a tradition that does not relate to your ethnic background; it does mean that in order to be respectful towards that tradition, you need to study it in depth and respect its original sources and context. If it is possible to receive transmission of that tradition from one of its keepers, then so much the better.

However, if an aspect of the tradition that you have received is actively harmful, then it is legitimate to change it, in my view. An obvious example is the tradition of marriage. In the past, the definition of marriage included polygamy. Some people regarded this as injurious to the individuality of the additional wives, and so polygamy became widely frowned-upon. It also included a woman being required to marry a man who raped her; this was obviously harmful, so the practice has been discontinued in most cultures. Until the early 20th century, it was extremely difficult to obtain a divorce, which meant that many people were trapped within failed marriages; again, this was regarded as harmful, so marriage was redefined as something that could be terminated. In countries where same-sex marriage is unavailable, same-sex couples are harmed by their exclusion from the possibility of being married, so they want the law changed so they can get married. Some have argued that this is a redefinition of marriage; maybe it is, but marriage has been redefined many times before, and it is still popular. The story of the evolution of marriage shows that it is possible to modify a custom to include more people, or to reduce the harm that it may cause, without changing the basic features of the tradition.

In English, we use the word 'tradition' in two distinct ways. There is tradition in the sense of an entire set of practices, beliefs, and values – a cohesive **religious tradition**. Examples include the Wiccan tradition, the Mennonite tradition, and the Quaker tradition.

There is a tradition in the sense of **a traditional practice** or ritual, such as marriage, initiation, invocation, a Passover Seder, lighting lamps for Diwali, decorating a Christmas tree, and so on.

What is the function of tradition?

Traditional practices function to bring groups together by acting out their shared values, commemorating previous generations, acting out their mythology and stories, and reinforcing group identity. Examples include the Passover Seder – a beautiful and effective ritual for commemorating past generations, teaching the story of the Exodus from Egypt to future generations, reinforcing the identity and values of the group, and transmitting Jewish values and culture to the next generation.

Other traditional practices (such as marriage) function to make a connection between the individual and the tribe. When you get married, you affirm the relationship with your partner in front of your tribe (family and friends) and your deities or deity. When you undergo a rite of passage (e.g. Bat Mitzvah, Bar Mitzvah), you make the transition from child to adult, and your connection to your community or tribe is reaffirmed. When you get initiated into Wicca, you make the transition from uninitiated to initiated, and you become a full member of the Wiccan community.

Traditions that affirm identity and community can be a wonderful and life-affirming thing. They make us feel whole and loved and part of something bigger than ourselves.

Traditions can harm or heal

Some traditional practices are obviously harmful – examples include foot-binding, female genital mutilation, and so on. Other traditional practices are disputed, because they are regarded as harmful by one community, but helpful by another (e.g. male circumcision).

Other practices are widely regarded as desirable but may exclude some categories of people – the obvious example being marriage. I would argue that a traditional practice that excludes a whole category of people is broken, and needs to change to include that category, provided that making that change harms no-one. (Clearly, a child or an animal cannot meaningfully consent to marriage, so that rules out underage spouses and bestiality, because being forced into an arrangement to which you cannot consent is obviously harmful).

In my video on *Gender and Sexuality in Wicca* [98], I said, "If a tradition is broken, then it needs fixing". I was referring to harmful traditional practices, or practices that exclude entire categories of people, not to an entire religious tradition. However, if you equate a particular practice or set of practices with the whole of your tradition, or as the most important part of your tradition, and that set of practices excludes a whole category of people, then maybe your entire religious tradition *does* need re-examining.

In that video, I argued that certain traditional practices within Wicca, such as those that appear to value heterosexuality more than other sexual orientations, or that prevent LGBTQIA+ people from doing certain magical

---

[98] https://www.youtube.com/watch?v=b0ePZAFjUAY

activities together, harm LGBTQIA+ people by excluding us from those practices. They also fail to represent the lived reality of gender and sexual diversity, and they may be preventing everyone within Wicca from experiencing the full spectrum of magical possibilities available to us.

Why might traditions change?

Traditions evolve and change all the time in response to the changing needs of the community. This applies both to religious traditions as a whole, and to traditional practices within them.

If a traditional practice excludes a whole category of people because of their core identity, then surely that it needs to be expanded to include them. There is no need to abolish the practice for the people for whom it works. The obvious example here is Wiccan initiation. For most people, male / female initiation works just fine. If you are cisgender and heterosexual, there is no reason to change how you will be initiated. But what if a person is transgender? Should they be initiated by someone of the opposite gender identity to themselves, or someone of the opposite physical sex? Or should they be allowed to choose? What about genderqueer people? What about those who are exclusively attracted to members of the same sex? This depends on whether you think initiation depends on polarity, and what you think polarity is, and how you think it is created. Is it created by erotic attraction, biological characteristics, or other differences?

Dialogue with tradition

In Judaism, mitzvot (plural of mitzvah) are a ritual means of maintaining the Jewish person's covenant with God.

Halakhah is the Jewish law and discussions around it. This debate, and the texts produced from it, are known as midrash. Aggadah or Haggadah are stories from the scriptures, and midrash aggadah is the rabbinical discussion of the meaning and implications of these stories. It was agreed in the second century CE that all scriptural exegesis should promote a humane outcome and be decided on Earth. [99] The story goes that there was a group of rabbis debating a passage of scripture, and Rabbi Eliezer was so convinced that he was right that he sought the authority of the Divine to back him up. This was provided in the form of a heavenly voice (the Bat Qol) but the other rabbis pointed out that as the Torah is now an earthly document, it is up to people on Earth to interpret it.

A similar process happens in Islam: there are hadith (sayings of the Prophet, which have different categories), sunnah (traditional practices), and there is a strong tradition of discussion about the meanings and implications of these for Muslim life (a fatwa is a non-binding opinion given by an imam on a question of interpretation of Muslim law). The process of discussing and interpreting Islamic law is called fiqh.

So, in Judaism and Islam, discussions about the impact, meaning, interpretation, and implementation of the norms and practices of their tradition happen all the time, and their traditions evolve. In Christianity, such discussions often resulted in violent schism, persecution of heretics, and rigid enforcement of orthodoxy, though even there, traditions also evolved.

---

[99] www.myjewishlearning.com/article/bat-kol-a-divine-voice/

Pagans who have escaped from Christianity often regard discussions of tradition in much the same way. They regard tradition as set in stone, and any departure from it as a heresy (this usually means you are expected to start a whole new tradition). As the Wiccan community discusses our traditions more online, people are realizing that different lineages do things differently, and that is just fine.

What would a Wiccan dialogue with tradition look like? We do not have a single unified Book of Shadows; there are different Books in different lineages, and there are many different interpretations of the rituals and writings passed down to us by the early Wiccans. We are unlikely to end up with categories resembling mitzvot, midrash, haggadah, and halakhah, and I do not think we should try to do so. (It is probably worth mentioning that throughout this section, when I say Wicca, I mean initiatory Wicca; I am not excluding eclectic Wiccans, but much of this discussion is irrelevant to them.)

A first step in such a dialogue could be to discuss the purpose of Wiccan traditions. Traditions should be a joyful and life-enhancing thing, not something that makes people unhappy. It is generally agreed that the purpose of Wicca is to deepen the practitioner's relationship with Nature; another common goal is the discovery of the authentic self. You can probably find someone who disagrees with these goals in some way, but they are fairly widely accepted.

Given these goals, we can examine a traditional practice to see if it helps or hinders progress towards these goals. The relatively neutral question of whether a wand can be made of plastic can be decided according to these criteria. Plastic is a human-made material and has a very tenuous relationship with the natural world (being made from oil). Metals are also wrought by humans, but they are usually not hugely transformed from their natural state (even in the case of alloys). Another way of looking at a question like this is to ask whether the proposed innovation helps or hinders the creation of magic and mystery. I generally assume that magical energy can more easily be transmitted along wood or metal, because wood has a grain, and metal transmits electricity; whereas plastic has neither of these of these qualities.

Another uncontroversial example is how you sweep a circle before a ritual. The purpose of sweeping the space is to get rid of any negative vibes in the space (as well as any physical dirt on the floor). When I sweep a circle, I sweep all the dirt into the middle, and then sweep it out of the door, just as you do when you are sweeping the kitchen floor. Some people sweep only around the edge of the circle, which does not make sense to me.

When it comes to more controversial topics, such as the role and purpose of gender and sexuality in Wicca, we can apply the same criteria to discussions of what to change and how much to change it. Does the proposed change (e.g. not making everyone stand alternately male and female in circle) help or hinder our stated magical goals?

We know from numerous scientific studies that biological sex is not binary (there are many intersex conditions, and there is more than one biological marker that can be used to decide which biological sex someone is). We know from numerous sociological studies of past and present cultures that gender is not binary. That being the case, an insistence on a binary definition of gender in a Wiccan circle makes no sense in the context of a stated goal to deepen our relationship with Nature. It does not work in a magical sense, because it ignores the many different types of polarity that are available.

In Judaism, when a mitzvot does not fit a modern context, the rabbis work out a new interpretation of that mitzvot that works in the modern context. If something that made sense to someone in the 1950s, 1960s, or 1970s no longer makes sense to us in the light of new understandings, we are at liberty to come up with a new interpretation of the concept that encompasses the new understanding.

If we truly want to decolonize our practice, this means examining every part of it to check for assumptions that we have unwittingly imported from a Christian understanding of religious practice. Even if you came from an atheist background, you have probably picked up all sorts of assumptions about how religion works that are broadly based on a Christian set of assumptions.

It is worth noting that in ancient paganisms, a *haeresis* (from which we get the word heresy) was a school of thought. The word was morally neutral: it did not mean an erroneous school of thought, just a different school of thought. Similarly, in Hinduism, there are many different schools and approaches (Bhaktivedanta, Brahmo Samaj, Shaktiism, Shivaism, devotion to Vishnu, and many more). These can have sharp disagreements with each other, but they are all regarded as forms of Hinduism and viewed as being within the Hindhu dharma.

We can have a diversity of thought and practice within

initiatory Wicca (even within the same tradition of initiatory Wicca) without the need for creating schism and insisting that the variation in practice should result in a new tradition. It is noticeable that this schismatic tendency has happened the most in the USA. I think this is for two reasons. The first is that the USA was founded by a group of people with a rigid adherence to a specific orthodoxy (Puritanism) which has also resulted in many schisms over points of doctrine and practice. The second is that we are seeing a version of diaspora effect, where a group of people who practice a religion in a different culture than the one where that religion arose tend to be much more rigid in their interpretation of that religion's rules and norms.

Rather than dismissing others' interpretations of traditions as wrong or heretical, we should enter into a dialogue about the meaning of the tradition or text, and how it can best be expanded or modified, both to ensure that the goal of these traditional practices is fulfilled, and to ensure that it includes people who might otherwise be excluded by it.

What are valid criteria for changing a traditional practice?

If the traditional practice is actively harmful to a large group of people (examples include child marriage, genital mutilation, and foot binding) either physically or psychologically, then it needs to be modified or abolished.

If the traditional practice excludes a category of people because of their innate characteristics (e.g. not allowing same-sex couples to get married, or refusing Wiccan initiation to people with a disability), then it needs to be expanded to include that category, provided that it does not harm anyone else.

If the traditional practice affirms the identity of your group at the expense of making derogatory claims about other groups, then it needs to be changed so that it is not derogatory towards the identity of another group. An example might be a Christian affirmation that they are 'not like the heathen', or that they renounce 'wicked idolatry'. The Vatican officially dropped a part of the Catholic liturgy that said something rude about the Jews, for example.

If it is claimed that the traditional practice excludes a category of people because of an acquired characteristic that is not part of their core identity, then we need to think a bit harder about modifying it. For example, I would argue strongly that the Wiccan practice of working skyclad is empowering and life-affirming and enhances group trust, but some people claim that it is harmful for people who have been raped or molested. I would certainly not want to add to their trauma by insisting that they work skyclad, but I would want to encourage them to work towards a state of trust and self-confidence where they felt able to work skyclad.

What are valid criteria for retaining a practice unchanged?

Is the practice life-affirming? Does everyone in your group or religious tradition feel included in it? Does it affirm the core identity of everyone in your group? Does it express and affirm the core values of your group or religious tradition? Does it help to transmit your values, beliefs, stories, and identity to new members of the group? Does it accurately describe a key magical or cosmological concept or experience? Does it help rather than harm? If the answer to all or most of these questions is yes, then congratulations, you have a worthwhile traditional practice.

Does it work? Does it get you nearer your goal?

What other criteria can we use? The most obvious criterion would be whether the practice works or not, and whether it is harmful or helpful. If it does not work for you, can you tweak something to make it work, either in yourself or in the practice? What is causing it not to work? If it is harming you in some way, then what are the barriers (in the practice or in yourself) that are making it harmful to you? If they cannot be overcome, then just stop doing the practice. For example, some of the stretchier yoga exercises may be contraindicated for people with Ehlers-Danlos Syndrome. Some people find the idea of nudity and scourging so triggering that they cannot overcome their aversion to them. Such people will clearly need to find a coven that will accommodate their preferences and prior experiences. It may be that they would benefit from overcoming their aversion to the practice - but it is up to them to decide when and how they will do that.

Another way to evaluate a practice would be to measure it against the goal of your tradition. For instance, one of the stated goals of Wicca is to feel connected to Nature. Does the practice help you to feel more connected to Nature? If it does not, and it makes you feel excluded, and it is because of the way the practice is framed, can the concept behind the practice be changed or expanded to include you?

My personal goal as a witch is to be the best witch that I

can be, which includes physical, spiritual, mental, and psychic excellence. There are many things that I am *not* excellent at (like keeping my house tidy, or doing a daily practice), so clearly this is an ideal rather than the reality, but it is good to have a goal to work towards.

When I choose a spiritual practice, or design a ritual, I do so in the hope that it will create *eudaimonia* or flourishing among the participants and empower people to grow and develop. To reach our goal of connectedness with Nature (the community of other-than-human persons), we will need to create good ritual, and good traditions that provide a foundation of healing and safety and well-being to participants. That does not necessarily mean harking back to what was done five hundred years ago, or even fifty years ago. The rituals of the past were needed and healing and transformative then and may still be valuable in many ways. If the rituals still work to connect people with something greater than themselves, then there is no need to change them. But if for some reason they fail to fulfil that purpose, then we need to look at why that is, and fix it.

Tradition is a vehicle or a container for transmitting what worked in the past, in the hope and expectation that it will continue to work and be valuable in the future. But it must live and breathe and grow if it is to continue to be valuable.

Tradition is valuable as a way to pass on techniques and concepts and stories and values - but it is for the sake of the ideas being passed on that we maintain the tradition, not for the sake of doing it that way because we have always done it that way.

A living tradition is a coherent and cohesive system, like a living organism, or a complex ecosystem, or a beautiful clock. Tolkien once compared the Catholic Church to a great old tree growing through time, with curiously shaped branches due to particular historical accidents; and he compared the Reformation to an attempt to chop down that tree and plant a sapling in its stead. But a big old gnarly tree could certainly do with a bit of pruning, and if we want the sapling of the witchcraft revival to grow into venerable trees, we might need to do a bit of judicious pruning.

What is the core mystery?

Some people have claimed that the central mystery of Wicca is heterosexual love, or "fertility" (a much-misused word), or even polarity. I think the point of a mystery is that it is ineffable, and each person experiences it in their own way.

I think that the central mystery of the Craft is love, in all its forms. The love of lover and beloved; the love of friends; the love of kin; love towards all beings, including animals and birds and plants. And I think the ultimate polarity is spirit and matter, and that the purpose of the Great Work is to bring more spirit into matter; to bring spirit and matter into ever greater union. All acts of love and pleasure are rituals that work towards this ultimate union (represented in Judaism by the union of Yahweh and the Shekhinah, and in Hinduism by the union of Shiva and Shakti).

And that, for me, is why my Craft must be inclusive of all sexual orientations and not merely focused on heterosexual love: because "all acts of love and pleasure are Her rituals", and if we do not celebrate love in all its forms, then the

Great Work of uniting spirit and matter ever more closely cannot be attained.

Discussion

What is the function and purpose of tradition?

What is the goal of your inner work?

What are the core aspects and practices of your tradition? How are they helpful? Is there a group of people who feel excluded by these practices?

Do your rituals and practices help or hinder your progress towards your goal?

Exercises

Meditate on your tradition in the form of a tree. Where are its roots? How has it grown? What are its fruits? Does it need pruning?

Draw a mandala or a mindmap representing your tradition, putting in the key aspects and practices and values.

19. What is a witch?

The marks of the witch are vitality and wildness, joyful celebration of life, connection with Nature, and liberation from oppression.

The deities of the witches are rebels and liminal figures, living on the margins, out in the wildwood, rebelling against authority: Lucifer, Aradia, Pan, Herne the Hunter, Hecate, Diana. They bring visions and dreams, ecstatic communion with the depths, the release of orgasm, the cry of the wild curlew.

The animals and birds beloved by witches are often seen as sinister by 'civilised' people: the frog, the toad, the bat, the hare, the owl, the cat. These are our familiars and our friends.

We are rooted in place and in the land. We are the friends of the twisted hawthorn tree, the mysterious sacred spring, the forgotten shrine, and the standing stone. We listen to the sighing of the rivers, the whispers of the trees, and the subtle signs of the mountains.

We descend into the depths of the underworld, returning with hidden knowledge; we commune with the ancestors and the dead; we ride out with the wild hunt and the faery rade into the outermost reaches of the sky. We fly to the Sabbat along the spirit paths, illuminated by the light of the Moon, which alchemically transforms everything to silver, the metal of the Moon.

We deal in herbs and have knowledge of healing, but also know how to bring down the oppressors and drag them from their places of power. We have the secret knowledge of controlling the wind by means of knots. We sail in a sieve across the stormiest seas and can make a boat from a discarded eggshell.

We are your fever-dreams of sexual orgies; we are the moment of climax. We are the salt that gives flavour to everything; we are the bearers of light. We are at home in the dark forest and the high wild moorland; we dwell in the liminal places, in the last house in the village, at the promontory and the water's edge.

We come in many shapes and colours, short and tall, dark and pale, willowy and plump, earthy and ethereal, swift and steady. The witch may be known by the flint that strikes the spark of divinity in the inmost core of the soul, and not by any outward sign or mark.

We are the guests at the mystic marriage of darkness and light. We are power contained and power released; we are the wielders of the energy of the pentacle. We are the iron in the soul and the fire in the blood. We are the grain of sand, the irritant in the oyster that makes the pearl.

We are our Craft and the secret matter of our Art. We are the *prima materia*, the basis of the Work, the lead, metal of Saturn, lord of time and death, that we shall transform into gold, the metal of the Sun.

We are the queer ones, who move between the worlds, walking the hidden ways, shaping reality, bending normality, weaving spells and visions. We are full of life, full of song, full of magic.

We are the ones who whisper spells and cantrips, enchantments and charms. We are the dreamers of a new day, those who carefully construct snares and nets for the oppressors. Like the keepers of a secret flame, we have fed and tended the dream of freedom.

We have always been with you, the hidden children of the Goddess. The goddess who comforts the oppressed, the mother of Earth who gives abundance and blessing and milk and honey; the Moon who sheds her healing tears upon the Earth; the secret teacher of the magic arts.

We are the witches.

Appendix I: Model guidelines for group discussion

These are presented as a template or resource for your own use, and can be used for face-to-face groups, or online. They were developed by the Inclusive Wicca Discussion Group.

Get participants to suggest their own guidelines and write them up on a flipchart. If they omit any items from this list, you can suggest them. That way, people feel that they own the guidelines.

When using them online, it is better to post the core guidelines and then ask if anyone wants to add anything.

The guidelines

Focus on arguments, not people (no *ad hominem* attacks)

Address others respectfully

Avoid stereotyping of other groups

Do not discriminate or be judgemental

There are no "stupid" questions or answers

Assume good faith by participants in discussions

Do not assume that you know what someone else means by what they have written / said

New members are encouraged to contribute

Keep it confidential who said what

Do not reveal personal information outside the group

Appendix II: A coming out ritual

A few years ago, someone asked, why isn't there a Pagan coming-out ritual? When do straight people come out as straight? Maybe one day in the future, when people do not assume that you are straight by default, there will be either be coming-out rituals for everyone, or no need of a coming-out ritual. There ought to be a coming-of-age ritual, though.

There have been criticisms of the notion of coming-out, both in terms of the notion of "out" — perhaps we're coming into being visible, instead of out of being hidden — and in terms of the notion of a closet, in that being closeted as a way to avoid stigma is becoming unnecessary in most social contexts.

A coming-out ritual

The circle or sacred space is opened in the appropriate manner for the tradition celebrating. If quarters are called, then they are addressed in a non-gender-binary way, e.g. Mighty Ones of the [direction], Powers of the [element]. All those gathered to celebrate bring a scarf. Preferably red, orange, yellow, green, blue, indigo, violet. The one who has recently come out as LGBTQIA wears a cloak and a veil.

Celebrant 1: Today we have gathered to celebrate the coming out of [name] as [identity]. (1)

> He/she/they (2) has/have been hidden,
> like a bulb hidden in the earth, waiting to put forth
> the first green shoots in Spring.
> He/she/they has/have been hidden, like a bud
> waiting for the first rays of the Sun to open.
> He/she/they has/have been hidden, like a shy

animal in their burrow,
Waiting for the dusk to emerge and explore.
He/she/they has/have been hidden,
Like a butterfly in the chrysalis,
Waiting for the right time to emerge.

Celebrant 2:   But now [name] has come out,
And emerges into the world like a bulb putting
forth a green shoot,
Like a flower opening to the sun,
Like an animal emerging from the burrow,
Like a butterfly emerging from the chrysalis!
Come out, [name], and be welcome in your full
glory.

All: Come out! Come out! Come out!

*(The outcomer now emerges from the cloak and the veil,
and steps forward)*

All: Hail and welcome!

*(Each person now steps forward and places a coloured scarf
around the outcomer's neck, either offering their own personal
blessing, or saying "I welcome you in your full glory as a
[lesbian/gay/bisexual/transgender/intersex/asexual/other] (3)
person, and celebrate your unique beauty and strength")*

Celebrant 1:   By coming out of the closet, you have come
into the queer community.

All: Welcome in!

Celebrant 2:   By coming out of the closet, you have come
into the Pagan (4) community. Paganism encourages
us to find our true and authentic self, and to be that

Yvonne Aburrow

to the best of our ability. By coming out as
[identity], you have revealed more of your true self,
both to yourself and to others.

Celebrant 1: There are as many ways to be queer as there
are queer people, but we now present to you ten
queer archetypes (5), who may help you and guide
you on your way.

The Catalyst: I am the catalytic transformer.
(Lights a flame)
I bring change.
I hunger and thirst for social justice.
I light the fire in the human heart,
The fire that rages against injustice,
The flame that burns bright to herald a new dawn.

The Mirror: I am a mirror, presenting an inverted image
to society.
(Holds up a mirror)
I am the Molly and the Drag Queen.
I am the one who queers everything.
I comfort the afflicted and afflict the comfortable.
I overthrow power structures with my parodies.

The Shaman: I am the queer shaman, (beats drum)
The consciousness scout.
I find the way between the worlds,
I travel the roads of the dead.
I am a child of the Moon,
A devotee of her mysteries.

The Trickster: I am the Trickster,

(presents the outcomer with a flower)
The eternally playful one.
I am Peter Pan, always youthful.
My tricks expand your consciousness,
My dreams bring sparkle to the world.

The Beautiful One: I am the keeper and maker of beauty,
(sprinkles glitter)
Making music, and art, and sacred drama.
I am the queer eye, discerning beauty wherever it roves.
I am the one who makes all things beautiful.

The Caregiver: I am the one who cares,
(Caresses the outcomer)
For the suffering, the lost, and the outcast.
I bring joy to those who are on the edge,
Lost in the liminal spaces.

The Mystic: I am the mystic one,
(holds wand/thyrsis/caduceus)
The in-between one,
The shaman, the traveller between the worlds.
I travel between the seen and the unseen,
I mediate between the worlds of flesh and spirit.

The Consecrated One: My sexuality is holy,
(sprinkles blessed water or mead)
My being is holy, and I stand before the divine ones,
And lead the people towards the union of matter and
spirit.

The Androgyne: I am the Divine Androgyne,

(holds wand and chalice in each hand)
Including and transcending all genders.
I am change, and I am growth.
I am space and time.
I am spirit and matter.
I am the inbreath and the outbreath.

The Gatekeeper: I am the gatekeeper, (makes gesture of opening doors)
Who stands at the door of the sacred realm,
Welcoming all who come to enter the portal,
The door to the unseen realms.
I welcome you to the place between the worlds.

All: Hail and welcome, [name of outcomer]

(The ritual is concluded with cakes & wine, mead, an eisteddfod, or whatever the closing appropriate to the tradition.)

Notes

(1) replace with lesbian, gay, bisexual, transgender, queer, intersex, asexual, or other, as appropriate

(2) use the pronoun of the outcomer here

(3) delete as appropriate

(4) use Heathen, Druid, Wiccan, polytheist, Feri, etc if preferred

(5) http://www.tommoon.net/articles/spiritmatters4.html

Appendix III:
Rite of farewell (for leaving a coven)

I wrote this ritual more than a decade ago, so I cannot remember if we used it in this exact form, but I think it is important to have rituals to mark changes in your group. Just as you welcome new people with initiations and other commitment ceremonies, it makes sense to offer some sort of closure when they leave.

Start with brief explanation of reasons for leaving & reactions from those remaining.

Set up the circle in the usual way for your tradition.

Each covener charges a pebble or other gift with blessings for the leaver.

The leaver stands before the altar and says:

> Farewell. I go to follow the path of the Hedge Witch / Hearth Fire / [name of the other coven]

(Hedge Witch if working solitary; Hearth Fire if not planning to practice the Craft; name of other coven if joining another coven; if this is a temporary absence, add "for a while")

The leaver stands before the temple guardian(s) and says:

> Hail and Farewell.

The leaver stands before the coven and says:

> I will not be walking by the same path as you,
> but I will be travelling on the same journey.

I pledge not to reveal the secrets of this coven, [coven name],
and always to honour the divine in each one of you.
Farewell.

The coveners respond, one by one, giving their pebble/gift and personal words of blessing to the leaver:

I pledge to honour and comfort you,
and to help you on your path.
I honour the divine within you. Farewell.

The leaver consecrates a cup of wine and addresses either the gods of the Craft or the patron deities of the coven:

Lady of the Moon, Horned One,
what I do now and henceforth is in your honour.
May I be granted the inner peace and knowledge
that is the measure of one who follows you.
Though I am moving to a different path,
I know that you are with me.

The leaver drinks from the cup and turns to the coven:

I pledge this cup to you all in token of Farewell.

All drink from the cup. All coveners say:

Farewell, and blessings on your journey.

Appendix IV: Witchcraft Traditions

When Gerald Gardner (or one of the New Forest Coven) coined the term "the Wica" (originally spelt with one c), it seems to have been intended to refer to all witches [100]. Subsequently, the term has come to be used by some people to mean only witches initiated into Gardnerian and Alexandrian Wicca, and has been used by others to mean anybody who identifies as Wiccan, and a whole spectrum of meanings between those two terms. This can make it confusing for people to understand what is meant by any individual using the term Wicca.

In an attempt to clear up the confusion, Gardnerians and Alexandrians in North America (by which they mean anyone who can trace their initiatory lineage back to Gardner or Sanders respectively) have started referring to themselves as "British Traditional Wicca". This seems to have happened in part because there are so many other traditions which are called Wiccan, but who cannot necessarily trace their lineage back to Gardner or Sanders. The term "British Traditional Wicca" has not been widely adopted in Britain, where there are fewer variant traditions of Wicca. In Britain, people generally refer to Gardnerian and Alexandrian Wicca as "initiatory Wicca" but even this term is misleading, as there are other witches with a

---

[100] Yvonne Aburrow (2015), *Wicca: History, Belief, and Community.* (An interview with Ethan Doyle White, author of *Wicca: History, Belief, and Community in Modern Pagan Witchcraft.*) http://dowsingfordivinity.wordpress.com/2015/09/wicca-history-belief-and-community/

lineage and initiations who identify as Wiccan in the UK. The terminology remains fluid and confusing.

There is a major distinction between folkloric witchcraft traditions and Wiccan traditions. Folkloric witchcraft does not identify as Wiccan; it tends to be happy to explore Luciferian and Christian mysteries alongside Pagan mysteries. Wiccans tend to focus on the Horned God and the Moon Goddess, and do not use the term "the Devil". Wiccan covens are usually led by a high priestess and a high priest. Folkloric witchcraft covens generally have a Magister and a Maid. Therefore, I have indicated in this list whether a tradition is witchcraft or Wicca.

Please do not be offended if I have not included your tradition in this list. There are so many traditions of witchcraft that it is difficult to list them all. I have listed the traditions in this appendix in alphabetical order, so as not to imply a hierarchy. Some of the traditions in this section are listed because they have similar names to each other, and this can cause confusion. There is a partial list on Wikipedia of some of the larger Wiccan traditions.

https://en.wikipedia.org/wiki/Category:Wiccan_traditions
https://en.wikipedia.org/wiki/Wicca

1734 witchcraft
The 1734 tradition was founded by Joe Wilson after a lengthy correspondence with Robert Cochrane, founder of the Clan of Tubal Cain. It is a folkloric craft tradition. It often uses riddles to convey its mysteries.

http://www.1734.com/
http://1734-witchcraft.org/

Alexandrian Wicca

Alexandrian Wicca was founded by Alex Sanders in the 1960s. Sanders was initiated into Gardnerian Wicca, though whether he got second degree or not is disputed. It tends to include more ideas from ceremonial magic than Gardnerian Craft. In the UK and Europe, Gardnerian and Alexandrian initiates may visit each other's circles without the need for re-initiation.

Clan of Tubal Cain

A folkloric witchcraft tradition. The Clan are the lineage bearers of the Robert Cochrane tradition through Evan John Jones. The Clan is also known as the People of Goda. They are a closed Initiatory group aligned to the Shadow Mysteries within the Luciferian stream dedicated to experiential gnosis. The sacred tenets of the Clan of Tubal Cain are Truth, Love and Beauty.

https://clantubalcain.com
http://www.clanoftubalcain.com

Dianic Wicca

A feminist and women-centred form of Wicca founded by Z Budapest in 1971. Men are not included in this form of witchcraft, and it generally excludes transgender women from its circles as well. Dianic Wiccans are generally Goddess monotheists, honouring the Goddess as the source of all life.

Feri Tradition

A form of American Traditional Witchcraft derived from the teachings of Victor and Cora Anderson and passed down through their various initiates. Feri seeks to transform the individual through practices of ritual magic, meditation, and energy work. The influences of the tradition include Huna, Conjure, Voodoo, Tantra, Celtic folklore, Christian mysticism, Yezidi mythology, and Greek gnosis. The Feri Tradition split into two strands: one believes that the mysteries can only be taught in small experiential and initiatory groups; the other believes that witchcraft can be taught through classes in larger groups. The main point of contention in the split was the issue of charging money for training.

https://andersonfaery.org
http://faerytradition.org
http://www.feritradition.org

Gardnerian Wicca
Gardnerian Wicca was founded by Gerald Gardner in the early 1950s and traces its roots back to the New Forest Coven which included Dafo, Mother Sabine, and the Mason family. Much of its early liturgy was written by Doreen Valiente. There are numerous lineages within Gardnerian Wicca, with considerable variation in ethos between them. The emphasis of Gardnerian Wicca tends to be less ceremonial than Alexandrian Wicca.

http://british-wicca.com

Georgian Wicca
The Georgian Tradition was founded in 1970 by George (Pat) Patterson, Zanoni Silverknife, and Tanith. It began as a small coven in Pat's home in Bakersfield, CA. Pat received early teachings from members of a Celtic coven in Boston. In 1970, Pat began a magickal calling that resulted in Zanoni and Tanith finding him and helping to found the Georgian tradition. There are known Georgian covens in

British Columbia, California, Florida, Oregon, Colorado, Maryland, Michigan, Washington and Oklahoma.

http://georgianwicca.com

The inclusive Wicca tendency

The inclusive Wicca tendency (small i) is not a separate tradition but a tendency within existing traditions. Any Wiccan may identify as inclusive and work to make their practice more inclusive of LGBTQIA+ people, disabled people, and of Black people, Indigenous people, and People of Colour. An inclusive approach to Wicca encompasses eco-spirituality, science, attitudes to truth, the sacred, sexuality, consent culture, group dynamics, coven leadership, ritual, ethics, and Wiccan theology and practice, tradition, and magic, and how these concepts can be explored as part of a liberal religious approach to Wicca.

www.inclusivewicca.org

Inclusive Wicca Tradition (Australia)

Inclusive Wicca was founded by Amethyst Treleven after she had spent several years learning the Craft from a variety of different sources. Having been initiated into three different traditions, and having completed a doctorate degree on Wicca that allowed her to be involved with a great many different Pagan practitioners, she saw both the good and the not so good of Wicca. She wanted more for herself and she wanted more for her fellow Wiccans.

www.oakandmistletoe.com/what-is-inclusive-wicca/

McFarland Dianic Wicca

An offshoot of Dianic Wicca that is usually open to transgender women and to cisgender and transgender men. McFarland Dianic is a Neopagan tradition of goddess worship founded by Morgan McFarland and Mark Roberts which, despite the shared name, has a different theology and in some cases accepts male participants. The McFarland tradition is largely based on the book *The White Goddess* by Robert Graves. While some McFarland covens will initiate men, the leadership is limited to female priestesses. Like other Dianic traditions, McFarland Dianic covens are feminist.

Minoan Brotherhood

The Minoan Brotherhood was founded as a response to the heterosexist culture of most forms of Traditional Witchcraft prevalent in the 1970s. Edmund M. Buczynski founded the Brotherhood in 1975 in New York City. Eddie was an Elder of the Gardnerian and New York Welsh Traditions, and a founding Elder of the Wica Tradition. The Minoan Brotherhood is a men's initiatory tradition of the Craft celebrating life, men who love men, and magic. It mainly draws on Cretan, Aegean, and Ancient Near Eastern mythology.

http://minoan-brotherhood.org

Minoan Fellowship

The Minoan Fellowship is an offshoot of the Minoan Sisterhood, and is open to women and men of any sexual orientation. (The Minoan Brotherhood does not recognise it as part of their tradition.) The Fellowship seeks to be inclusive of all genders and sexual orientations.

Minoan Sisterhood

The Minoan Sisterhood began in 1976. At that time, a small group of priestesses in the Wica Tradition began working with materials devised by Eddie Buczynski. Lady Rhea and Lady Miw-Sekhmet used this material as to build the Women's mysteries which formed the basis of the Minoan Sisterhood. Their work resulted in the founding of the first Grove of the Minoan Sisterhood in New York City. The Sisterhood is open to any woman, and emphasizes Women's Mysteries. The Minoan Brotherhood and Minoan Sisterhood are sibling paths in the Minoan Tradition, each with its own Mysteries and rites. A third path within the Minoan Tradition is the Cult of Rhea, also known as the Cult of the Double Axe, which represents a meeting ground between the two traditions.

www.minoaneleutheria.org/faq.php

Mohsian Wicca

The Mohsian Tradition of Wicca was founded in the early 1960s by Bill and Helen Mohs. Mohsian is comprised of many threads from British Traditional and other sources. Much of their ritual is derived from early Gardnerian and Alexandrian, including passages from a British Celtic (Pagan, not Wiccan) tradition called Y Plant Bran. Many of their spells and rituals were given to Bill and Helen by Joe Wilson, founder of the 1734 Tradition. Another source is the Boread Tradition as transmitted by Thomas Giles, and there is even a snippet from NROOGD, used with the permission of one of its founders.

Progressive Wicca

Progressive Wicca was started in the early 1990s by Karin Rainbird, Tam Campbell, and David Rankine. It was a tendency within Gardnerian and Alexandrian Wicca, and emphasised valuing the contributions of all members of the coven, ensuring that all members received thorough training, and tended to have a stronger emphasis on environmentalism. Progressive Wiccans are happy to experiment and incorporate more eclectic material into their rituals.

www.sacred-texts.com/bos/msg0015.htm

Progressive Witchcraft

Progressive Witchcraft emerged from Progressive Wicca, and was made famous by Janet Farrar and Gavin Bone in their book of the same name. Its ethos is egalitarian, exploratory, and experimental. Janet and Gavin have started their own witchcraft tradition whose initiation rituals and tenets are distinct from Gardnerian and Alexandrian Wicca.

www.callaighe.com

The Nameless Arte

Not so much a tradition as a collection of individuals exploring folkloric witchcraft in a similar manner. Many of them were inspired by the books of Nigel Pennick such as *The Secrets of East Anglian Magic*. It has no singular book, but for the collective embodied wisdom of its adherents. It can never be fully pinned down, as it constantly evolves and adapts to the requirements of the time.

www.theprismaticgarden.com/nameless-arte

Reclaiming

Reclaiming is a community of people working to unify spirit and politics. Their vision is rooted in the religion and magic of the Goddess, the Immanent Life Force. They see their work as teaching and making magic: the art of empowering themselves and each other. In their classes, workshops, and public rituals, they train their voices, bodies, energy, intuition, and minds. They use the skills that they learn to deepen their strength, both as individuals and as community, to voice their concerns about the world in which we live and bring to birth a vision of a new culture. Founded around 1980 in the San Francisco Bay Area, the Reclaiming tradition now includes several dozen regional communities across North America and in Europe and Australia. The founder of Reclaiming, Starhawk, was trained in the Feri Tradition by Victor and Cora Anderson.

www.reclaiming.org

Spectrum Gate Mysteries

Spectrum Gate Mysteries is an initiatory religious ritual system that embraces all genders, sexes, and sexual preferences. They believe there are infinite ways to connect with each other and with the divine, and they strive to support all of them. Their system is orthopraxic, not orthodoxic; there are no mandated beliefs, and practitioners are encouraged to find their own meaning in the liturgy and ritual. Their system is based on Traditional Wicca, and borrows heavily from Blue Star Wicca, but it is not a Wiccan tradition.

https://spectrumgatemysteries.wordpress.com

Swedish Faery Wicca

This is an eclectic and egalitarian initiatory tradition in Sweden, based on Gardnerian and Alexandrian Wicca. It is LGBT-inclusive. It should not be confused with the Feri Tradition, which is a separate and unrelated tradition.

Roses, Too!

A tradition of eclectic Feminist Witchcraft, founded in 1993 in the Delaware Valley (Philadelphia, PA area).

https://sites.google.com/site/stasasministry/roses-too-tradition

The Unnamed Path

A shamanic path for men who love men, the Unnamed Path is a four-fold spiritual tradition revealed to us from the Ancestors of Men-who-love-men. It is also inclusive towards transgender men and nonbinary people. It is rooted in age-old techniques practiced around the world that foster relationships with the Divine, the ancestors, the spirits in the land, and each other. Eduardo 'Eddy' Gutiérrez (1976-2014), whose magical name was Hyperion, founded The Unnamed Path and hosted the popular podcast *The Unnamed Path*. He discovered and named the important magical concept of resonance, where two people who are similar to each other make energy together by bringing their energies into phase with each other.

http://unnamedpath.com

Further reading

Yvonne Aburrow (2020), *Dark Mirror: the inner work of witchcraft*, The Doreen Valiente Foundation in association with the Centre for Pagan Studies.

Yvonne Aburrow (2014), *All Acts of Love and Pleasure: inclusive Wicca*, Avalonia Books.

Conner, Randy P., David Sparks, and Mariya Sparks (1997), *Cassell's Encyclopedia of Queer Myth, Symbol and Spirit: Gay, Lesbian, Bisexual and Transgender Lore*. London and New York: Cassell.

Christine Hoff Kraemer and Yvonne Aburrow, eds (2016), *Pagan Consent Culture: Building Communities of Empathy and Autonomy*, Asphodel Press.

http://www.paganconsentculture.com

Taylor Ellwood, Brandy Williams, Crystal Blanton, *Bringing Race to the Table: Exploring Racism in the Pagan Community*. Immanion Press.

Tara 'Masery' Miller, ed., *Rooted in the Body, Seeking the Soul - Magic Practitioners Living with Disabilities & Illness*. Immanion Press.

Starhawk (1982, 1988. 1997), *Dreaming The Dark: Magic, Sex, and Politics*. Boston: Beacon Press.

Taylor Ellwood, Shauna Aura Knight (eds), *The Pagan Leadership Anthology: An Exploration of Leadership and Community in Paganism*. Immanion Press.

Chapter 1

Clarissa Pinkola Estés (1992), *Women who run with the Wolves: Myths and Stories of the Wild Woman Archetype*, Ballantine Books.

Barbara Graham (1994), *Women Who Run With the Poodles: Myths and Tips for Honoring Your Mood Swings*. Avon Books.

David Smail (1998), *Taking care: An Alternative to Therapy*. Constable and Robinson.

David Webster (2012), *Dispirited: How Contemporary Spirituality Makes Us Stupid, Selfish and Unhappy*. John Hunt Publishing.

Chapter 3

Robert Augustus Masters (2013), *Spiritual Bypassing: Avoidance in Holy Drag*.
http://robertmasters.com/writings/spiritual-bypassing/

Ingrid Mathieu (2011), "Beware of spiritual bypass". *Psychology Today*.
https://www.psychologytoday.com/blog/emotional-sobriety/201110/beware-spiritual-bypass

David Smail (1987), *Taking Care: An Alternative to Therapy*. Karnac Books.

Thorn Mooney (2018), *Traditional Wicca: A Seeker's Guide*. Llewellyn.

David Webster (2016), *Dispirited: How Contemporary Spirituality Makes Us Stupid, Selfish and Unhappy*.

Chapter 5

Yvonne Aburrow (2014), *All Acts of Love and Pleasure: inclusive Wicca*, chapter 20: "Eco-spirituality and embodiment". Avalonia Books.

Yvonne Aburrow (2014), *All Acts of Love and Pleasure: inclusive Wicca*, chapter 23: "Witchcraft and activism". Avalonia Books.

Barry Patterson (2007), *The Art of Conversation with The Genius Loci*. Holmes Publishing Group.

Peter Grey (2013), *Apocalyptic Witchcraft*. Scarlet Imprint.

Rebecca Solnit (2005), *Hope in the dark: The Untold History of People Power*. (Also published as *Hope in the Dark: Untold Histories, Wild Possibilities*.) Nation Books.

Christopher Orapello and Tara-Love Maguire (2018), *Besom, Stang and Sword: A Guide to Traditional Witchcraft, the Sixfold Path, and the Hidden Landscape*. Weiser Books.

Rhyd Wildermuth and Alley Valkyrie, *A Pagan Anti-Capitalist Primer*. Gods & Radicals, available from https://godsandradicals.org/a-pagan-anti-capitalist-primer/

Christopher Scott Thompson (2016), *Pagan Anarchism*. Gods & Radicals.

Chapter 9

Religion and mental health

Thorn Mooney (2015), *Wicca and Depression*, http://www.patheos.com/blogs/oathbound/2015/08/wicca-and-depression/

Asa West (2015), *Don't Listen to Your Gut: Practicing Witchcraft with Anxiety and OCD*, http://www.patheos.com/blogs/shekhinahcalling/2015/08/21/dont-listen-to-your-gut-practicing-witchcraft-with-anxiety-and-ocd/

Marg Herder, *The Long Overdue Conversation About Mental Illness*, http://www.patheos.com/blogs/emergentvillage/2015/08/the-long-overdue-conversation-about-mental-illness/

Heron Michelle, *She Who is Without Oddness, Cast the First Stone*, http://www.patheos.com/blogs/agora/2015/08/witch-on-fire-she-who-is-without-oddness-cast-the-first-stone/

The history of madness and psychiatry

David Smail, *Taking Care: An Alternative to Therapy*

Michel Foucault, *Madness & Civilization: A History of Insanity in the Age of Reason*

Support groups

The Critical Psychiatry Network,
http://www.critpsynet.freeuk.com/antipsychiatry.htm

The Hearing Voices Network,
http://www.hearing-voices.org/

Chapter 12

Eric Berne (1964), *Games People Play: The Psychology of Human Relationships*.

Yvonne Aburrow (2014), *All Acts of Love and Pleasure: inclusive Wicca*, chapter 21: "Running a coven". Avalonia Books.

Chapter 13

Robert K Greenleaf (1970), *The Servant as Leader*.

James McGregor Burns (1978), *Leadership*. Harper Perennial Political Classics.

Bernard M. Bass (1985), *Leadership and Performance Beyond Expectations*.

MindTools.com, *Leadership Styles: Choosing the Right Approach for the Situation*.
https://www.mindtools.com/pages/article/newLDR_84.htm

Chapter 17

Bringing Race to the Table: Exploring Racism in the Pagan Community (edited by Crystal Blanton, Taylor Ellwood, Brandi Williams, 2015)

Shades of Faith: Minority Voices in Paganism, by Crystal Blanton (2011)

Bridging the Gap: Working Within the Dynamics of Pagan Groups and Society, by Crystal Blanton (2010)

Pain and Faith in a Wiccan World: Spirituality, Ethics and Transformation, by Crystal Blanton

Shades of Ritual: Minority Voices in Practice (edited by Crystal Blanton)

Unsettling Canada: A National Wake-Up Call, by Art Manuel, Grand Chief Ronald M. Derrickson (2015)

The Reconciliation Manifesto: Recovering the Land, Rebuilding the Economy by Art Manuel and Grand Chief Ronald Derrickson (2017)

Indigenous Writes: A Guide to First Nations, Métis, and Inuit issues in Canada, by Chelsea Vowel (2016)

The Inconvenient Indian: A Curious Account of Native People in North America, by Thomas King, Lorne Cardinal, et al.

Web resources

You can find more resources, articles, and a glossary of terms at the inclusive Wicca website:

Ethnicity and anti-racism:
http://www.inclusivewicca.org/p/ethnicity-and-anti-racism-systemic.html

Intersectional feminism:
http://www.inclusivewicca.org/p/intersectional-feminism-reflections-on.html

Cultural appropriation:
http://www.inclusivewicca.org/p/blog-page_27.html

Inclusive Wicca:
http://www.inclusivewicca.org/p/inclusive-wicca-articles.html

Queering Paganism:
http://www.inclusivewicca.org/p/queering-paganism-absolute-dangers-of.html

Civil courage:
http://www.inclusivewicca.org/p/leaflet-no.html

Thanks

Thanks to everyone whose conversations led me to a deeper understanding of the inner work.

Thanks to my initiators, without whom I would not have embarked on this journey.

Thanks to Julie Payne and Emlyn Price of the Doreen Valiente Foundation for publishing the new, revised, and expanded edition of these books.

Many thanks to Dalia Heiser, for all the help with ebook formatting issues.

Thanks to Dalia Heiser, Jake Leo, Julie Payne, Emlyn Price, Darren Jones, Helix, Vernon Marshall, Jim Blair, Sarah Tinker, Sue Woolley, Linda Haggerstone, Alder Lyncurium, Brian Paisley, Kumar Devadasan, Mhairi Strauss, Anna Hammarlund, Anya Read, Brian Paisley, Francois Schaut, Lirilin Lee, Susan Harper, for sharing ideas and techniques.

Thanks to Steve Dee for the awesome foreword, and to Geraldine Beskin, Lydia Knox, Tim Landry, Misha Magdalene, Sabina Magliocco, Thista Minai, Julia Phillips, Lucya Starza, and Morgana Sythove for reviews and feedback.

And thanks to my beloved Bob, the members of my coven, and the members of the Inclusive Wicca Discussion Group, for your encouragement and enthusiasm.

Any errors or omissions in the text are mine.

Yvonne Aburrow

The Doreen Valiente Foundation
and
The Centre for Pagan Studies

The Doreen Valiente Foundation is a charitable trust dedicated to the preservation and protection of material relating to Pagan practices, spirituality, and religion. The Foundation is dedicated to researching and interpreting this material and making both the research and the material accessible to the public for the benefit of wider education and the advancement of knowledge in this unique landscape of living cultural and religious heritage.

The Foundation was established in 2011 and received legal ownership of Doreen Valiente's entire legacy of artefacts, books, writings, documents, manuscripts and copyrights under a deed of trust that permanently prevents the sale or splitting up of the collection and prohibits the making of profit through the exploitation of the collection. This means that every penny earned by the Foundation (including the publishers' proceeds of the sale of this book) is spent on pursuing its goals and charitable objects as above.

The Foundation is working towards the establishment of a permanent museum to house the collection, and the physical creation of a Centre for Pagan Studies, which is the organisation of which Doreen was patron shortly before her death in 1999. The Foundation succeeded in campaigns to have Heritage Blue Plaques placed on the former homes of Doreen Valiente and Gerald Gardner. The DVF and CFPS also organise conferences, talks, and exhibitions as well as engaging with the global community in matters of religious history and spiritual heritage.

More information about Doreen Valiente, the Doreen Valiente Foundation, and The Centre for Pagan Studies, including membership, donations, events, and activities, and purchase of books, can be found at:

www.doreenvaliente.org

www.centre-for-pagan-studies.com

CPSIA information can be obtained
at www.ICGtesting.com
Printed in the USA
LVHW081638230123
737760LV00016B/1206